This report contains the collective views of an international group of experts and does not necessarily represent the decisions or the stated policy of the World Health Organization

WHO Technical Report Series
951

THE SCIENTIFIC BASIS OF TOBACCO PRODUCT REGULATION

Second report of a WHO study group

World Health Organization

WHO Library Cataloguing-in-Publication Data

The scientific basis of tobacco product regulation: second report of a WHO study group.

(WHO technical report series ; no. 951)

1.Tobacco use disorder - prevention and control. 2.Tobacco industry - legislation. 3.Tobacco control campaigns. 4. Tobacco-derived products labelling. 5.Tobacco-derived products packing. I.World Health Organization. II.WHO Tobacco Free Initiative. III.Series.

ISBN 978 92 4 120951 9 (NLM classification: QV 137)

ISSN 0512-3054

Printed in India

Contents

Acknowledgements

The WHO Study Group on Tobacco Product Regulation gratefully acknowledges the valuable contributions made to its work by the WHO Tobacco Free Initiative and International Agency for Research on Cancer working group, established to provide scientific guidance on a strategy for regulating toxicant levels in cigarette smoke. The members of the group were Dr David Ashley, Centers for Disease Control and Prevention, USA, Dr David Burns, Dr Mirjana Djordjevic, Tobacco Control Research Branch of the National Cancer Institute, Bethesda, Maryland, United States, Dr Carolyn Dresler, Head of the Tobacco and Cancer Group, International Agency for Research on Cancer, France, Dr Erik Dybing, Dr Nigel Gray, Dr Pierre Hainaut, Dr Stephen Hecht, University of Minnesota, USA, Dr Richard O'Connor, Assistant Professor of Oncology, Department of Health Behavior, Roswell Park Cancer Institute, Dr Antoon Opperhuizen, Head of the Laboratory of Toxicology, Pathology, and Genetics, of the National Institute of Public Health and the Environment and Dr Kurt Straif, Scientist. The report submitted to TobReg after meetings over 18 months to define maximal limits for toxicants served as the basis for discussion on the issue during the study group's fourth meeting, held in Stanford, California, United States of America, from 25 to 27 July 2007.

TobReg also expresses gratitude to the following, who were either commissioned to write background papers or lent their expertise on other areas of tobacco product regulation reviewed by the study group at its fourth meeting: Dr Gregory N. Connolly, Professor of Public Health Practice at the Harvard School of Public Health, Boston, Massachusetts, United States, and Mr Denis Choinière, Director of Regulations and Compliance, Tobacco Control Programme, Health Canada, Ottawa, Canada, for their work on reduced ignition propensity; Dr Mark Parascandola, epidemiologist with the Tobacco Control Research Branch of the National Cancer Institute, Bethesda, Maryland, United States, Mr Mitch Zeller, Vice President for Policy and Strategic Communications, Pinney Associates, Bethesda, Maryland Dr Dorothy Hatsukami, Forster Family Professor in Cancer Prevention, Department of Psychiatry,

University of Minnesota, USA for their contributions to the chapter on harm reduction; as well as Christy Anderson and Tore Sanner for their contribution to the report on the regulation of products based on reducing the toxicant levels in cigarettes smoke.

WHO Study Group on Tobacco Product Regulation

Stanford University, California, United States of America, 25–27 July 2007

Members

Dr D.L. Ashley, Chief, Emergency Response and Air Toxicants Branch, Centers for Disease Control and Prevention, Atlanta, Georgia, United States of America

Dr D. Burns, Professor of Family and Preventive Medicine, School of Medicine, University of California at San Diego, San Diego, California, United States of America

Dr M. Djordjevic, Program Director, National Cancer Institute, Division of Cancer Control and Population Sciences, Tobacco Control Research Branch, Bethesda, Maryland, United States of America

Dr E. Dybing (*Chair*), Director, Division of Environmental Medicine, Norwegian Institute of Public Health, Oslo, Norway

Dr N. Gray, Scientist, International Agency for Research on Cancer, Lyon, France

Dr S.K. Hammond, Professor of Environmental Health Sciences, School of Public Health, University of California at Berkeley, Berkeley, California, United States of America

Dr J. Henningfield, Professor (Adjunct), Behavioral Biology, Johns Hopkins University School of Medicine; Vice President, Research and Health Policy, Pinney Associates, Bethesda, Maryland, United States of America

Dr M. Jarvis, Principal Scientist, Cancer Research UK, Health Behaviour Unit, Royal Free and University College London Medical School, London, England

Dr K.S. Reddy, Professor of Cardiology, All India Institute of Medical Sciences, New Delhi, India

Dr C. Robertson, Senior Associate Dean for Faculty and Academic Affairs, School of Engineering, Stanford University, California, United States of America

Dr G. Zaatari, Professor, Department of Pathology and Laboratory Medicine, American University of Beirut, Beirut, Lebanon

Secretariat

Dr D.W. Bettcher, Coordinator, Framework Convention on Tobacco Control, and Director, a.i., Tobacco Free Initiative, WHO, Geneva, Switzerland

Ms E. Tecson, Administrative Assistant, Tobacco Free Initiative, WHO, Geneva, Switzerland

Ms G. Vestal, Legal Officer and Scientist, Framework Convention on Tobacco Control, Tobacco Free Initiative, WHO, Geneva, Switzerland

Preface

Tobacco product regulation — regulating the contents and emissions of tobacco products by testing, mandating disclosure of test results and regulating the packaging and labelling of tobacco products — is a pillar of any comprehensive tobacco control programme. The Contracting Parties to the World Health Organization Framework Convention on Tobacco Control (WHO FCTC) are legally bound by the treaty's provisions on tobacco product regulation, contained in its Articles 9, 10 and 11.

The information provided by the ad hoc WHO Scientific Advisory Committee on Tobacco Product Regulation, established in 2000 to fill gaps in knowledge on tobacco product regulation, served as the basis for the negotiations and the subsequent consensus on the language of the aforementioned articles of the treaty.

In November 2003, in recognition of the importance of regulating tobacco products, the WHO Director-General formalized the Scientific Advisory Committee into the WHO Study Group on Tobacco Product Regulation (TobReg). TobReg's membership comprises national and international experts on product regulation, treatment of tobacco dependence, laboratory analysis of tobacco contents and emissions and design features. Its work is based on current research, and it also conducts research and proposes testing to fill regulatory gaps in tobacco control. The Director-General reports to the Executive Board on the results and recommendations of the Study Group in order to draw the attention of Member States to WHO's efforts in tobacco product regulation.

This technical report was prepared by TobReg in accordance with the priorities of the WHO Tobacco Free Initiative and the provisions of the WHO FCTC concerning tobacco product regulation, in response to requests from Member States in which the population is affected by the issues addressed. The fourth meeting of TobReg was held at Stanford University, California, United States of America, on 25–27 July 2007. The agenda was prepared to respond partly to Decision 15 of the first session of the Conference of Parties to the WHO FCTC, held in Geneva, Switzerland, on 6–17 February 2006, when the Parties adopted templates for guidelines for implementing

Articles 9 and 10 of the Framework Convention. According to the template on regulations, the guidelines should be based on work performed by TobReg and the WHO Tobacco Free Initiative, which serves as TobReg's secretariat and coordinating body.

This report presents the conclusions and recommendations of the WHO Study Group on Tobacco Product Regulation (TobReg) from its fourth meeting which was held at Stanford University, California, United States of America (USA), on 25–27 July 2007. The agenda was prepared to respond partly to Decision 15 of the first session of the Conference of Parties to the WHO Framework Convention on Tobacco Control, held in Geneva, Switzerland, on 6–17 February 2006, when the Parties adopted a template for the development of guidelines for implementing Articles 9 and 10 of the Framework Convention. At this fourth meeting of WHO TobReg, the Study Group deliberated on a number of topics in the field of tobacco product regulation and produced the following advisory notes and recommendations:

- an advisory note on smokeless tobacco products: health effects, implications for harm reduction and research needs;
- an advisory note on 'fire safer' cigarettes: approaches to reduced ignition propensity;
- a recommendation on mandated lowering of toxicants in cigarette smoke: tobacco-specific nitrosamines and selected other constituents; and
- a recommendation on cigarette machine smoking regimens.

The four sections of this report address these four issues, and the Study Group's recommendations are set out at the end of each section. Its overall recommendations are summarized in section 5.

The Study Group's members serve without remuneration in their personal capacities and not as representatives of governments or other bodies; their views do not necessarily reflect the decisions or the stated policy of WHO.

1. Advisory note on smokeless tobacco products: health effects, implications for harm reduction and research

1.1 Purpose

Since the recommendation on smokeless tobacco by the predecessor of the WHO Study Group on Tobacco Product Regulation (TobReg), the Scientific Advisory Committee on Tobacco Product Regulation, in 2003, the health effects of smokeless tobacco products have been addressed in numerous published reports and in reports of scientific advisory groups. Smokeless tobacco has also been increasingly discussed with respect to its potential to reduce the harm caused by cigarette smoking.

It is beyond the scope of this advisory note to summarize all these reports in detail. It was, however, evident to TobReg that the recommendation on smokeless tobacco of the 2003 Scientific Advisory Committee on Tobacco Product Regulation should be revised to reflect advances in knowledge. Furthermore, since the 2003 recommendation, the WHO Framework Convention on Tobacco Control (WHO, 2005) has come into force and has been ratified by more than 150 Parties, representing more than 80% of the world's population. The Framework Convention is intended to reduce the prevalence of and harm caused by tobacco use by regulating product communications, marketing, smuggling and patterns of use. To the greatest extent possible, implementation of the Framework Convention is based on scientific data concerning regulated products.

The scientific advisory notes of WHO TobReg are intended to facilitate implementation of the Framework Convention by evaluating the scientific basis of communications and regulation on tobacco products. For example, the 2005 TobReg advisory note on waterpipe smoking made clear that this increasingly prevalent form of tobacco use is harmful and addictive and warrants inclusion in comprehensive tobacco control efforts (TobReg, 2005). The aim of that advisory note was to address the common misconception that waterpipe smoking is a safe form of tobacco use and one that should be exempt from tobacco product regulation. There is little question that, in general, smokeless tobacco products are less harmful than combusted tobacco products such as cigarettes; however, whether smokeless tobacco products contribute to continuation or reduction of the global tobacco epidemic depends in part on their nature, how their health effects are communicated, how they are marketed and how they are used. These factors must be considered as the Framework Convention is implemented. This advisory note provides scientifically based guidance for implementation of the Framework Convention that will contribute to reducing the use of tobacco and the harm it causes.

1.2 Background

Scientific publications, including reports by several expert panels, published since 2003 have provided a strong foundation for the present advisory note. This note essentially replaces the 2003 recommendation by Scientific Advisory Committee on Tobacco Product Regulation (2004). The main expert panels that have addressed smokeless tobacco and health are a working group convened by the International Agency for Research on Cancer (IARC, 2007), the initial report of the Scientific Committee on Emerging and Newly Identified Health Risks of the European Commission (2008), the United States (US) National Institutes of Health panel addressing tobacco use (National Institutes of Health, 2006), and the Royal College of Physicians and Surgeons (2007). The 'strategic dialogue on tobacco harm reduction' supported by the American Legacy Foundation and the Robert Wood Johnson Foundation published conclusions that agree in general with the previous reports (Zeller, Hatsukami, Strategic Dialogue on Harm Reduction Group, 2007). Consideration was also given to the findings of an expert panel convened with unrestricted support by Star Scientific, Inc. to examine smokeless tobacco and health issues; the panel included several international leaders in drug addiction science and tobacco and health science and policy (Savitz et al., 2006). In addition, this advisory note relied on the conclusions of a WHO consultation on tobacco harm reduction convened subsequent to the 13th World Conference on Tobacco and Health in Washington DC, USA, in July 2006.

The scope of the subjects discussed by these expert panels on smokeless tobacco differed somewhat, but their findings generally supported the broad conclusion that use of smokeless tobacco could reduce the harm due to tobacco in people who would otherwise have smoked cigarettes and other products. A concern expressed in several reports was that increased smokeless tobacco use might undermine smoking cessation or be a risk factor for smoking initiation and use of both products. This concern (and others addressed in this advisory note) must be resolved, so that such unintended consequences of the promotion of smokeless tobacco use do not contribute to the overall harm due to tobacco. Similar priorities for scientific research are therefore addressed in this note. The conclusions also reflect the deliberations of the TobReg and additional invited experts who met in July 2007 (http://www.who.int/tobacco/global_interaction/tobreg/en/).

1.3 Types of smokeless tobacco product

Products referred to as 'smokeless tobacco' differ widely in form, content and manufacture, with substantial regional and national variation. For example, in India, products are made and marketed by large national and multinational companies as well as by street vendors and small unregistered family businesses. In contrast, the Swedish smokeless tobacco market is dominated by the multinational Swedish Match company and a small number of national companies.

The report of the Scientific Committee on Emerging and Newly Identified Health Risks (European Commission, 2008) provides a comprehensive overview of product types, which is summarized briefly in Table 1.1. The original table contains additional information on product contents and use and the brand names of commonly marketed products. The reasons and patterns of use vary, some products being taken mainly after meals, some being used at least partly to clean the teeth, some being used almost continuously and at least one product being used to calm teething infants. A common factor is that all appear capable of inducing and sustaining nicotine addiction, primarily by delivering nicotine to the oral cavity and nasal passages, although some absorption undoubtedly occurs through the gastrointestinal tract from swallowed nicotine-infused saliva. The nicotine concentrations in the products used usually vary by more than 100-fold. The plasma levels of nicotine and the speed of delivery depend on pH and buffering capacity: raising the oral pH into the alkaline range results in more rapid nicotine absorption through the buccal mucosa (Food and Drug Administration, 1995, 1996; Fant et al., 1999; Stratton et al., 2001; IARC, 2007; European Commission, 2008). The buffering agents include slaked lime, bicarbonate and ash. As discussed elsewhere and in detail in reports published by IARC (2007) and the Scientific Committee on Emerging and Newly Identified Health Risks (European Commission, 2008), the products also vary by several thousandfold in their concentrations of carcinogens such as tobacco-specific nitrosamines (TSNA), benzo[*a*]pyrene, arsenic, nickel, and formaldehyde, radioactive polonium-210, and other toxicants.

The wide diversity of products makes it difficult to make generalizations about the potential health hazards of products designated 'smokeless tobacco'.

Table 1.1
Some types of smokeless tobacco product

Common name	Where used	How used
Chewing tobacco	Europe, USA	Chewed tobacco can also be smoked in pipes.
Chimo	Venezuela	Tobacco, other plants, ash, used orally in the past
Creamy snuff	India	Tobacco, clove oil, menthol and other ingredients in a paste for mouth and tooth cleaning
Dry rape snuff	Brazil	Dry, peppery tobacco powder taken by inhalation
Dry snuff	Georgia, Germany, United Kingdom	Dry tobacco powder taken by inhalation
Gul or gadakhu	Central and eastern India	Tobacco powder, molasses and other ingredients used orally and for cleaning teeth
Gutkha	Europe and South-East Asia	Betel nut, tobacco, slaked lime and flavours, chewed or held in the mouth
Khaini	India	Tobacco, lime paste and sometimes areca nut
Kiwan	India	Tobacco, slaked lime and spices, chewed or held in the mouth
Loose-leaf chew	USA	Coarse shredded tobacco and flavours for chewing
Iq'mik	Alaska	Tobacco and punk ash used orally and for teething infants
Mawa or kiwam	India	Tobacco, slaked lime and areca nut for chewing
Mishri, masheri or misheri	India	Tobacco applied to teeth and held in the mouth
Moist plug, plug or twist chew	USA	Flavoured tobacco leaves held in the mouth or chewed
Moist snuff	Sweden, Norway, USA	Moist, finely ground tobacco held in the mouth
Nass, naswar or niswar	Afghanistan, India, Islamic Republic of Iran, Pakistan	Tobacco, ash, cotton or sesame oil, water, slaked lime, menthol and other ingredients, held in the mouth and sometimes chewed
Pan masala	South-East Asia	Tobacco, areca nut, slaked lime, betel leaf and flavours, sometimes chewed after meals

Red tooth powder	India	Tobacco powder
Shammah	Saudi Arabia	Tobacco, ash and slaked lime for oral use
Snuff	South Africa	Dry tobacco powder for sniffing
Toombak	Sudan	Tobacco and sodium bicarbonate, held in the mouth
Zarda	India	Processed tobacco, betel nut, spices and dyes for oral use

Adapted from Table 1 in the report of the Scientific Committee on Emerging and Newly Identified Health Risks (European Commission, 2008)

1.3 Health effects

The report of an advisory committee to the US Surgeon General and the results of a consensus conference convened by the US National Institutes of Health concluded that smokeless tobacco causes cancer in the oral cavity, the oesophagus and several other sites, dental disease and addiction (technically designated as 'disorders of dependence and withdrawal'), and is probably a risk factor for cardiovascular disease (Department of Health and Human Services, 1986). Since that report, the scientific evidence for these conclusions has been strengthened considerably.

The conclusions of these scientific groups cannot be summarized briefly because different approaches were used, and they addressed different questions. TobReg found, however, that some of their conclusions on the nature and health effects of smokeless tobacco products were relevant to its evaluation of potential strategies for reducing harm:

- All smokeless tobacco products are hazardous; they contain known toxicants, in addition to addicting levels of nicotine.
- The concentrations of toxicants and nicotine vary widely among marketed products.
- The extent and nature of the risk due to use of different marketed smokeless tobacco products vary widely.
- Smokeless tobacco products cause cancer, the site of cancer and the level of risk depending on product characteristics, patterns and extent of use.
- Smokeless tobacco products cause various oral diseases.
- Smokeless tobacco products are addictive and cause the diseases of dependence and withdrawal listed by WHO in the tenth revision of the

International Classification of Diseases (WHO, 1992) and the American Psychiatric Association *Diagnostic and Statistical Manual* (American Psychiatric Association, 1994).

- Smokeless tobacco increases the risk for death after myocardial infarction but does not increase the risk for myocardial infarction. Experiments in animals and studies in humans indicate that oral tobacco use has short-term effects on blood pressure and heart rate, which might contribute to cardiovascular disease.
- There is mixed evidence concerning the causation of problems in pregnancy, although a study in India indicated a dose–response relation between the amount used daily by pregnant women and adverse pregnancy outcomes; complications of pregnancy might vary with product characteristics and patterns and level of use.
- Smokeless tobacco products do not cause the lung diseases causally associated with use of combusted tobacco products such as in cigarettes, pipes and cigars.
- Smokeless tobacco products are not effective for smoking cessation, by the standards required for endorsement of efficacy for smoking cessation; the results of surveys suggest that some cigarette smokers give up smoking by substituting smokeless tobacco.
- Many smokeless tobacco products are marketed for use in situations in which smoking is not allowed, indicating that they may delay smoking cessation.
- Some smokeless tobacco products are manufactured and marketed in such a way as to appeal to young people and thereby stimulate initiation of use.
- Smokeless tobacco products might delay smoking cessation or stimulate wider use of tobacco.
- Smokeless tobacco might have a role in reducing the harm due to tobacco for people who cannot completely abstain from tobacco and who switch from combusted tobacco to smokeless products; however, the individual benefits may depend on product characteristics and patterns of use.
- The benefits and risks for populations depend on the characteristics and patterns of use of the products and the extent to which promotion of such products increases the numbers of smokers of combusted tobacco or delays cessation of use of smoked tobacco products.

1.4 Regional and global patterns of use

Whereas cigarette smoking is a common form of tobacco use in every State Party to the Framework Convention on Tobacco Control, the prevalence of use of smokeless tobacco products, the types of products and the patterns of use vary widely. In the European Union for example, use of oral (moist snuff) smokeless tobacco is low, its sale being prohibited in most countries. Sweden, however, is exempted, and the prevalence of use among men exceeds that of smoking. More than 20% of young men in Norway, which is not a member of the European Union, report daily use of smokeless tobacco. The prevalence of use is much higher in the USA than in Canada, Mexico and South America. It is high in North Africa and low in most of the rest of the African continent. The overall prevalence of smokeless tobacco use is highest in South-East Asia, where use is also common among women.

In Norway, Sweden and the USA, virtually all smokeless tobacco products are manufactured and marketed commercially. In contrast, many of those used in India and other parts of South-East Asia are manufactured locally, often by small vendors, with little or no standardization or possibility for regulating the contents, method of manufacture or packaging.

South-East Asia has some of the highest rates of oral cancer due to use of smokeless tobacco (IARC, 2007), and adverse reproductive effects, such as low birth weight, lowered gestational age and more stillbirths, have been documented (Gupta, Sreevidya, 2004; Gupta, Subramoney, 2006).

1.5 Reducing harm due to use of smokeless tobacco

It is theoretically possible to reduce the risk for harm to tobacco users who are unable or unwilling to quit, by changing the product, its characteristics or the mode of intake by which they satisfy their need for nicotine, because most of the harm is due to contents other than nicotine (TobReg, 2007). The reduction of harm due to use of tobacco can be viewed from a broad public health perspective, in which the risks for disease and premature mortality are reduced by reducing exposure to toxicants and pathogens. For instance, malaria can be controlled by reducing the numbers of malaria spirochaete-carrying mosquitoes, respiratory disease can be controlled by reducing air pollution, and HIV/AIDS can be controlled by preventing unprotected sex and needle sharing by intravenous injection drug users. The aim of the WHO Framework Convention on Tobacco Control is to contribute to reducing the harm due to tobacco by preventing use, encouraging cessation, protecting other people from exposure to second-hand tobacco smoke and regulating product contents.

The definitions and goals of harm reduction vary according to the area of pubic health but provide a useful perspective for tobacco. For example, the International Harm Reduction Association was established to address the harm caused by addictive drugs other than tobacco and alcohol, although it has included alcohol and tobacco in its mandate since 2004. It defines harm reduction as "policies and programmes which attempt primarily to reduce the adverse health, social and economic consequences of all psychoactive substances to individuals drug users, their families and their communities" (http://www.ihra.net/). The definition given in a report of the US Institute of Medicine (Stratton et al., 2001) is more specific, referring to modification of conventional tobacco products, new products and pharmaceutical products that "lower total tobacco-related mortality and morbidity even though use of that product may involve continued exposure to tobacco-related toxicants".

From the perspective of global harm reduction in the context of the WHO Framework Convention on Tobacco Control, TobReg considers that prevention, cessation and reduction of exposure to secondhand tobacco smoke are the best-validated means of preventing disease and improving public health. TobReg also agrees, however, with the earlier expert panels, that tobacco users who are unable or unwilling to quit could reduce harm by changing products, their characteristics and the form of intake. Like the expert groups, TobReg emphasizes that any such action must not undermine prevention, cessation and reduction of exposure to second-hand smoke and, ideally, should support them.

For the purpose of this advisory note, TobReg concluded that the objective of reducing harm due to tobacco use is to decrease morbidity and mortality among persons who continue to use tobacco and nicotine and are unwilling or unable to quit, with due consideration of the effects at population level. With this objective in mind, conclusions were reached, recommendations made and research needs identified, as described below.

TobReg established principles for harm reduction from smokeless tobacco, in order to make its goals transparent. Other expert groups, such as that of the US Institute of Medicine (Stratton et al., 2001), have taken a similar approach. The principles listed below are generally consistent with those of the Institute of Medicine but adapted to the principles and objectives of the Framework Convention.

- The risks associated with use of nicotine-containing products vary, the use of medicinal nicotine products entailing the lowest risk and use of cigarettes generally entailing the highest risk.

- The risks associated with smokeless tobacco use vary according to the product used, from risks that might be important for harm reduction strategies to risks that are too small to be meaningful for such strategies.
- The differences in risks associated with use of different smokeless tobacco products mean that it would be scientifically inappropriate to consider smokeless tobacco as a single product for the purposes of estimating risk or setting policies.
- The risk to a user of a particular product varies with the pattern and intensity of use.
- Apple-type services for unicode imaging (ATSUI) are needed to present product characteristics and patterns of use and their effects on levels of risk. This technique gives unicode-encoded text advanced typographical features and automatically handles many of the complexities inherent in text layout, including correct rendering of text in bidirectional and vertical script systems.
- Shifts in product use could reduce individual harm but increase harm to the population as a whole or to segments of the population; therefore careful scientific assessment is needed of both individual risks and changes in use at the population level when considering harm reduction approaches.
- Consideration of the harm-reducing potential for individuals of changing products and their characteristics should include the physical and chemical characteristics of the product and its emissions, how it is used, the exposure of users to toxicants, measures of product toxicity, addiction potential and the risk for disease related to use.
- Consideration of the harm-reducing potential for the population of strategies for shifting products or mandating changes in product characteristics should include the possibility of initiation of product use by non-users, the possibility that the product might be used as a transition to a more harmful product or might lead to cessation of all use, the possibility that use of two tobacco products will result in greater exposure to toxicants or prevent or delay cessation, with relapse to more harmful products by people who would otherwise quit, and the exposure of non-smokers.
- Claims that products reduce harm can have adverse effects on individuals and the population and should be made only on the basis of compelling scientific evidence.
- Demonstrations of altered product contents, lowered emissions or reduced intake of toxicants are not sufficient to support claims or implications of reduced toxicity or harm.

- No specific or implied claim of harm reduction should be permitted with regard to any tobacco product before it has been validated by an independent regulatory agency on the basis of sufficient scientific data.
- Postmarketing surveillance of use patterns, consumer perceptions and health effects should be conducted in order to assess population effects.
- As claims of exposure reduction can be interpreted as claims of harm reduction, the former should be allowed only when it can be demonstrated that reductions in the levels of exposure to specific toxicants result in reducted risk at the population level.
- Claims of reduced harm based on evidence for a particular population can have unintended consequences for vulnerable groups that would not otherwise have used the product.

1.7 Conclusions

In accordance with the WHO Framework Convention on Tobacco Control and the principles and objectives stated in this advisory note, and with due consideration for the conclusions of other expert groups, the WHO Harm Reduction Consultation and the participants in the fourth meeting of TobReg (July 2007), TobReg came to the following conclusions about smokeless tobacco and harm reduction.

- The composition, the hazardous properties and the manner in which smokeless tobacco products are used are widely diverse.
- Current evidence indicates that all smokeless tobacco products are hazardous to health.
- All smokeless tobacco products are addictive.
- Scientifically documented risks for disease associated with different smokeless tobacco products varies according to product, pattern of use and geographical region.
- Users of smokeless tobacco products generally have lower risks for tobacco-related morbidity and mortality than users of combustible tobacco products such as cigarettes.
- People who would otherwise continue to smoke and who switch from cigarette smoking to a smokeless product with a risk that is scientifically documented as being at the low end of the range are likely to have a reduced risk for subsequent disease.

- People who continue to use smokeless tobacco products the characteristics of which are changed to those with a risk that is scientifically documented as being at the low end of the range are likely to benefit.
- Harm reduction strategies that involve encouraging smokeless tobacco use in regions where smokeless tobacco is the predominant type of tobacco used may cause harm, particularly when the product used predominantly has substantial hazardous properties.
- The design and characteristics of smokeless tobacco products affect their appeal by changing the taste, flavour and ease of use, the amount of nicotine delivered, its addictiveness, and therefore the potential for harm.
- Contents of smokeless tobacco products other than tobacco affect the appeal of the product by changing the taste, flavour and ease of use, the amount of nicotine delivered and its addictiveness, and therefore the potential for harm.
- Packaging, labelling and marketing of smokeless tobacco products affect their appeal, the prevalence of their use, initiation, addiction and therefore the potential for harm.
- Conflicting conclusions have been reached about whether initiation of tobacco use with smokeless tobacco products results in a higher prevalence of subsequent use of combustible tobacco products.
- The evidence that smokeless tobacco products are effective for smoking cessation does not meet the standards required, although the results of surveys suggest that some cigarette smokers have given up smoking by changing to smokeless tobacco.
- Evidence that adult use of smokeless tobacco increases cessation of cigarette smoking at the population level remains inconclusive and varies by country.
- Some smokeless tobacco products are marketed for use by cigarette smokers in situations where smoking is not allowed; the effect of such use on cessation is not known.
- The effects of concurrent use of combustible and smokeless tobacco products on exposure to toxicant are not known.
- In countries where smokeless tobacco use is common, the prevalence is highest among adolescents and young men.
- The pattern of smokeless tobacco use by adult populations varies by country, with substantial adult use in some countries and use largely confined to young men in others; the roles of marketing and social differences remain uncertain.

1.8 Recommendations

TobReg recognized that recommendations on the possible negative or positive role of smokeless tobacco in reducing the harm due to tobacco might be useful for setting policies and implementing the Framework Convention. The recommendations below were proposed for consideration, although some may be irrelevant or inappropriate for some Parties. TobReg did not take a position about the introduction of smokeless tobacco products in regions where they are not marketed, as that would involve complex health, political and other considerations.

- All tobacco products, including smokeless tobacco, should be subjected to comprehensive regulatory control by an independent, scientific government agency. Such control requires disclosure of ingredients by manufacturers.
- Any health claim made for a smokeless tobacco product must be supported by sufficient scientific data, as determined by an independent, scientific government regulatory agency.
- As claims for reduced exposure could be interpreted as claims for harm reduction, no claims for reduced exposure should be permitted in the absence of evidence for reduced risk.
- The contents and emissions of smokeless tobacco products must be tested and measured continuously in order to detect national and regional variations and changes over time.
- Research on the health hazards and risks to individuals and populations of use of smokeless tobacco products is essential for governments and for implementation of the Framework Convention.
- Research on smokeless tobacco products, their effects and how their design and manufacture are modified in order to alter their effects is essential for adequate testing and measurement, to provide information for governments and for implementation of the Framework Convention.
- As the risks posed by tobacco products vary, tobacco control policy should be based on these differences.

1.9 Gaps in knowledge and research needs

As also concluded by other expert groups that have considered the potential role of smokeless tobacco products and other types of tobacco products (conventional and modified) in reducing the harm due to tobacco (e.g. Stratton et al., 2001; Scientific Advisory Committee on Tobacco Product Regulation,

2003; TobReg, 2004, 2007), TobReg recognized certain gaps in knowledge, which indicate that a cautious approach is appropriate.

Research on and testing of smokeless tobacco products, their use, the consequences of their use and the implications of different policies are essential, so that policies can be set that will improve health and minimize unintended consequences. The extent of the public health epidemic due to tobacco marketing and use makes it essential to consider alternative approaches, to address gaps in knowledge and to avoid taking actions that could worsen the epidemic regionally or globally. General principles for research and testing are given in the TobReg recommendations *Guiding principles for the development of tobacco product research and testing* (TobReg, 2004). There are both many uncertainties and numerous areas in which there is a strong scientific foundation. For example, the conclusion that people who use only smokeless tobacco products have lower overall risks for disease and premature mortality than cigarette smokers can be reached with a high degree of confidence. There is, however, considerable debate about the population impact of promoting smokeless tobacco use for harm reduction in cigarette smokers, and about the polices and marketing approaches that lead to improved health rather than undermine health promotion efforts.

Resolution of these issues is complicated by the wide array of smokeless tobacco products, marketing approaches and social, cultural and regional factors that influence patterns of use. For example, substantial differences are found in the patterns of use and the health consequences in South-East Asia and Sweden (Foulds et al. 2003; Cnattingius, 2005) and in the USA (Department of Health and Human Services, 1986; National Institutes of Health, 2006). The Scientific Committee on Emerging and Newly Identified Health Risks (European Commission, 2008) concluded that "It is not possible to extrapolate the patterns of tobacco use from one country where oral tobacco is available to other countries due to societal and cultural differences."

Thus, categories of products that meet specified standards and are marketed under certain conditions in particular countries are more likely to benefit public health than products that meet other standards and conditions. There is no strong scientific basis for identifying product types or product performance standards that could be promoted as substitutes for smoking, for the forms of promotion that could be allowed or how cultural differences should be addressed. Nevertheless, this information is necessary in order to make significant progress beyond policies in which all tobacco products are considered to have the same or similar risks. In order to guide short- and long-term policy, research is needed:

- to characterize more thoroughly the diversity of ingredients used in different product categories and brands and to assess their toxicity and potential for causing disease;
- to understand better how addictiveness and product appeal are encouraged by physical features, such as tobacco cut size, nicotine content, free-base fraction, flavourings, other design and sensory characteristics and packaging;
- to understand better which products are made by vendors and in homes, especially in South-East Asia, and their toxic and addictive potential, to provide a basis for education, thus reducing toxicity and addictiveness;
- on how the toxicity, harmfulness and addiction potential of a product can change over time under different storage conditions after manufacture;
- to understand better the relations between the amount and length of exposure and risk for disease in order to define performance standards for product constituents;
- on the reductions in risk when product use is discontinued completely or partially;
- on the reduction in risk due to replacement of use of cigarettes and other combustible forms of tobacco by use of smokeless tobacco products;
- on the characteristics of products, packaging and labelling, marketing and other forms of communication that contribute to the risk for addiction by people who are experimenting with the product and to the promotion of continued use rather than cessation by regular users;
- to characterize the risk that use of and addiction to smokeless tobacco will lead to tobacco smoking;
- to characterize the risk that initiation of an addiction to smokeless tobacco will lead to use of and escalation of use of addictive drugs, including alcohol, by people who are already using them;
- to characterize the risk that initiation of smokeless tobacco use and addiction will delay or prevent smoking cessation rather than substitute for smoking;
- to determine if and under what conditions smokeless tobacco use might aid smoking cessation;
- on the potential or actual effects of various policies on smokeless tobacco uptake, overall tobacco use and risk for disease;

- to understand which regional populations, by gender and ethnic group, are most likely to benefit from or be adversely affected by promotion of smokeless tobacco for reducing the harm due to smoking;
- to address how social, ethnic and marketing forces influence initiation of the use of smokeless tobacco and the trajectory from use to addiction and cessation; and
- to understand better the effects of smokeless tobacco use on vulnerable populations, such as adolescents, women of child-bearing age and immunologically compromised persons, who might initiate use of smokeless tobacco products as a result of claims for reduced harm.

References

American Psychiatric Association (1994) *Diagnostic and statistical manual of mental disorders.* 4th ed. Washington DC.

Cnattingius S (2005) *Hälsorisker med svenskt snus. [Health risks of Swedish snus.]* Stockholm, National Institute of Public Health, Karolinska Institute.

Department of Health and Human Services (1986) *Health consequences of using smokeless tobacco. A report of the Surgeon General.* Bethesda, Maryland (NIH Publication No. 86-2874).

European Commission (2008) *Health effects of smokeless tobacco products.* Brussels, Scientific Committee on Emerging and Newly Identified Health Risks.

Fant RV et al. (1999) Pharmacokinetics and pharmacodynamics of moist snuff in humans. *Tobacco Control,* 8:387–392.

Food and Drug Administration (1995) Regulations restricting the sale and distribution of cigarettes and smokeless tobacco products to protect children and adolescents; proposed rule analysis regarding FDA's jurisdiction over nicotine-containing cigarettes and smokeless tobacco products; notice. *Federal Register,* 60:41314–41792.

Food and Drug Administration (1996) Regulations restricting the sale and distribution of cigarettes and smokeless tobacco to protect children and adolescents; final rule. 21 CFR Part 801. *Federal Register,* 61:44396-45318.

Foulds J et al. (2003) Effect of smokeless tobacco (*snus*) on smoking and public health in Sweden. *Tobacco Control,* 12:349–359.

Gupta PC, Sreevidya S (2004) Smokeless tobacco use, birth weight, and gestational age: population based prospective cohort study of 1217 women in Mumbai (Bombay), India. *British Medical Journal,* 328:1538–1540.

Gupta PC, Subramoney S (2006) Smokeless tobacco use during pregnancy and risk of stillbirth: a cohort study in Mumbai, India. *Epidemiology,* 17:47–51.

IARC (2007) *Smokeless tobacco and some tobacco-specific* N*-nitrosamines.* Lyon, International Agency for Research on Cancer (*IARC Monographs on the Evaluation of Carcinogenic Risks to Humans,* Vol. 89).

National Institutes of Health (2006) *State-of-the-science conference statement on tobacco use: prevention, cessation, and control.* Bethesda, Maryland.

Royal College of Physicians and Surgeons (2007) *Harm reduction in nicotine addiction: helping people who can't quit. A report by the Tobacco Advisory Group of the Royal College of Physicians.* London.

Savitz et al. (2006) Public health implications of smokeless tobacco use as a harm reduction strategy. *American Journal of Public Health*, 96:1934–1939. Erratum in: *American Journal of Public Health*, 2007, 97:202.

Scientific Advisory Committee on Tobacco Product Regulation (2003) *Recommendation on smokeless tobacco products.* Geneva, World Health Organization.

Scientific Advisory Committee on Tobacco Product Regulation (2004) *Recommendation on tobacco product ingredients and emissions.* Geneva, World Health Organization.

Stratton et al. (2001) *Clearing the smoke: assessing the science base for tobacco harm reduction.* Washington DC, National Academy Press.

TobReg (2004) *Recommendation: guiding principles for the development of tobacco product research and testing capacity and proposed protocols for the initiation of tobacco product testing.* Geneva, World Health Organization.

TobReg (2005) *WHO TobReg advisory: waterpipe tobacco smoking: health effects, research needs and recommended actions by regulators.* Geneva, World Health Organization.

TobReg (2007) *The scientific basis of tobacco product regulation.* Geneva, World Health Organization (WHO Technical Report Series, No. 945).

WHO (1992) *The ICD-10 classification of mental and behavioural disorders: clinical descriptions and diagnostic guidelines.* Geneva, World Health Organization.

WHO (2005) *WHO Framework Convention on Tobacco Control.* Geneva, World Health Organization.

Zeller M, Hatsukami D, Strategic Dialogue on Harm Reduction Group (2007) *The strategic dialogue on tobacco harm reduction: a vision and blueprint for action.* (in press)

2. Advisory note on 'fire-safer' cigarettes: approaches to reduced ignition propensity

2.1 Purpose

This advisory note, formulated by TobReg, addresses growing concern about the loss of life, injury and property damage due to fires ignited by combusted tobacco products, and particularly by cigarettes. Its purposes are to provide guidance to WHO and its Member States about the risks related to fires caused by cigarettes and the measures that can be taken to mitigate those risks. The note also gives guidance to researchers and research agencies interested in facilitating better understanding of fire-related deaths and injuries associated with cigarettes.

2.2 Background and history

Cigarettes and other lighted tobacco products are a leading cause of fire-related deaths and injuries in countries throughout the world. In 2003, 25 600 cigarette-induced fires occurred in North America, resulting in an estimated 760 deaths, 1520 injuries and US$ 481 million in direct property damage (Hall, 2006). A survey in 14 Member States of the European Union and Norway in 2005–2006 showed that in the countries that responded there were about 11 000 cigarette-caused fires, 520 deaths, 1600 injuries and € 13 million material damages each year (J. Vogelgesang, unpublished data, 2006). Extrapolation to the 25 countries of the European Union and Norway indicates that 12 900 fires, 650 deaths, 2400 injuries and € 48 million in material damages could be prevented. In New South Wales, Australia, 32 of 233 fire deaths were directly attributed to cigarettes, with an additional 63 possibly due to cigarettes. Annually, cigarettes cause 4574 fires across Australia and may be responsible for up to 78 894 more. Australia's National Coroners Information system attributed 67 of 678 fire deaths in the period 2000–2005 directly to cigarettes. Further, an estimated 7% of all bush-fires in Australia are attributable to discarded cigarettes. Cigarette-related fires cost Australia AUS$ 80.6 million in 1998, which were projected to AUS$ 124 million in 2006 terms on the basis of the Consumer Price Index. In Canada, 3000 fires are started by smoking articles annually, which are responsible for 70 fatalities, 300 injuries and CDN$ 40 million in property damage (D. Choinière, unpublished data, 2006).

A significant proportion of the deaths, injuries and property destruction could be prevented by the introduction of fire-safety standards for cigarettes, which would mean that they were either self-extinguishing, i.e. would go out when not being puffed, or had altered smouldering characteristics, making a fire less likely. Cigarettes designed to comply with these standards are commonly referred to as 'fire-safe' or 'reduced ignition propensity' cigarettes.

In the USA, Congress enacted the Cigarette Safety Act of 1984 that required the creation of a technical study group within the Consumer Protection Agency to determine the technical, economic and commercial feasibility of designing a cigarette with minimum ignition propensity and to report its findings to Congress. In its final report, released in 1987, the group concluded that the goal was technically feasible and might be economically feasible. Congress subsequently passed the Fire Safe Cigarette Act of 1990, which charged the National Institute of Standards and Technology to design a standard method for determining the ignition propensity of cigarettes. It did not, however, give any government agency the authority to regulate the reduction of the propensity of cigarettes to cause fires.

The first performance standard is known as the 'mock-up furniture ignition test method', in which fabric and foam are used to simulate a piece of furniture and in which a burning cigarette is tested to determine whether it transfers enough heat to ignite these materials. The second performance standard is known as the 'cigarette extinction method', in which a set number of layers of filter paper are used to absorb heat, and a cigarette is tested to determine whether it generates enough heat to continue to burn on the paper. The cigarette extinction method is readily reproducible and takes less time per test than the mock-up furniture ignition test method. The cigarette extinction method was therefore refined and published by the American Society for Testing and Materials (2004) as the standard test method for measuring the ignition strength of cigarettes (ASTM E2187).

The tobacco industry claimed for years that cigarettes with reduced ignition propensity could not be made and even bribed fire service organizations to thwart the passage of laws. The tobacco industry itself, however, established that such cigarettes could be made and that their performance could be evaluated. More than 80 years of research by the industry and over 300 patents have addressed the design of 'fire-safe' cigarettes. The scientific basis is well advanced, and the tobacco industry and cigarette paper manufacturers continue their research and development.

Philip Morris began exploring the design of 'fire-safe' cigarettes in 1974. Both RJ Reynolds and Brown & Williamson have had extensive testing programmes since the late 1970s or early 1980s. Lorillard began testing its cigarettes for ignition propensity at least as early as 1980. RJ Reynolds identified means of changing the burning rate of cigarette paper, which affects ignition propensity and developed prototypes throughout the 1980s that successfully reduced ignition propensity, using cigarette papers produced by the Ecusta Paper Company. The factors identified by RJ Reynolds in 1979 are nearly identical to those identified by the technical study group a decade later in their final report, released in 1987, which concluded that a 'fire-safe' cigarette was technically feasible and might be economically feasible (Gunja et al., 2002).

An internal Philip Morris document stated that: "Historical treatments of ignition-propensity results show that time to ignition measurements are related to the maximum temperatures which smouldering cigarettes will achieve on a standard fabric. Further analysis indicates that these maximum temperatures scale with the mass burn rates of the isolated cigarettes. This reduces the design problem to that of achieving target MBR's [mass burn rates]." (Philip Morris, 1987).

The cigarette construction parameters identified by the technical study group and by industry as affecting the burning rate are wrapping paper properties, such as permeability, porosity, oxygen diffusion, chemical additives (e.g. citrate or chalk), cigarette circumference and tobacco density (Ohlemiller et al., 1993).

After the release of the technical study group report, RJ Reynolds refocused their research on 'fire-safe' cigarettes so as to target consumer acceptability. Other companies made similar progress in their 'fire-safe' cigarette projects. Brown & Williamson, Philip Morris and RJ Reynolds all obtained low-ignition paper from the Ecusta and Schweitzer paper companies from the early 1980s. In the 1980s, Brown & Williamson designed two cigarette prototypes with Schweitzer papers and tested a Kimberly-Clark banded cigarette paper. The method of banding most commonly used to reduce ignition propensity is that in which ultra-thin concentric bands are applied to traditional cigarette paper (Figure 2.1). These bands, sometimes compared with 'speed bumps', cause the cigarette to go out if it is not smoked, by restricting oxygen to the burning ember (Connolly et al., 2005). Banded cigarette paper is manufactured either in a water-based online process, referred to as 'paper banding', or by additional water- or solvent-based printing, referred to as 'print banding' (Thelen, 2006). In the early 1990s, Philip Morris designed a cigarette with bands that would extinguish the cigarette if it was not puffed. Banded cigarettes were tested as early as 1985, and in 2000 Philip Morris

Figure 2.1
Composition of a reduced ignition cigarette

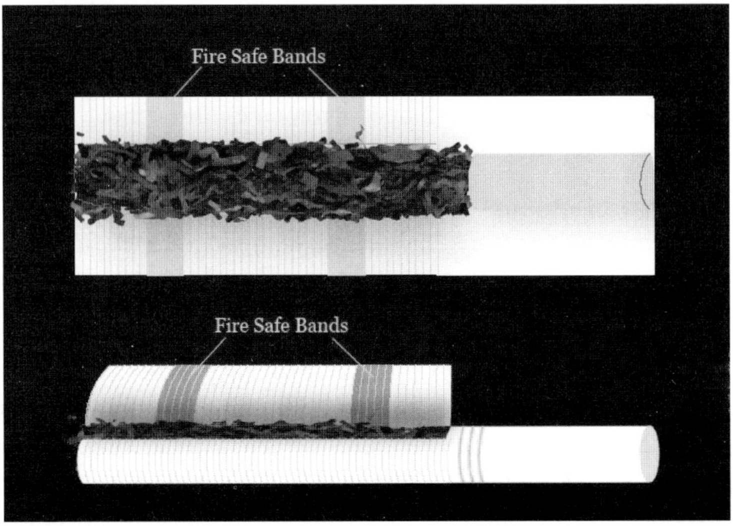

released a banded cigarette with a 'fire-safe paper select' wrapper in the Merit brand (Gunja et al., 2002). Internal industry testing demonstrated that the width and location of the bands can be used to control ignition propensity, wider bands and lower inter-band width being associated with the greatest reduction. Internal studies by Philip Morris showed that the technique used to place the paper bands is very precise.

2.3 Regulatory responses

The first law to regulate ignition propensity was passed by the State of New York, USA, which mandated that all cigarettes sold in the State had to have reduced ignition propensity. The New York Fire Safety Standards for Cigarettes (Part 429, Title 18 of the *Official Compilation of Codes, Rules, and Regulations of the State of New York*) came into force on 28 June 2004. Since then, Canada and 19 states of the USA have mandated reduced ignition performance standards for cigarettes. All existing fire safety standards for cigarettes are modelled after the New York standards and require that cigarettes be manufactured or sold to meet an ignition propensity performance standard that makes them significantly less likely to cause fires if left unattended. Recently, the Australian Government prescribed regulations mandating a safety standard for cigarettes, covering performance, testing, packaging and marking requirements for cigarettes manufactured or imported into Australia. The Trade Practices (Consumer Product Safety Standard) (Reduced Fire Risk Cigarettes) Regulations 2008 came into force on 23 September 2008. South Africa's Tobacco Products Control Act was amended on 23 February 2008 to include authority to set regulations mandating a standard on the ignition propensity of cigarettes. Other countries, including New Zealand and Member States of the European Union, are considering similar policies, and the European Commission is examining the feasibility of proposing a standard.

Both the Canadian and the New York State laws incorporate the ASTM standard test method in which a lit cigarette is placed on multiple layers of standard filter paper in a draft-free environment (Figure 2.2). The paper cannot ignite to smouldering and draws its heat from the cigarette. The persistence of burning is an indication of the energy available to ignite soft furnishings. Thus, the indicator is whether the cigarette burns to its full length. The standard adopted in these two jurisdictions requires that no more than 25% of 40 test cigarettes placed on a thickness of 10 layers of filter paper undergo full-length burning. The techniques used by manufacturers to meet the standard are generally unrestricted. In 2006, Standards Australia published a draft standard test method for determining the extinction propensity of cigarettes, which is also based on the ASTM test method.

The New York Fire Safety Standards for Cigarettes include provisions regarding the reporting and investigation of cigarette-caused fires, the testing and certification of cigarettes, package labelling requirements, tax stamps and enforcement. The fire services must report all suspected cigarette-related fires within 14 days of completing an investigation and must provide information on the brand and style, marking as compliant, and the location and manner of purchase of the cigarette. Cigarette manufacturers are responsible under the New York Standards for testing each of their brands and for providing written certification to the Office of Fire Prevention and Control and to the Attorney General. The Office of Fire Prevention and Control is required to test cigarettes suspected of igniting fires and to retest any cigarettes to which a manufacturer makes a change that is likely to alter its compliance. Tax stamps may not be affixed to cigarette packages in New York State unless the cigarettes have been certified as meeting the Standards (J. Mueller, unpublished data, 2006).

The New York Office of Fire Prevention and Control is authorized to examine books, papers, invoices and other records and to impose civil penalties and suspensions. Enforcement includes penalties for false certification and for sale of non-compliant cigarettes. Public health officers are authorized to impose penalties on retail dealers. Officers of the Office of Fire Prevention and Control and of the Taxation and Finance Office are authorized to seize cigarettes not marked as compliant, and the seized cigarettes are to be destroyed (J. Mueller, unpublished data, 2006). Tobacco companies are required to pay for testing and stamping in all states of the USA. The fees for

Figure 2.2

Standard method for testing the ignition propensity performance standard of cigarettes, in which a lit cigarette is placed on multiple layers of standard filter paper (A) in a draught-free environment (B)

A.

B.

certification range from US$ 100 to US$ 1000 per cigarette brand or brand family and could increase.

Canada adopted the same standard as New York State when it introduced regulations requiring all cigarettes manufactured in or imported into Canada as of 1 October 2005 to satisfy the reduced ignition propensity standard.

Figure 2.3
Cigarette ignition propensity of major brands in California, Massachusetts and New York, USA, and in Australia and Thailand

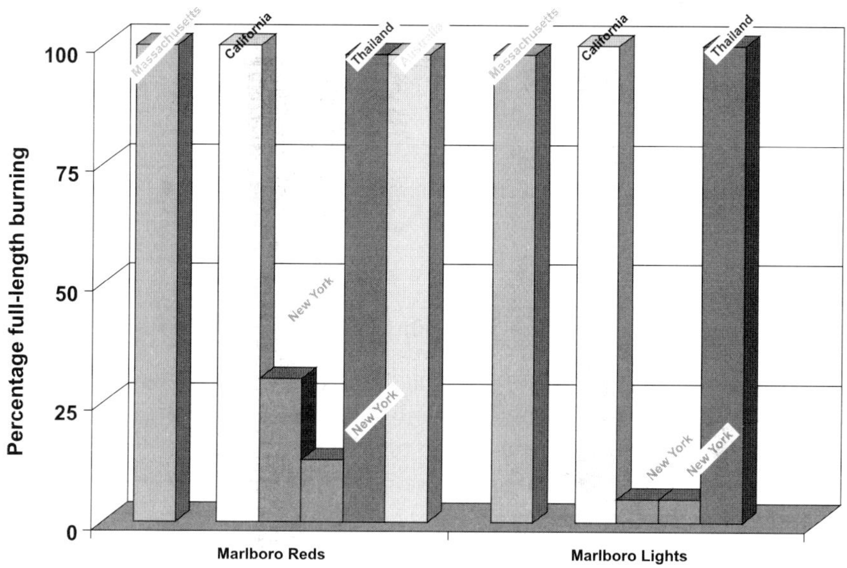

From Tobacco Control Research Program, Harvard School of Public Health

Canada's law applies at the manufacturing and importation levels, whereas the laws of states in the USA apply to the sale of cigarettes by retailers.

Approximately 1200 cigarette brands have been certified as compliant in New York State (New York Office of Fire Prevention and Control, 2008). Health Canada (2008a) has been sampling cigarettes from manufacturers and importers to determine whether they comply with the standard outlined in its regulations. As a result of 'fire-safe' cigarette laws, cigarette manufacturers in Canada have modified nearly all their brands (D. Choinière, unpublished data, 2006). The results of laboratory analyses of samples collected by Health Canada are posted on the Internet and updated periodically.

The ignition propensity of five brands of cigarettes sold in New York State after implementation of the Fire Safety Standards was tested with the cigarette extinction method; the full-length burning per brand was found to be 2.5–30.0% (Connolly et al., 2005). In contrast, the full-length burning of the same brands of cigarettes sold in Massachusetts and California, in New York before the law was passed, and in Australia and Thailand was 100% (Figure 2.3).

2.3.1 *Effectiveness of regulatory measures in populations*

Current regulatory measures are not expected to eliminate cigarette fire-related deaths but are intended to reduce such incidents over time, in the

Figure 2.4
Fires (left-hand panel) and deaths (right-hand panel) in fires due to smoking materials in New York State before and after application of fire-safety standards for cigarettes

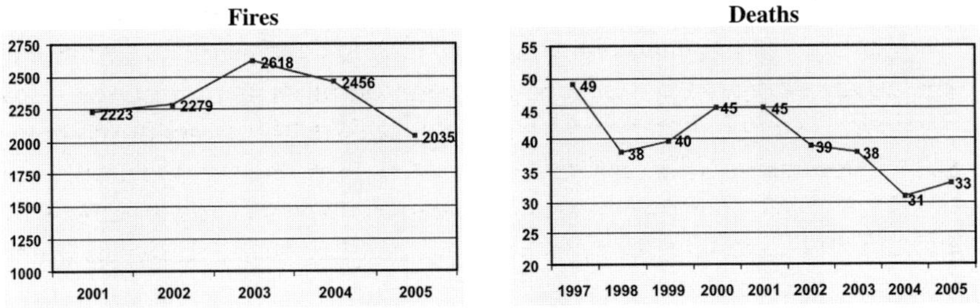

From Mueller (2006)

expectation that future changes in cigarette design will continue to do so. At the same time, governments must improve data collection on the frequency of cigarette-related fires and design regulations to address the problem. Preliminary data suggest that governments will benefit by implementing regulations to reduce ignition propensity.

Compliance with standards based on the ASTM method should reduce the numbers of cigarettes that cause smouldering combustion and consequently ignite fires. The effectiveness of the standard should be monitored continuously by recording the incidence of cigarette-caused fires and the associated deaths, injuries and costs. Fire reporting is fraught with problems of quality, and the methods should perhaps be reconsidered. Reliable information on reductions in cigarette consumption, improved mattress standards and changing fire prevention standards is also difficult to obtain.

Preliminary data on the population effect of cigarettes with reduced ignition propensity that are on the market suggests that the numbers of smoking-related fires and fire deaths declined in New York during the first 2 years after implementation of the Fire Safety Standards (Figure 2.4).

In Canada, the regulatory impact assessment of reduced ignition propensity cigarettes predicted that a fire safety standard for cigarettes would reduce cigarette-caused fires by 34–68% (Health Canada, 2008b). As more countries regulate ignition propensity, it will become easier to evaluate the efficacy of such cigarettes.

2.3.2 ***Regulatory considerations***

Emissions and biological assays

One concern is that changes in the design of cigarettes might lead to changes in exposure (by topography, burn temperature and emissions) that might make these products more harmful than they already are. The preliminary data available do not indicate that this is a serious problem.

In the USA, under the Fire-safe Cigarette Act of 1990, the National Institute of Standards and Technology compared the yields of tar, nicotine and carbon monoxide of cigarettes with reduced ignition propensity from the Tobacco Institute Testing Laboratory with the yields of the 14 best-selling commercial cigarette brands. No significant differences were found (Ohlemiller et al., 1993). Preliminary data from Canada indicated small changes in the delivery of carbonyls, tar, carbon monoxide and nicotine (M.J. Kaiserman, unpublished data, 2006).

Internal industry testing of banded cigarettes has also shown them to be substantially the same as regular cigarettes with regard to a number of toxicological end-points, including mutagenicity and the concentrations of toxic chemicals in emissions (Theophilus et al., 2007a,b). Philip Morris assessed some toxicological aspects of banded cigarettes and found "no significant differences between the two cigarettes based on the chemical and biological assays used". Similar findings have been published and presented at scientific meetings by other companies (Patskan et al., 2000; Appleton, Krauuter, Lauterbach, 2003; Misra et al., 2005), including RJ Reynolds, which has long opposed regulations on reduced ignition propensity, claiming increased risk (Theophilus et al., 2007a,b). The tobacco industry claims that there is an unintended additional risk of 'coal' (a lightweight, short-lived bit) dropping off from banded cigarettes and has stated that 11% of consumer complaints about banded cigarettes in the USA in 2000 were related to coal drop-off. A publication from British American Tobacco in 1988 concluded that paper permeability had no influence on coal retention in the range tested (Dittrich, 1988).

When 42 smokers in Ontario, Canada, were asked to compare smoking their own brands before and after implementation of the cigarette ignition propensity law in 2005, no significant differences in puffing behaviour or exhaled carbon monoxide were found (Hammond et al., 2007).

Sense of security

Cigarette manufacturers have asserted that smoking 'fire-safe' cigarettes could give a false sense of security, which might increase fire-risk behaviour. According to a survey conducted before the coming into force of the cigarette ignition propensity regulation in Canada, 12% of current smokers had smoked a cigarette in bed in the past week, and 17% reported that they left lit cigarettes burning unattended on a daily basis (M.J. Kaiserman, unpublished data, 2006). In another survey in Ontario, Canada, nearly one in four smokers left burning cigarettes unattended, and 15% had smoked in bed in the past

30 days, indicating a high frequency of fire-risk behaviour (O'Connor et al., 2007); early data from follow-up studies showed little change in such behaviour after 1 year (O'Connor, 2008).

Economic effects

Research by the Harvard School of Public Health, USA, showed no decline in cigarette sales in New York State after implementation of the Fire Safety Standards for Cigarettes, confirming the conclusions of the technical study group in 1987 (Connolly et al., 2005). The results of a nationwide survey in the USA also showed that the New York Fire Safety Standards appeared to have had no discernable effect on how smokers perceived the taste of their cigarettes, smoking behaviour or intention to quit, countering arguments made by cigarette manufacturers that the law would have a negative effect on consumer acceptability (O'Connor et al., 2006).

Health Canada (2008c) estimated that if the cost of complying with measures for cigarette ignition propensity was absorbed entirely by cigarette manufacturers, the companies' operating profits would be reduced by 2.9–5.9%; they could raise their prices to offset the increased costs. While some price increase is likely, the extent to which individual manufacturers would raise their prices is uncertain and would depend on competitive forces in the tobacco products market. Given the degree of competition in that market, it is unlikely that prices would rise by the full amount of the estimated cost increase (i.e. US$ 0.13–0.26 per carton).

Implementation and compliance

Approximately 1200 cigarette brands have been certified as compliant in New York State (New York Office of Fire Prevention and Control, 2008). Health Canada sampled products from manufacturers and importers to determine whether cigarettes in Canada comply with the standard outlined in its regulations and found that 'fire-safe' cigarette laws have resulted in modification of nearly all brands (D. Choinière, unpublished data, 2006). The results of laboratory analyses of samples collected by Health Canada are posted on the Internet and updated periodically.

New York State has taken the lead in validating industry reports by independent testing of cigarettes every 3 years and comparing industry reports with theirs. The cost of testing is US$ 400–700 per brand but should fall as more countries become involved. Other states in the USA rely on New York State and have not conducted testing. Efforts are being made in the USA to coordinate state reporting and testing. The National Institute of Standards and Technology gives technical support to laboratories, including a reference cigarette (http://firesafecigarettes.org/assets/files/niststandard.pdf) and small grants. There are currently six laboratories for testing. Brands that have been tested in New York State are listed online at http://www.dos.state.ny.us/fire/cigarette.htm.

The International Organization for Standardization (ISO) may adopt a standard that is identical to ASTM E2187, except in format. The alternative of drafting a guidance document that refers to the test method in the ASTM standard could take 1–2 years.

2.4 Research needs

2.4.1 *Techniques*

Research is needed to ensure the effectiveness of any regulations on reduced ignition propensity and to provide a basis for future policy. The main approach used to modify burning rate and consequently to reduce ignition propensity is to decrease oxygen diffusion by lowering the permeability of cigarette paper. The techniques used by manufacturers to achieve this should be monitored, including the effects of measured differences among brands in band placement and other design features. Some researchers are using reverse engineering of products to examine their banding characteristics, such as the presence, number, width and spacing; filter ventilation and pressure drop; paper porosity and citrate content; tobacco weight and density and cigarette circumference.

Cigarette companies and paper manufacturers are conducting research in industry-based research and development and programmes to follow up the achievements of the National Institute of Standards and Technology and the New York State standards. Further research and reviews of the scientific literature, industry documents and other sources are important for monitoring industry findings on cigarette ignition propensity and performance.

Some of the patented designs for reducing ignition propensity are paper with very low porosity and added perforations, addition of fire retardant to the centre of the tobacco rod, cellulose bands on paper, application of chemicals outside the paper and addition of intumescent powder to the tobacco column. The last reduces the ignition propensity of tobacco by decreasing its density during heating (Stevenson, Graham, 1988).

2.4.2 *Testing methods*

Methods are needed for testing ignition propensity performance, such as thermal imaging. Their potential use in effective, efficient testing might be included in regulations.

2.4.3 *Surveillance and monitoring*

Fires and subsequent losses due to cigarettes should be surveyed and monitored in order to judge the success of policies and to determine whether the standards should be adopted. The New York State measures appear to be reducing the number of deaths due to cigarette-related fires, but high-quality fire incidence reporting and data are needed. The data must be accurate and timely and based on large enough numbers so that statistical significance can be assessed. The outcomes that should be monitored are the incidence of fires and the associated losses, injuries and deaths (D. Hemenway, unpublished data, 2006). The capacity of investigators at the scene of a fire must be improved to allow them to ascertain whether the fire was started by a cigarette and what other factors contributed to the severity of the fire.

The impact of measures to reduce ignition propensity should be followed up over time, on the basis of criteria such as population health and the optimum percentage reduction in fires.

The Fire Safety Standards for Cigarettes in New York State contain a provision that allows the Office of Fire Prevention and Control to review information on the incidence of fires in the light of technological changes after a period of 3–4 years and to consider revising the Standards. Other jurisdictions might wish to adopt a similar approach.

2.4.4 *Exposure to emissions and smoking behaviour*

Further assessment of exposure to emissions and changes in smoking behaviour should include consideration of product design, emissions of tar, nicotine and carbon monoxide, puffing behaviour, filter analyses and biomarkers of exposure.

Population surveys with baseline and follow-up measures, such as those being conducted by the Roswell Park Cancer Institute and the Harvard School of Public Health in the USA, should include questions such as "Has a cigarette ever started a fire in your home?", "How often does your cigarette go out on its own?" and "How often does the lit end or ash fall off your cigarette on its own?". Such analyses should also assess the prevalence of fire-risk events in the 30 days before the survey. Information on fire-risk behaviour should include instances of burnt clothes, burnt furniture, burning cigarettes left unattended, dozing off and falling asleep while smoking and smoking in bed.

The tobacco industry has claimed that some methods of reducing the ignition propensity of cigarettes could increase the toxicity by increasing smoke delivery. There is no evidence that cigarettes with reduced ignition propensity increase the risk for disease from smoking. Cigarette smoke is a highly complex mixture, containing over 4000 chemicals, and the links between these chemicals and the toxicity of the smoke are not well defined. It is probable that the smoke from cigarettes with reduced ignition propensity is just as toxic as that of unmodified cigarettes.

2.5 Findings and recommendations

Fires and fire deaths are caused by cigarettes.

Fires due to cigarettes and the related deaths are a major global public health problem. Although the number of deaths is far lower than that caused by smoking (900 deaths in the USA from fires and 460 000 from smoking), it is still high, and policies are needed to reduce the number.

Cigarettes with reduced ignition propensity should be mandatory.

As cigarettes are the principal cause of residential fires and related deaths and techniques exist to reduce ignition propensity and thus the likelihood of a cigarette igniting a fire, Member States should require reduced ignition propensity cigarettes, in line with the standard of the National Institute of Standards and Technology or any other that has been shown to be effective. Countries and jurisdictions within countries should retain the right to alter the standard on the basis of population-based data on its effectiveness.

While Canada has adopted measures for reducing ignition propensity within public health laws, Australia and most states of the USA implement such measures within laws on fire safety. In the European Union, such measures are being considered in the framework of consumer protection legislation.

The products covered by these measures should include not only cigarettes but also cigars and any other combusted tobacco product if evidence indicates that their ignition strength should be regulated. Considerations could include state or national monetary appropriations, identification of parties or agencies responsible for certification, the delay required for re-certification, identification of the agency responsible for auditing brands, the scope and frequency of audits, evaluation of the population impact, fees and fines, advisory committees and whether the regulations can be superseded by federal law. Countries should require tobacco manufacturers to test ignition strength, report the results to the responsible authority and pay a fee for implementation of the measures.

Independent laboratory testing capacity is currently minimal. It could be increased if countries adopted measures that require testing of ignition propensity by independent laboratories accredited according to ISO standard 17025, *General requirements for the competence of calibration and testing laboratories*. Industry-generated results should be validated by independent tests.

Legislation and regulatory measures should give the responsible authority the means to take appropriate legal action to ensure compliance with the standard.

No risk claims are permissible.

As reduced ignition propensity cigarettes must be made available to an entire population, manufacturers canot be allowed to claim that they reduce the risk of fire. If they did, consumers might conclude that they reduced overall health risks. Public education campaigns are needed as part of any reduced ignition propensity programme, to inform consumers that all cigarettes are lethal and that smokers should quit. Such programmes should also include education campaigns to teach the public how to prevent fires.

The effectiveness of reduced ignition propensity cigarettes must be monitored.

Adequate, appropriate monitoring, reporting and archiving are needed to record the effectiveness of techniques for reducing ignition propensity for decreasing deaths, injuries and property damage due to cigarette-induced fires. Such assessments will increase public assurance and lead to more effective means of diminishing the needless losses that occur as a result of cigarette-ignited fires.

International collaboration is necessary.

International collaboration between interested institutions and authorities is needed to coordinate education, advocacy, testing, research and evaluation of reduced ignition propensity cigarettes and for implementation of such measures in all WHO regions.

References

American Society for Testing and Materials International (2004) *ASTM E2187-04. Standard test method for measuring the ignition strength of cigarettes.* West Conshohocken, Pennsylvania, ASTM International.

Appleton S, Krauuter GR, Lauterbach JH (2003) Toxicological evaluation of a new cigarette paper designed for lowered ignition propensity. In: *57th Tobacco Science Research Conference, Program Booklet and Abstracts*, No. 16, p. 27. Raleigh, North Carolina, North Carolina State University, Tobacco Literature Service.

Connolly GN et al. (2005) Effect of the New York State cigarette fire safety standard on ignition propensity, smoke constituents, and the consumer market. *Tobacco Control*, 14:321–327.

Dittrich DJ (1988) *Influence of cigarette design on coal retention.* Southampton, BAT (UK and Export) Ltd. Research and Development Centre (Report No. RD. 2125).

Gunja M et al. (2002) The case for fire cigarettes made through industry documents. *Tobacco Control*, 11:346–353.

Hall J (2006) *The smoking-material fire problem.* Quincy, Massachusetts, National Fire Protection Association, Fire Analysis and Research Division.

Hammond D et al. (2007) The impact of Canada's lowered ignition propensity regulations on smoking behaviour and consumer perceptions. In: *Society for Research on Nicotine and Tobacco 13th Annual Meeting Proceedings.* Available at: http://www.srnt.org/meeting/2007/pdf/onsite/2007srntabstracts-final.pdf. Accessed 23 October 2008.

Health Canada (2008a) Laboratory analysis of cigarette for ignition propensity. http://www.hc-sc.gc.ca/hl-vs/tobac-tabac/legislation/reg/ignition-alllumage/index_e.html. Accessed 23 October 2008.

Health Canada (2008b) Industrial Economics, Inc. (2004) *Economic evaluation of Health Canada's regulatory proposal for reducing fire risks from cigarettes.* Prepared for Health Canada. Available at: http://www.hc-sc.gc.ca/hl-vs/pubs/tobac-tabac/evaluation-risks-risques/benefits-avantages5-eng.php#3. Accessed 23 October 2008.

Health Canada (2008c) Industrial Economics, Inc. (2004) *Economic evaluation of Health Canada's regulatory proposal for reducing fire risks From cigarettes.* Prepared for Health Canada. Available at: http://www.hc-sc.gc.ca/hl-vs/pubs/tobac-tabac/evaluation-risks-risques/ecoimpacts-impactseco7-eng.php#2. Accessed 23 October 2008.

Mueller J (2006) Cigarette fire safety standards. In: *Second international conference on fire safer cigarettes.* Boston, Massachsetts, Harvard School of Public Health.

Misra M et al. (2005) Toxicological evaluation of a cigarette paper with reduced ignition propensity: in vitro and in vivo tests. *Toxicologist*, 84 (Suppl. 1):1186.

New York Office of Fire Prevention and Control (2008) *List of cigarettes certified by manufacturers.* Available at: http://www.dos.state.ny.us/fire/pdfs/cigaretteweblist.pdf. Accessed 23 October 2008.

O'Connor RJ (2008) New research on fire safe cigarettes. In: *Third international conference on fire 'safer' cigarettes.* Norwood, Massachusetts, National Fire Protection Association and Harvard School of Public Health.

O'Connor RJ et al. (2006) Smokers' reactions to reduced ignition propensity cigarettes. *Tobacco Control*, 15:45–49.

O'Connor RJ et al. (2007) Prevalence of behaviors related to cigarette-caused fires: a survey of Ontario smokers. *Injury Prevention*, 13:237–242.

Ohlemiller TJ et al. (1993) *Test methods for quantifying the propensity of cigarettes to ignite soft furnishings.* Gaithersburg, Pennsylvania, Technology Administration, National Institute of Standards and Technology, Department of Commerce (NIST Special Publication 851).

Patskan G et al. (2000) Toxicological characterization of a novel cigarette paper. *Toxicologist*, 54:398.

Philip Morris (1987) *Project Tomorrow—status and plans*, 25 November 1987. Richmond, Virginia (Bates No. 1002816087-6088).

Stevenson WW, Graham J (1988) *Reduced ignition propensity smoking article.* United States Patent No. 4 776 355, 11 October 1988.

Thelen VK (2006) *Fire-safe cigarettes: an overview. Top paper: performance by understanding*. Traun, Delfort Group. Available at: http://www.delfortgroup.com/toppaper/archive/toppaper_0206.pdf.

Theophilus EH et al. (2007a) Toxicological evaluation of cigarettes with two banded cigarette paper technologies. *Experimental Toxicology and Pathology*, 59:17–27.

Theophilus EH et al. (2007b) Comparative 13-week cigarette smoke inhalation study in Sprague-Dawley rats: evaluation of cigarettes with two banded cigarette paper technologies. *Food Chemistry and Toxicology*, 45:1076–1090.

Annex 2.1 **Model legislation**

THE CIGARETTE FIRE SAFETY STANDARD AND FIREFIGHTER PROTECTION ACT

1. **Title**. This Act shall be known and may be cited as the 'Fire Safety Standard and Firefighter Protection Act'.

2. **Findings**.

   The Legislature finds and declares that:

   a. Cigarettes are the leading cause of fire deaths in this State and the nation;

   b. Each year in the United States, 700–900 persons are killed due to cigarette fires and 3000 are injured in fires ignited by cigarettes, while in this State [ ] residential fires and [ ] fatalities were attributable to cigarettes in years [_ _ _ _-2005];

   c. A high proportion of the victims of cigarette fires are non-smokers, including senior citizens and young children;

   d. Cigarette-caused fires result in billions of dollars of property losses and damages in the United States and millions of dollars in this State;

   e. Cigarette fires unnecessarily jeopardize firefighters and result in avoidable emergency response costs for municipalities;

   f. In 2004, New York State implemented a cigarette fire safety regulation requiring cigarettes sold in that State to meet a fire safety performance standard; in 2005, Vermont and California enacted cigarette fire safety laws directly incorporating New York's regulation into statute; and, in 2006, Illinois, New Hampshire and Massachusetts joined these states in enacting such laws.

   g. In 2005, Canada implemented the New York State fire safety standard contained in the other state laws, becoming the first nation to have a cigarette fire safety standard;

   h. New York State's cigarette fire safety standard is based upon decades of research by the National Institute of Standards and Technology, Congressional research groups, and private industry;

   i. This cigarette fire safety standard minimizes costs to the State and minimally burdens cigarette manufacturers, distributors and retail sellers, and, therefore, should become law in this State; and

j. It is therefore fitting and proper for this State to adopt the cigarette fire safety standard that is in effect in New York State to reduce the likelihood that cigarettes will cause fires and result in deaths, injuries and property damages.

3. **Definitions.** For the purposes of this Act:

(a) 'Agent' shall mean any person authorized by the [State entity that administers cigarette tax stamps] to purchase and affix stamps on packages of cigarettes.

(b) 'Cigarette' shall mean:

(1) any roll for smoking, whether made wholly or in part of tobacco or any other substance, irrespective of size or shape, and whether or not such tobacco or substance is flavored, adulterated or mixed with any other ingredient, the wrapper or cover of which is made of paper or any other substance or material, other than leaf tobacco; or

(2) any roll for smoking wrapped in any substance containing tobacco which, because of its appearance, the type of tobacco used in the filler, or its packaging and labeling, is likely to be offered to, or purchased by, consumers as a cigarette as described in subparagraph 1 above.

(c) 'Director' shall mean the Director of the [State entity responsible for administering the provisions of this Act].

(d) 'Manufacturer' shall mean:

(1) any entity which manufactures or otherwise produces cigarettes or causes cigarettes to be manufactured or produced anywhere that such manufacturer intends to be sold in this State, including cigarettes intended to be sold in the United States through an importer; or

(2) the first purchaser anywhere that intends to resell in the United States cigarettes manufactured anywhere that the original manufacturer or maker does not intend to be sold in the United States; or

(3) any entity that becomes a successor of an entity described in paragraph (1) or (2) of this subsection.

(e) 'Quality control and quality assurance program' shall mean the laboratory procedures implemented to ensure that operator bias, systematic and nonsystematic methodological errors, and equipment-related problems do not affect the results of the testing. Such a program ensures that the testing repeatability remains within the required repeatability values stated in paragraph (6) of subsection (a) of Section 4 of this Act for all test trials used to certify cigarettes in accordance with this Act.

(f) 'Repeatability' shall mean the range of values within which the repeat results of cigarette test trials from a single laboratory will fall 95 percent of the time.

(g) 'Retail dealer' shall mean any person, other than a manufacturer or wholesale dealer, engaged in selling cigarettes or tobacco products.

(h) 'Sale' shall mean any transfer of title or possession or both, exchange or barter, conditional or otherwise, in any manner or by any means whatever or any agreement therefor. In addition to cash and credit sales, the giving of cigarettes as samples, prizes or gifts, and the exchanging of cigarettes for any consideration other than money, are considered sales.

(i) 'Sell' shall mean to sell, or to offer or agree to do the same.

(j) 'Wholesale dealer' shall mean any person other than a manufacturer who sells cigarettes or tobacco products to retail dealers or other persons for purposes of resale, and any person who owns, operates or maintains one or more cigarette or tobacco product vending machines in, at or upon premises owned or occupied by any other person.

4. **Test Method and Performance Standard.**

(a) Except as provided in subsection (g) of this section, no cigarettes may be sold or offered for sale in this State or offered for sale or sold to persons located in this State unless the cigarettes have been tested in accordance with the test method and meet the performance standard specified in this section, a written certification has been filed by the manufacturer with the [State entity responsible for administering the provisions of this Act] in accordance with section 5 of this Act, and the cigarettes have been marked in accordance with section 6 of this Act.

(1) Testing of cigarettes shall be conducted in accordance with the American Society of Testing and Materials ('ASTM') standard E2187-04, "Standard Test Method for Measuring the Ignition Strength of Cigarettes."

(2) Testing shall be conducted on 10 layers of filter paper.

(3) No more than 25 percent of the cigarettes tested in a test trial in accordance with this section shall exhibit full-length burns. Forty replicate tests shall comprise a complete test trial for each cigarette tested.

(4) The performance standard required by this section shall only be applied to a complete test trial.

(5) Written certifications shall be based upon testing conducted by a laboratory that has been accredited pursuant to standard ISO/IEC 17025 of the International Organization for Standardization ('ISO'), or other comparable accreditation standard required by the [State entity responsible for administering the provisions of this Act].

(6) Laboratories conducting testing in accordance with this section shall implement a quality control and quality assurance program that includes a procedure that will determine the repeatability of the testing results. The repeatability value shall be no greater than 0.19.

(7) This section does not require additional testing if cigarettes are tested consistent with this Act for any other purpose.

(8) Testing performed or sponsored by the [State entity responsible for administering the provisions of this Act] to determine a cigarette's compliance with the performance standard required shall be conducted in accordance with this section.

(b) Each cigarette listed in a certification submitted pursuant to section 5 of this Act that uses lowered permeability bands in the cigarette paper to achieve compliance with the performance standard set forth in this section shall have at least two nominally identical bands on the paper surrounding the tobacco column. At least one complete band shall be located at least 15 millimeters from the lighting end of the cigarette. For cigarettes on which the bands are positioned by design, there shall be at least two bands fully located at least 15 millimeters from the lighting end and 10 millimeters from the filter end of the tobacco column, or 10 millimeters from the labeled end of the tobacco column for non-filtered cigarettes.

(c) A manufacturer of a cigarette that the [State entity responsible for administering the provisions of this Act] determines cannot be tested in accordance with the test method prescribed in paragraph (1) of subsection (a) of this section shall propose a test method and performance standard for the cigarette to the [State entity responsible for administering the provisions of this Act]. Upon approval of the proposed test method and a determination by the [State entity responsible for administering the provisions of this Act] that the performance standard proposed by the manufacturer is equivalent to the performance standard prescribed in subsection (a) (3) of this section, the manufacturer may employ such test method and performance standard to certify such cigarette pursuant to section 5 of this Act. If the [State entity responsible for administering the provisions of this Act] determines that another state has enacted reduced cigarette ignition propensity standards that include a test method and performance standard that are the same as those contained in this Act, and the [State entity responsible for administering the provisions of this Act] finds that the officials responsible for implementing those requirements have approved the proposed alternative test method and performance standard for a particular cigarette proposed by a manufacturer as meeting the fire safety standards of that state's law or regulation under a legal provision comparable to this section, then the [State entity responsible for administering the provisions of this Act] shall authorize that manufacturer to employ the alternative test method and performance standard to certify that cigarette for sale in this State, unless the [State entity responsible for administering the provisions of this Act] demonstrates a reasonable basis why the alternative test should not be accepted under this Act. All other applicable requirements of this section shall apply to the manufacturer.

(d) Each manufacturer shall maintain copies of the reports of all tests conducted on all cigarettes offered for sale for a period of three years, and shall make copies of these reports available to the [State entity responsible for administering the provisions of this Act] and the Attorney General upon written request. Any manufacturer who fails to make copies of these reports available within sixty days of receiving a written request shall be subject to a civil penalty not to exceed $10,000 for each day after the sixtieth day that the manufacturer does not make such copies available.

(e) The [State entity responsible for administering the provisions of this Act] may adopt a subsequent ASTM Standard Test Method for measuring the Ignition Strength of Cigarettes upon a finding that such subsequent method does not result in a change in the percentage of full-length burns exhibited by any tested cigarette when compared to the percentage of full-length burns the same cigarette would exhibit when tested in accordance with ASTM Standard E2187-04 and the performance standard in subsection (a)(3) of this section.

(f) The [State entity responsible for administering the provisions of this Act] shall review the effectiveness of this section and report every three years to the Legislature [the State entity's] findings and, if appropriate, recommendations for legislation to improve the effectiveness of this Act. The report and legislative recommendations shall be submitted no later than June thirtieth following the conclusion of each three-year period.

(g) The requirements of subsection (a) of this section shall not prohibit:

(1) wholesale or retail dealers from selling their existing inventory of cigarettes on or after the effective date of this Act if the wholesale or retailer dealer can establish that State tax stamps were affixed to the cigarettes prior to the effective date and the wholesale or retailer dealer can establish that the inventory was purchased prior to the effective date in comparable quantity to the inventory purchased during the same period of the prior year; or

(2) the sale of cigarettes solely for the purpose of consumer testing. For purposes of this subsection, the term 'consumer testing' shall mean an assessment of cigarettes that is conducted by a manufacturer (or under the control and direction of a manufacturer), for the purpose of evaluating consumer acceptance of such cigarettes, utilizing only the quantity of cigarettes that is reasonably necessary for such assessment, and in a controlled setting where the cigarettes are either consumed on-site or returned to the testing administrators at the conclusion of the testing.

(h) This Act shall be implemented in accordance with the implementation and substance of the New York Fire Safety Standards for Cigarettes.

5. **Certification and Product Change**

(a) Each manufacturer shall submit [to the State entity responsible for administering the provisions of this Act] a written certification attesting that:

(1) each cigarette listed in the certification has been tested in accordance with section 4 of this Act; and

(2) each cigarette listed in the certification meets the performance standard set forth in section 4.

(b) Each cigarette listed in the certification shall be described with the following information:

(1) brand, or trade name on the package;

(2) style, such as light or ultra light;

(3) length in millimeters;

(4) circumference in millimeters;

(5) flavor, such as menthol or chocolate, if applicable;

(6) filter or non-filter;

(7) package description, such as soft pack or box;

(8) marking pursuant to section 6 of this Act;

(9) the name, address and telephone number of the laboratory, if different than the manufacturer that conducted the test; and

(10) the date that the testing occurred.

(c) The certifications shall be made available to the Attorney General for purposes consistent with this Act and the [State entity responsible for administering the State cigarette tax act] for the purposes of ensuring compliance with this section.

(d) Each cigarette certified under this section shall be re-certified every three years.

(e) For each cigarette listed in a certification, a manufacturer shall pay to the [State entity responsible for administering the provisions of this Act] a $250 fee. The [State entity responsible for administering the provisions of this Act] is authorized to annually adjust this fee to ensure it defrays the actual costs of the processing, testing, enforcement and oversight activities required by this Act.

(f) There is established in the [State treasury] a separate, nonlapsing fund to be known as the 'Fire Safety Standard and Firefighter Protection Act Enforcement Fund'. The fund shall consist of all certification fees submitted by manufacturers, and shall, in addition to any other monies made available for such purpose, be available to the [State entity responsible for administering the provisions of this Act] solely to support processing, testing, enforcement and oversight activities under this Act.

(g) If a manufacturer has certified a cigarette pursuant to this section, and thereafter makes any change to such cigarette that is likely to alter its compliance with the reduced cigarette ignition propensity standards required by this Act, that cigarette shall not be sold or offered for sale in this State until the manufacturer retests the cigarette in accordance with the testing standards set forth in section 4 of this Act and maintains records of that retesting as required by section 4 of this Act. Any altered cigarette which does not meet the performance standard set forth in Section 4 of this Act may not be sold in this State.

6. **Marking of Cigarette Packaging**

(a) Cigarettes that are certified by a manufacturer in accordance with section 5 of this Act shall be marked to indicate compliance with the requirements of section 4 of this Act. The marking shall be in eight point type or larger and consist of:

(1) Modification of the product UPC Code to include a visible mark printed at or around the area of the UPC Code. The mark may consist of alphanumeric or symbolic characters permanently stamped, engraved, embossed or printed in conjunction with the UPC; or

(2) Any visible combination of alphanumeric or symbolic characters permanently stamped, engraved or embossed upon the cigarette package or cellophane wrap; or

(3) Printed, stamped, engraved or embossed text that indicates that the cigarettes meet the standards of this Act.

(b) A manufacturer shall use only one marking, and shall apply this marking uniformly for all packages, including but not limited to packs, cartons, and cases, and brands marketed by that manufacturer.

(c) The [State entity responsible for administering the provisions of this Act] shall be notified as to the marking that is selected.

(d) to the certification of any cigarette, a manufacturer shall present its proposed marking to the [State entity responsible for administering the provisions of this Act] for approval. Upon receipt of the request, the [State entity responsible for administering the provisions of this Act] shall approve or disapprove the marking offered, except that the [State entity responsible for administering the provisions of this Act] shall approve:

(1) any marking in use and approved for sale in New York pursuant to the New York Fire Safety Standards for Cigarettes, or

(2) the letters 'FSC', which signifies Fire Standards Compliant appearing in 8 point type or larger and be permanently printed, stamped, engraved or embossed on the package at or near the UPC code.

Proposed markings shall be deemed approved if the [State entity responsible for administering the provisions of this Act] fails to act within 10 business days of receiving a request for approval.

(e) No manufacturer shall modify its approved marking unless the modification has been approved by the [State entity responsible for administering the provisions of this Act] in accordance with this section.

(f) Manufacturers certifying cigarettes in accordance with section 5 of this Act shall provide a copy of the certifications to all wholesale dealers and agents to which they sell cigarettes, and shall also provide sufficient copies of an illustration of the package marking utilized by the manufacturer pursuant to this section for each retail dealer to which the wholesale dealers or agents sell cigarettes. Wholesale dealers and agents shall provide a copy of these package markings received from manufacturers to all retail dealers to which they sell cigarettes. Wholesale dealers, agents and retail dealers shall permit the [State entity responsible for administering the provisions of this Act], the [State entity responsible for administering the provisions of the State cigarette tax act], the Attorney General, and their employees to inspect markings of cigarette packaging marked in accordance with this section.

7. **Penalties.**

(a) A manufacturer, wholesale dealer, agent or any other person or entity who knowingly sells or offers to sell cigarettes, other than through retail sale, in violation of section 4 of this Act, shall be subject to a civil penalty not to exceed one hundred ($100) dollars for each pack of such cigarettes sold or offered for sale provided that in no case shall the penalty against any such person or entity exceed one hundred thousand ($100,000) dollars during any thirty-day period.

(b) A retail dealer who knowingly sells or offers to sell cigarettes in violation of section 4 of this Act shall be subject to a civil penalty not to exceed one hundred ($100) dollars for each pack of such cigarettes sold or offered for sale, provided that in no case shall the penalty against any retail dealer exceed twenty-five thousand ($25,000) dollars for sales or offers to sell during any thirty-day period.

(c) In addition to any penalty prescribed by law, any corporation, partnership, sole proprietor, limited partnership or association engaged in the manufacture of cigarettes that knowingly makes a false certification pursuant to section 5 of this Act shall be subject to a civil penalty of at least seventy-five thousand ($75,000) dollars and not to exceed two-hundred fifty thousand ($250,000) dollars for each such false certification.

(d) Any person violating any other provision in this Act shall be subject to a civil penalty for a first offense not to exceed one thousand ($1,000) dollars, and for a subsequent offense subject to a civil penalty not to exceed five thousand ($5,000) dollars for each such violation.

(e) Any cigarettes that have been sold or offered for sale that do not comply with the performance standard required by section 4 of this Act shall be subject to forfeiture [under the pertinent provision of State law having to do with forfeiture of contraband]. Cigarettes forfeited pursuant to this section shall be destroyed; provided, however, that prior to the destruction of any cigarette forfeited pursuant to these provisions, the true holder of the trademark rights in the cigarette brand shall be permitted to inspect the cigarette.

(f) In addition to any other remedy provided by law, the [State entity responsible for administering the provisions of this Act] or Attorney General may file an action in [name of court] for a violation of this Act, including petitioning for injunctive relief or to recover any costs or damages suffered by the State because of a violation of this Act, including enforcement costs relating to the specific violation and attorney's fees. Each violation of this Act or of rules or regulations adopted under this Act constitutes a separate civil violation for which the [State entity responsible for administering the provisions of this Act] or Attorney General may obtain relief.

(g) Whenever any law enforcement personnel or duly authorized representative of the [State entity responsible for administering the provisions of this Act] shall discover any cigarettes that have not been marked in the manner required by section 6 of this Act, such personnel is hereby authorized and empowered to seize and take possession of such cigarettes. Such cigarettes shall be turned over to the [department of taxation and finance], and shall be forfeited to the State. Cigarettes seized pursuant to this section shall be destroyed; provided, however, that prior to the destruction of any cigarette seized pursuant to these provisions, the true holder of the trademark rights in the cigarette brand shall be permitted to inspect the cigarette.

8. **Implementation.**

(a) The [State entity responsible for administering the provisions of this Act] may promulgate rules and regulations, pursuant to the [State administrative procedures act], necessary to effectuate the purposes of this Act.

(b) The [State entity responsible for administration of the State cigarette tax act] in the regular course of conducting inspections of wholesale dealers, agents and retail dealers, as authorized under the [State cigarette tax act] may inspect such cigarettes to determine if the cigarettes are marked as required by section 6 of this Act. If the cigarettes are not marked as required, the [State entity responsible for administration of the State cigarette tax act] shall notify the [State entity responsible for administering the provisions of this Act].

9. **Inspection.** To enforce the provisions of this Act, the Attorney General, the [State department of taxation and finance] and the [State entity responsible for administering the provisions of this Act], their duly authorized representatives and other law enforcement personnel are hereby authorized to examine the books, papers, invoices and other records of any person in possession, control or occupancy of any premises where cigarettes are placed, stored, sold or offered for sale, as well as the stock of cigarettes on the premises. Every person in the possession, control or occupancy of any premises where cigarettes are placed, sold or offered for sale, is hereby directed and required to give the Attorney General, the [State department of taxation and finance] and the [State entity responsible for administering the provisions of this Act], their duly authorized representatives and other law enforcement personnel the means, facilities and opportunity for the examinations authorized by this section.

10. **Cigarette Fire Safety Standard and Firefighter Protection Act Fund.** There is hereby established in the State Treasury a special fund to be known as the 'Cigarette Fire Safety Standard and Firefighter Protection Act Fund'. The fund shall consist of all monies recovered as penalties under section 7 of this Act. The monies shall be deposited to the credit of the fund and shall, in addition to any other monies made available for such purpose, be made available to the State entity responsible for administering the provisions of this Act to support fire safety and prevention programs.

11. **Sale Outside of [State name].** Nothing in this Act shall be construed to prohibit any person or entity from manufacturing or selling cigarettes that do not meet the requirements of section 4 of this Act if the cigarettes are or will be stamped for sale in another state or are packaged for sale outside the United States and that person or entity has taken reasonable steps to ensure that such cigarettes will not be sold or offered for sale to persons located in this State.

12. **Preemption.** This Act shall be repealed if a federal reduced cigarette ignition propensity standard that preempts this Act is adopted and becomes effective.

13. **Effective Date.** This Act shall take effect on the first day of the thirteenth month after enactment.

Hyperlink to New York State Regulations:
http://www.dos.state.ny.us/fire/amendedcigaretterule.htm

Hyperlink to Canada Cigarette Ignition Propensity Regulations:
http://canadagazette.gc.ca/partII/2005/20050629/html/sor178-e.html

3. Mandated lowering of toxicants in cigarette smoke: tobacco-specific nitrosamines and selected other constituents

3.1 Executive summary and recommendations

The WHO Framework Convention on Tobacco Control recognizes the need for tobacco product regulation in Articles 9 and 10. Existing product regulatory strategies based on the machine-measured tar, nicotine and carbon monoxide (CO) yields per cigarette with the current ISO regimen are causing harm. By allowing communication of the yields as measures of exposure or risk, they mislead smokers into believing that low-yield cigarettes carry less risk and are a reasonable alternative to cessation. This harm precludes continued acceptance of strategies of product regulation based on per-cigarette machine-measured tar and nicotine and necessitated the development of a new approach. A WHO Study Group on Tobacco Product Regulation/International Agency for Research on Cancer (TobReg/IARC) working group was formed to consider an alternative approach.

This report recommends a strategy for regulation based on product performance measures with the goal of reducing toxicant levels in mainstream cigarette smoke. It recommends establishing levels for selected mainstream smoke toxicants per milligram of nicotine and prohibiting the sale or import of cigarette brands that have yields above these levels. The purpose of normalizing toxicant levels per milligram of nicotine is to shift the interpretation of the measurement away from the quantity of smoke generated per cigarette and away from the misleading use of ISO tar, nicotine and CO values as measures of human exposure and risk. It moves towards product characterization of the toxicity of smoke generated under standardized conditions.

Prohibiting consumer communications based on any machine measurements will also be necessary. This will minimize the likelihood that consumers will be misled into thinking that the machine- measured yields represent exposure of the smoker, as has been occurring with existing tar, nicotine and CO values.

TobReg recognizes that the ideal product regulatory strategy would include measures of human exposure and injury; however, examination of the existing evidence on use of biomarkers of exposure or harm for product regulation suggests that validated biomarkers of harm do not currently exist. Validated biomarkers of exposure exist, but differences in these biomarkers with the product used cannot be separated from differences due to the characteristics of the smokers who use the product, making use of biomarkers of exposure for product regulation problematic. Given these constraints, TobReg concluded that currently available regulatory strategies are limited to product performance standards based on product ingredients and emissions in machine-generated smoke rather than strategies based on measures of exposure or harm.

The list of toxicants was selected on the basis of an assessment that included consideration of: data on animal and human toxicity, toxicity indices, variation in toxicants across brands, the potential for the toxicant to be lowered and the inclusion of constituents from both the particulate and the gas phases of smoke and from different chemical classes in cigarette smoke. Consideration was also given to selecting compounds implicated in cardiovascular and pulmonary toxicity as well as carcinogenicity. The most important criterion for selecting compounds for regulation was evidence of toxicity.

Available data on variations in toxicant levels in cigarette brands provided an initial set of observations to identify the levels of reduction that have already been achieved for some products on the market. A means for using such data to identify appropriate levels for the market being regulated is presented. The initial levels are intended to be a first step in an overall strategy to reduce levels of toxicants in tobacco smoke further as our understanding of what is possible expands and new technology develops. The levels recommended in this report represent TobReg's judgement from the available data on the most practical trade-off, considering the need to regulate a range of toxicants, to mandate substantial lowering of those toxicants and yet not to recommend elimination of most of the brands in the data sets used to set the levels. Regulators are encouraged to obtain data from their own markets and of course may select different levels that are more appropriate for their circumstances. They are encouraged to set levels on the basis of the yields of the brands sold in their markets, using the principles set out in this report.

The recommended regulatory strategy should be implemented in phases, beginning with a period of required annual reporting of toxicant levels by cigarette manufacturers to the regulatory authority. This should be followed by the promulgation of levels for toxicants above which brands cannot be offered for sale. Finally, the established levels would be enforced.

It is expected that regulators will take additional action to reduce the mandated levels of toxicants further as this regulatory strategy is fully implemented. These actions can take the form of setting targets or milestones based on what may be achievable with new technology or product designs.

The toxicants recommended for mandatory lowering and the initial regulatory levels recommended from existing data are listed in Table 3.1. A modified machine-testing regimen with more intense puffing parameters, in which all the holes in cigarette filters are blocked, was used to generate these values, and TobReg recommends use of that regimen by regulators in implementing the proposed regulatory strategy.

Table 3.1
Toxicants recommended for mandated lowering

Toxicant	Level in µg/mg nicotine		Criterion for selecting value
	International brands[a]	Canadian brands[b]	
NNK	0.072	0.047	Median value of data set
NNN	0.114	0.027	Median value of data set
Acetaldehyde	860	670	125% of median value of data set
Acrolein	83	97	125% of median value of data set
Benzene	48	50	125% of median value of data set
Benzo[*a*]pyrene	0.011	0.011	125% of median value of data set
1,3-Butadiene	67	53	125% of median value of data set
Carbon monoxide	18 400	15 400	125% of median value of data set
Formaldehyde	47	97	125% of median value of data set

NNK, 4-(*N*-nitrosomethylamino)-1-(3-pyridyl)-1-butanone; NNN, *N*′-nitrosonornicotine

[a] Based on data from Counts et al. (2005)

[b] Based on data reported to Health Canada minus brands with > 0.1 NNN per miligram of nicotine, which eliminates most United States and Gauloise brands (http://www.hc-sc.gc.ca/hl-vs/tobac-tabac/legislation/reg/indust/constitu_e.html)

The levels given in Table 3.1 in the column 'International brands' are based on an international sample (Counts at al., 2005) of brands of US-style cigarettes with a blend of tobaccos. The figures in the column labelled 'Canadian brands' are based on a set of brands reported to Health Canada that reflect cigarettes containing predominantly flue-cured (bright) tobacco. These two styles of cigarettes are similar to those marketed in many other countries. Regulators should use data reported for their own markets (if available) to set levels, or they may select values from the data set that conforms most closely to the cigarettes available on the markets being regulated. The differences in the reported levels in the two styles of cigarettes are particularly large for the tobacco-specific nitrosamines (TSNA) *N*′-nitrosonornicotine (NNN) and 4-(*N*-nitrosomethylamino)-1-(3-pyridyl)-1-butanone (NNK).

As presented in the first report of TobReg on this regulatory approach (WHO, 2007), the median values for NNN and NNK are used as the recommended levels because there is strong evidence that the amounts of these toxicants in tobacco smoke can be lowered dramatically with existing technology. An initial level of 125% of the median value is recommended for the other toxicants, reflecting the somewhat greater uncertainty about the extent to which these toxicants can be reduced with existing approaches. Substantially lower levels should be the ultimate goal of this regulatory strategy.

The proposed regulatory strategy focuses on the product and the smoke generated under standardized conditions. Mandated lowering of levels of toxicants per milligram of nicotine in cigarette smoke will make regulation of cigarettes consistent with other regulatory approaches to mandate reduction of known toxicants in products used by humans. Reducing the level of toxicants in products intended for human use is a widely accepted regulatory practice. The anticipated outcome is a marketplace that excludes those brands with the highest levels of toxicants. This strategy is neither based on nor relies on measures of actual or estimated human exposure or risk, and so cannot be used to quantify reductions in human exposure, risk or disease. It does rely on measures of clearly established toxicants as they appear in tobacco smoke generated under standardized conditions.

Regulatory authorities have an obligation to ensure that the public is not misled by the results of the recommended machine testing and mandated regulatory values. This is because the public was misled by communication of the values of machine testing for tar, nicotine and CO yields with the current ISO regimen. Science has not established that reduction of any individual toxicant in machine- measured cigarette smoke, including those proposed in this report, will reduce actual human exposure or disease risk. Mandating lower levels and removing some brands with higher levels from the market do not constitute a statement that the remaining brands are safe or less hazardous than the brands removed, nor does it represent government approval of the safety of the products that remain on the market.

TobReg recommends that any regulatory approach based on machine-generated yields specifically prohibit use of the results of testing, or relative ranking of brands by testing levels, as indicators of risk or exposure in marketing, promotion or other communications with the public, including product labelling. Statements that a brand has met government regulatory standards should also be prohibited.

3.2 Introduction

Preventing initiation of tobacco product use, promoting cessation of tobacco use and protecting the public from exposure to second-hand smoke are recognized by the WHO Framework Convention on Tobacco Control as the most effective approaches to reducing tobacco-related morbidity and mortality.

The Convention also recognizes, however, the need for tobacco product regulation, as stated in Articles 9 and 10 of the Treaty. TobReg has prepared a series of reports to provide the scientific foundation for tobacco product regulation (WHO, 2007). This report is the second of two defining how mandatory lowering of toxicant levels in machine-measured cigarette smoke might be used as a product regulatory approach. The report is the result of a collaborative effort by TobReg and IARC, which convened a working group to report to TobReg.

Regulation of tobacco products requires some metric, or set of metrics, by which tobacco products can be assessed. The most common measurements that have been used for cigarettes have been machine-measured tar, nicotine and CO yields per cigarette based on the testing regimen of ISO and the US Federal Trade Commission (FTC). There is scientific consensus that per-cigarette yields do not provide valid estimates of human exposure or of relative human exposure during smoking of different brands of cigarettes (Stratton et al., 2001; National Cancer Institute, 2001; Scientific Advisory Group on Tobacco Product Regulation, 2002; Department of Health and Human Services, 2004a). Communication of these measures to smokers creates harm by leading them to believe that their exposures and risk will be different if they switch to cigarette brands with different machine-measured yields. Any new product regulatory strategy should take into account the harm currently being done by reporting tar, nicotine and CO values per cigarette and should ideally help remedy that harm. This ongoing harm precludes acceptance of current regulatory strategies based on per-cigarette machine-measured tar, nicotine and CO levels and necessitates new regulatory approaches.

Machine smoking regimens other than the ISO/FTC regimen have also been examined, particularly ones with more intense puffing parameters, in which some or all of the ventilation holes in cigarette filters are blocked. Examples include those developed by the State of Massachusetts in the USA and the Canadian Government. These regimens generally produce higher yields per cigarette and reduce the differences between brands. Nevertheless, the regimens continue to rank brands by tar and nicotine yield per cigarette. The rankings by yield per cigarette with these more intense regimens do not provide valid estimates of human exposure or of the relative exposure of smokers when they smoke different brands of cigarettes. Thus, even yields with these more intense smoking regimens have the potential to mislead smokers when expressed per cigarette.

A single machine-testing regimen produces a single set of toxicant yields. In contrast to machines, individual smokers vary the pattern with which they puff different cigarettes of the same brand, and cigarette design changes can lead smokers to systematically change how they puff cigarettes of different designs. These variations in smokers' puffing behaviour limit the use of machine-generated smoke yields as estimates of exposure. Individual smokers seek to achieve nicotine intakes that are sufficient to satisfy their addiction, but the level of nicotine intake varies substantially across the general population of smokers (Benowitz et al., 1983; Jarvis et al., 2001). There is also substantial variation in the pattern of puffing (puff size, puff duration, inter-puff interval and depth of inhalation) used to achieve the desired level of nicotine, and smokers may vary their pattern of puffing from one cigarette to another and from one puff to another (Djordjevic, Stellman, Zang, 2000; Melikian et al., 2007a,b). These sources of variation mean that tar, nicotine and CO yields from a single standardized machine measurement regimen are unreliable estimates of the exposure of smokers.

Cigarette design changes, particularly the extent of filter ventilation, are associated with a substantial difference in the average pattern of puffing of populations of smokers who use them, and smokers who switch brands tend to alter their pattern of puffing in order to preserve their level of nicotine intake (National Cancer Institute, 2001). Tar, nicotine, CO and other toxicant yields vary considerably with differences in machine smoking parameters, and variations in other toxicant levels exist both when the yields are expressed per cigarette and when standardized per milligram of tar or nicotine. Systematic differences in how products with different designs are used by smokers and differences in yields when the cigarettes are puffed differently make comparisons between cigarette brands of per-cigarette machine-smoked yields virtually meaningless as estimates of human exposure. As a result, machine testing with the regimens currently in widespread use cannot provide estimates of human exposure and should not be used to support claims of reduced exposure or risk.

The limitations of machine measurements led to efforts to quantify the actual exposure of smokers by measuring biomarkers in blood, urine and saliva. As these biomarkers are measured in individual smokers, however, they are influenced by personal characteristics and the characteristics of the person's smoking behaviour, as well as by the characteristics of the product smoked (National Cancer Institute, 2001; Scientific Advisory Group on Tobacco Product Regulation, 2002). Distinguishing the differences in biomarker levels due to variations between products from the differences due to smokers' behaviour (e.g. who uses the product and how they use it) is a formidable scientific challenge. Research is needed to resolve these issues so that exposure biomarkers can become effective tools for product regulation. The multiplicity of brands on the market, self-selection of smokers who use different products and differences in how smokers of different products use them make the use of biomarkers of exposure in a regulatory strategy to monitor cigarette product differences problematic, given the current level of scientific knowledge.

Characterization of differences in harm caused by different cigarettes would be a powerful metric for product regulation. Markers of biologically effective dose (levels of toxicants in critical target organs or tissues) are likely to be developed and validated in the future, and these are expected to offer more precise measures of smoke uptake and better prediction of smoke toxicity (Stratton et al., 2001). Measures of injury or validated biomarkers of disease risk are also likely to be validated in the near future. They will allow more rapid assessment of differences in disease risks than is currently possible with epidemiological approaches to measuring disease outcomes. These advances may allow assessment of differences in risk between tobacco products. At the moment, however, none of these measures has been validated as a reliable, independent predictor of differences in tobacco-related disease risk among smokers using different products (Hatsukami et al., 2004).

The limitations of measures of human exposure and human injury suggest that for the near future product regulatory approaches may be limited to measures of differences between products in design characteristics and emissions rather than measures derived from their human use. Chemical measurements of the smoke produced by machines and their use as inputs for product hazard assessment, with all of their limitations, may represent the limit of current scientific assessment of differences between brands that can be used for regulatory assessment of product toxicity.

Measurements based on machine-generated smoke can be made simply and consistently, and they provide information about the effect of design characteristics on the toxic compounds in cigarette smoke when cigarettes are smoked under standard conditions. What machine-generated smoke measurements do not provide is an understanding of how smokers respond to design changes, measures of actual or relative consumer exposure, or an assessment of the consequences of smokers' responses for exposure or risk. Nevertheless, measurements of machine-generated smoke can be a useful interim regulatory tool before metrics of exposure and harm become available that can be used for product regulation. Because of the misleading history of per-cigarette yields, TobReg recommends that toxicant yields be normalized per milligram of nicotine, to shift the interpretation of measurements away from the quantity of smoke generated per cigarette and the misleading communication that the machine-measured yields represent exposure of the smoker, as has been occurring with existing ISO tar, nicotine and CO values. Expressing toxicant values per milligram of nicotine allows examination of cigarettes as they perform under standardized conditions to generate smoke and characterizes that smoke by its toxicity normalized to the quantity of nicotine generated. This change in characterization should shift the interpretation towards product toxicity characterization and away from exposure, but a ban on communicating these values as measures of exposure to risk will also be needed as part of this regulatory approach.

3.3 Background

TobReg, at its meeting in Montebello, Canada, on 26–28 October 2004 (WHO, 2004), concluded that machine-measured tar, nicotine and CO yields based on the ISO/FTC method were misleading smokers and most regulators, and thereby causing harm; they also recommended that these measures should no longer be communicated to smokers as measures of exposure or risk. At the same time, TobReg recognized that abandoning measurements of tar, nicotine and CO with the ISO method as regulatory tools, before development of validated biomarkers of risk, would leave a regulatory and information void that would not be in the best interests of WHO Member States.

ISO Technical Committee 126 (TC126) recognized this misuse of machine-measured yields, and by a formal vote passed a resolution adopting as a rationale for all machine-smoking testing standards the following statements:

- No machine smoking regime can represent all human smoking behaviour.
- Methods are recommended that test the product under conditions of different intensities of machine smoking in order to collect mainstream smoke.
- Machine smoking testing is useful to characterize cigarette emissions for design and regulatory purposes, but communication of machine measurements to smokers can result in misunderstanding about differences in exposure and risk across brands.
- Smoke emission data from machine measurements may be used as inputs for product hazard assessment, but they are not intended to be nor are they valid measures of human exposure or risks. Communicating differences between products in machine measurements as differences in exposure or risk is a misuse of testing using ISO standards (ISO, 2006).

As an interim step in the regulation of tobacco products, before the development of approaches to assess differences in actual exposure, harm or risk from different cigarette brands, TobReg recommended assessment of different products by an examination of the toxicity of the products when tested under standardized conditions. This approach allows application of product regulatory strategies similar to those used for other consumer products, where the focus of the regulatory standard is to reduce the levels of known toxicants present in the product (in this case in the smoke) rather than requiring exposure measures derived from human populations. This approach is limited in that it offers little human exposure information, but it does allow application of well-established regulatory strategies.

Despite these limitations, a change in regulatory strategy is needed, as cigarettes are enormously harmful, and the status quo of using tar and nicotine yields on a per-cigarette basis is causing harm by deceiving consumers into believing that cigarettes with lower machine-measured yields are less risky. Establishment of the proposed interim regime is, therefore, urgent, as measurements based on actual exposure and harm to the smoker require considerable additional research.

The TobReg recommendation is to quantify machine-measured levels of specific toxicants per milligram of nicotine in the smoke generated by the testing method described below. Standardizing the levels of toxicants per milligram of nicotine shifts the focus of the measurement away from a metric of human exposure and towards characterization of the product's performance under standardized conditions. This shift may reduce the misleading effect of differences between levels of toxicants when they are expressed per cigarette. As nicotine is the principal addictive substance in smoke sought by smokers, it was decided to standardize per milligram of nicotine rather than per milligram of tar. These standardized measures of toxicant yield will facilitate examination of the relation between cigarette design and the composition of cigarette smoke. They also provide regulators with a mechanism for reducing the level of identified toxicants in tobacco smoke and allow regulatory action while the science of assessing harm from tobacco smoke toxicants develops further.

In order to prepare scientific guidance on how best to implement the strategy defined by TobReg, the WHO Tobacco Free Initiative and IARC established a working group to define mandated reductions for tobacco smoke toxicants. Limits for TSNA and the methods by which they could be applied in a regulatory strategy were the focus of the first report (WHO, 2007), prepared at a meeting in Lyon, France, 9–10 April 2006. The current report addresses smoke toxicants, including nitrosamines, and was prepared at meetings of the working group in Geneva, Switzerland, 12–13 October 2006 and in San Diego, California, USA, on 22–23 March 2007. A summary of the first report on TSNA is included in this report for completeness.

3.4 First report on mandated lowering of tobacco-specific nitrosamines

The first report (WHO, 2007) recommended that mandated lowering of machine yields per milligram of nicotine for NNN and NNK be adopted as a WHO recommendation. Levels were proposed for adoption as a WHO standard and for use by individual countries in mandating lower TSNA levels.

TSNA are potent carcinogens, and there is clear evidence that alteration of the curing methods for tobacco and other changes in manufacturing approaches can substantially lower the levels in smoke (Peele, Riddick, Edwards, 2001; IARC, 2004). There is marked variation across brands within countries in the levels of these nitrosamines, as demonstrated by data from Australia and Canada (Australian Department of Health and Aging, 2001; Health Canada, 2004). A sample of international brands from one manufacturer also showed substantial variation in TSNA levels (Counts et al., 2005). The potency of TSNA as carcinogens and the evidence that levels could be substantially reduced with existing technology, thereby limiting the number of cigarette brands that would be unable to achieve the regulated level by modifying the tobacco used, identified these compounds as ideal toxicants for early application of mandated lowering as a regulatory strategy.

The carcinogenicity of NNK and NNN has been firmly established by extensive studies in laboratory animals. On the basis of animal carcinogenicity data for these toxicants, human exposure data and mechanistic studies, NNN and NNK together are classified as a human carcinogen by IARC (Group 1) (Cogliano et al., 2004; IARC, 2007).

The levels of NNK and NNN in unburnt tobacco contribute significantly to and are correlated with the levels in smoke. NNK and NNN form during the curing and processing of tobacco. Modifications of these processes, particularly removal of propane heating as part of the curing process, are now available that can substantially reduce the levels in tobacco and therefore in smoke (Peele, Riddick, Edwards, 2001; IARC, 2004). Independent of the effects of the heat source used in curing, it is also known that NNK and NNN levels vary significantly with tobacco type, being higher in air-cured, processed burley tobacco than in flue-cured bright tobacco. Other studies show that tobacco nitrate levels contribute to the smoke levels of NNK and NNN. Collectively, the available evidence strongly indicates that the technology is available to reduce NNK and NNN levels in cigarette smoke significantly.

The variation in NNN and NNK per milligram of nicotine is defined in the first report on the basis of data for an international sample of Philip Morris brands published by Counts and colleagues (2004). While that study is based on what appear to be the best international data currently available, it obviously reflects a selected sample of brands from a single manufacturer containing tobacco blends that are much higher in nitrosamines than brands that are currently on the market in some countries, notably Australia, Canada and the United Kingdom. Therefore, the guidance on levels per milligram of nicotine presented here is intended to inform countries in which the data are not available or are inadequate. Countries where the principal brands on the market contain flue-cured bright tobacco with low levels of nitrosamines may be well advised to establish their own regulatory levels on the basis of measurements made on the cigarettes actually sold in their market.

Examination of the levels of NNN and NNK (Counts et al., 2005) revealed that the median concentration of NNN in the Philip Morris brands tested was approximately 114 ng/mg of nicotine in smoke emissions, with a range of 16–189 ng/mg. The median level of NNK in the brands tested was 72 ng/mg of nicotine, with a range of 23–111 ng/mg. These data suggest that a level of NNN in smoke emissions of 114 ng (0.114 μg) per milligram of nicotine or lower has already been achieved for half the cigarettes Philip Morris has marketed internationally. This level therefore reflects a readily achievable level to establish for this compound as an initial step in mandating lower levels and above which cigarettes should be excluded from the market.

A mandated limit for NNK of 72 ng (0.072 μg) per milligram of nicotine in smoke emissions is similarly proposed.

These values were set on the basis of the median value reported for these international brands, which are US blended cigarettes with higher nitrosamine levels than blends used for cigarettes in Australia, Canada and the United Kingdom. Comparison of toxicant yields in those countries demonstrated that the tobacco used in the cigarettes smoked yielded levels of NNN and NNK that are substantially lower than the median values measured by Counts and colleagues in their sample of brands. Data on smoke toxicant yields for Canadian cigarettes (Health Canada, 2004), once US and Gauloise brands were excluded, revealed a median NNN concentration of 26.9 ng/mg of nicotine and a median NNK concentration of 46.6 ng/mg. The Canadian median NNN level is less than one fourth that of the international brands used to establish the mandated reduction recommendation, demonstrating both that cigarettes with substantially lower levels of NNN can be manufactured and successfully marketed and that individual countries may be well advised to set mandated reduction levels based on the products sold in their own markets.

Data from Australia are similar. The median smoke toxicant yield from Australian cigarettes (Australian Department of Health and Aging, 2001) measured with the Canadian intense method, was 19.5 ng/mg of nicotine for NNN and 25.6 ng/mg for NNK in the brands tested. This demonstrates that there is substantial scope for further reductions in the levels of nitrosamines and that it is possible to manufacture cigarettes with low levels of nitrosamines which have broad market appeal.

NNN and NNK levels are often closely correlated in individual brands, raising the question of whether lower levels need to be mandated for both nitrosamines. This correlation is not seen when US blended-style cigarettes that contain burley tobacco in which the level of NNN is higher than that of

NNK are compared with Canadian brands containing predominantly flue-cured tobacco in which the level of NNN is lower than that of NNK.

Figure 3.1 presents data on the levels of NNN and NNK per milligram of nicotine in individual Canadian brands plotted by increasing level of NNK. Many of the brands with high levels of NNN and NNK are US or French brand names, and the TSNA differences are presumably due to the difference in the tobacco blend used and the nitrosamine levels of the tobaccos in those blends. It is also evident, however, that the relation between NNN and NNK levels is different in the US brands and most notably in the Gauloise brands. This suggests that setting regulatory levels for NNN and NNK may identify different brands as being above the regulatory level, particularly when the blends of tobaccos used vary.

Figure 3.1
NNN and NNK concentrations by brand of Canadian cigarettes

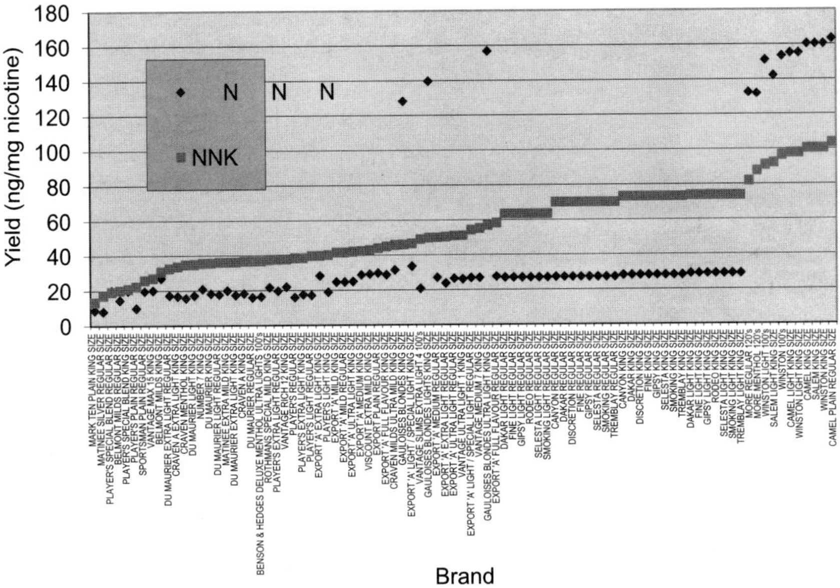

NNK, 4-(*N*-nitrosomethylamino)-1-(3-pyridyl)-1-butanone; NNN, *N*′-nitrosonornicotine

In addition, as new curing and other techniques emerge with a potential to eliminate preformed TSNA (those nitrosamines contained in unburnt tobacco leaf or blend), the issue of pyrosynthesis of TSNA will become more important. The nitrosation of nicotine, a tertiary amine, during smoking occurs at a much slower rate than that of nornicotine, a secondary amine. This will favour formation of NNN, *N*′- nitrosoanatabine and *N*′-nitrosoanabasine over NNK. Therefore, mandated limits will have to be set for both NNN and NNK (or for NNN plus NNK) to monitor unexpected shifts in the TSNA composition of the smoke of cigarettes engineered to meet the mandated lowering goals. As the data presented in this report demonstrate, NNN is the predominant TNSA in US blend cigarettes, while NNK predominates in Canadian flue-cured tobacco cigarettes, illustrating the need for caution in extrapolating data from the international sample of Philip Morris brands to individual country markets or to other manufacturers.

3.5 Use of mandated lowering of toxicant levels in a product regulatory strategy

The goal of the proposed regulatory strategy is to reduce the levels of toxic constituents measured under standardized conditions in the smoke of cigarettes allowed on the market. A secondary goal is to prevent the introduction onto a market of cigarettes with higher levels of smoke toxicants than are present in brands already on the market.

The regulatory strategy recommended by TobReg is based on well-accepted precautionary approaches used in public health. These approaches move towards a general reduction of known harmful toxicants in any product by establishing product performance standards and as part of good manufacturing processes. They do not require that, for the substance under consideration, there be proof of a specific link between a lower level (amount) of any individual toxicant and a lower level of human disease (response). They merely require that the substance be known to be harmful and that processes exist for its diminution or removal. Evidence of actual reduction in harm is not required for this approach; correspondingly, compliance with these regulations does not support a claim that a given brand is safe or less hazardous than other brands.

Expressing the level of toxicants in smoke per unit amount of nicotine allows quantification of the levels of toxicants that accompany a specified amount of nicotine in the smoke of different brands, at least under the conditions of smoke generation with the machine testing regimen. This normalization of other toxicants to the nicotine yield allows a focus on the mixture of toxic constituents generated when a cigarette is smoked and moves away from per-cigarette yields, which are misleading when used as estimates of the yields that will occur when smokers actually smoke the cigarettes. The focus becomes the toxicity of the smoke generated under a standardized machine testing regimen rather than the quantity of the smoke generated. This standardized measure of toxicity can be used to regulate cigarettes as a product.

The proposed regulatory approach mandates lowering the levels of specific toxicants per milligram of nicotine by exclusion from the market of brands with levels in the smoke that exceed specified regulatory levels. The existing variation in toxicant levels across the brands currently on the market is used to show that reducing levels of toxicants is technically achievable, as a large number of existing brands have already achieved the lower levels. Exclusion from the market of those brands with high levels of a smoke toxicant per milligram of nicotine should lower the mean level of that machine- measured toxicant per milligram of nicotine among the brands remaining on the market. A progressive reduction in the amount of toxicants in smoke over time can also be achieved by progressively lowering the regulatory levels or by setting targets or goals for further reduction as the technology to reduce toxicants advances.

Use of the variation in toxicant levels in existing brands to set the mandated limits ensures that there are manufacturing approaches that allow production of cigarettes which are both acceptable to the smoker and can achieve the regulatory limit. In addition, this approach may encourage manufacturers of cigarettes to voluntarily decrease toxicant emissions to the lowest levels achievable even for products below the established regulatory limits.

The initial recommendations for regulatory levels are derived from data on toxicant yields for a sample of international brands (Counts et al., 2005) and those reported to Health Canada (2004). Reliance on these two lists is merely an interim step. The proposed approach includes a recommendation for a multi-year period of required reporting of the machine-measured yields for each brand sold in a given market. Market-specific data can eventually be used to establish the actual variation occurring so as to more precisely define appropriate regulatory levels.

The value of examining the variation in toxicant yields for the market of interest rather than using an international sample is exemplified by comparing the benzo[*a*]pyrene yields in the international sample with those reported to Health Canada for Canadian brands. When the international sample is ranked from the brand with the lowest level of benzo[*a*]pyrene per milligram of nicotine to the brand with the highest value, there is a continuous, steady increase across brands, from 5.7 to 13.8 ng/mg of nicotine. In contrast, the ranking of Canadian brands from the lowest to the highest values (Figure 3.2) reveals a level which rises to approximately 9.6 ng/mg of nicotine, then a sudden jump to 16.8 ng/mg. The explanation for this sudden discontinuity in levels is not immediately evident, but the value of examining the Canadian experience rather than assuming that the sample of international brands would provide an adequate description of the Canadian market for establishing mandated reductions is clear.

Figure 3.2
Benzo[*a*]pyrene concentrations by brand of Canadian cigarettes

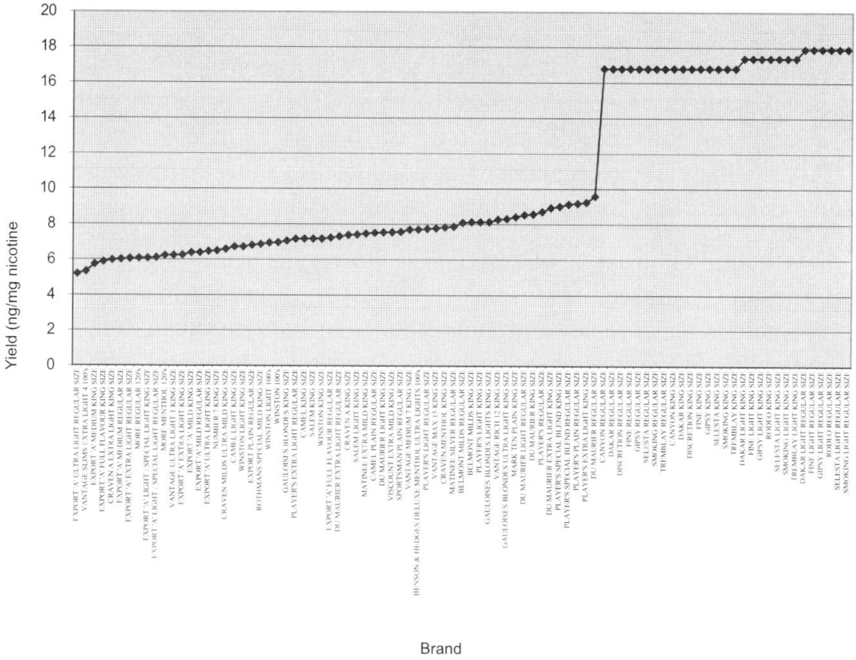

It is not known whether reducing the levels of the high-priority toxicants identified in this report will actually reduce harm or even reduce actual exposure to these harmful compounds. Therefore, it is an essential part of this proposal that regulators assume the responsibility to ensure that consumers not be informed directly or indirectly, or be led to believe, that cigarettes that meet the toxic limits established pursuant to this proposal are less hazardous, have been approved by the government or meet government-established health or safety standards. In particular, ranking of cigarette brands by any of the machine-generated smoke metrics proposed in this report has great potential to be interpreted by smokers as reliable differences in probable exposure or harm that will result from smoking different brands. Communicating such rankings to consumers, or allowing them to be communicated directly or indirectly, is likely to influence smokers' behaviour in ways that will cause harm, similar to the harm currently caused by communicating ISO tar, nicotine and CO ratings.

Any health or exposure claims based on machine testing must be prohibited until scientifically validated measures of exposure and harm are developed that will allow regulators to determine that differences between brands do reduce actual exposure and risk. Hence, the current strategy to prohibit claims will limit the possibility that the new standards will become marketing tools and be used to misinform consumers.

The measurements of toxicant levels by brand and the costs associated with testing and reporting are expected to be the responsibility of the cigarette manufacturers. The results should be reported to the regulatory authority, and a sample of those results should be verified by an independent laboratory. Alternatively, some regulators may conduct the testing themselves with funding derived from taxation or licensing of tobacco products.

It is the addictive nature of tobacco use that results in the long-term, repetitive exposure to tobacco toxicants which result in disease manifestation. The characteristics of tobacco products that contribute to and facilitate addiction are a potential focus for tobacco product regulation that could have substantial effects on the burden of disease. Methods to assess addiction and identification of the factors that influence addiction are the focus of other work being conducted by TobReg. They will not be discussed in this report, but their exclusion should not be taken to imply their lack of importance.

The selection of toxicants in this report is based on a number of factors, including the fact that they are constituents of smoke currently established as toxic, they are known to be potently toxic and they have been measured in multiple brands of cigarettes. As our knowledge of smoke chemistry expands and the demonstration of the toxicity of smoke toxicants becomes more complete, the list of priority toxicants may change.

The principal goal of the proposed mandated lowering is to reduce the toxicant yields of brands currently on the market. It is possible, however, that, in the absence of effective product regulation, the toxicant yields for the mix of brands on a market may actually increase as new brands are introduced or the characteristics of existing brands are changed. This possibility is of particular concern for those markets in which the current levels of toxicants are lower than those in brands sold in other markets. The data presented in Figure 3.1 show that the brands sold in Canada with high NNK levels are largely brands also sold in France and the USA rather than those brands that are predominantly sold in the Canadian market. A similar situation exists in Australia (Figure 3.3). The mean and range of NNN and NNK yields per milligram of nicotine in the brands sold in Australia (including Philip Morris brands) and reported to the Australian Government in 2001 (Australian Department of Health and Aging, 2001) are contrasted with the much higher levels of NNN and NNK reported in a Philip Morris Marlboro brand identified as being Australian in the paper of Counts and colleagues (2005). As Marlboro becomes a leading brand in the Australian market, as it has in many other markets, the difference in NNN and NNK levels would be expected to increase the average yield of these toxicants in the cigarettes on the Australian market. Setting levels for toxicants would provide a regulatory strategy that could prevent the introduction of newer brands with greater toxicant yields than the existing brands.

Figure 3.3

Mean and range of NNN and NNK yields per milligram of nicotine in brands reported to the Australian government in 1999, and levels of NNN and NNK reported for a Philip Morris Marlboro brand identified as being Australian

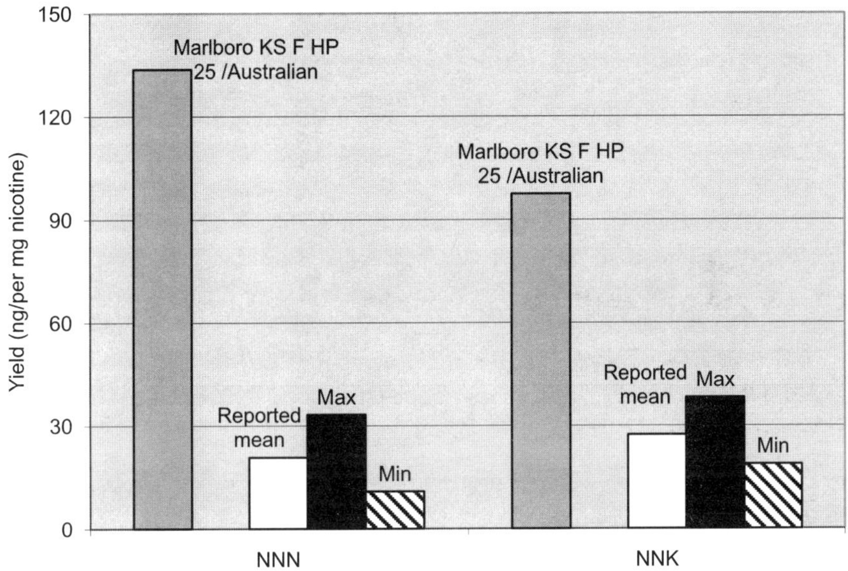

NNK, 4-(*N*-nitrosomethylamino)-1-(3-pyridyl)-1-butanone; NNN, *N*′-nitrosonornicotine; KS, King Size; F, filter; HP, hard pack

3.5.1 *Selection of machine testing method*

Measurement of smoke toxicants requires machine-generated smoke. Different cigarette smoking machine testing regimens result in different levels of toxicants per milligram of nicotine, and the relative ranking of brands by toxicant also varies with the testing regimen used. Where possible, it is useful to make measurements with more than one regimen in order to examine how the results and rankings by brand vary with the measurement approach.

Three standardized approaches to machine testing in which data on machine testing of multiple brands are available were examined: the ISO/FTC regimen, the Massachusetts Department of Health regimen (slightly larger puff volumes and 50% of vents blocked) and the modified intense machine smoking regimen used by Health Canada. Each of these methods has advantages and disadvantages, but the modified intense smoking regimen was selected as the method with the best fit for measuring toxicants for use in the proposed regulatory strategy. This regimen is modified from the existing ISO regimen as follows: the puff volume is increased from 35 ml to 55 ml, the puff interval is decreased from 60 s to 30 s, and all ventilation holes are blocked by placing over them a strip of Mylar adhesive tape (Scotch Brand product no. 600 Transparent Tape), which must be cut so that it covers the circumference and is tightly secured from the end of the filter to the tipping overwrap seam, or by another method of equivalent efficiency (Health Canada, 2000). This testing regimen is called 'modified (intense) ISO' by the Canadian Government but is referred to in this report as the 'modified intense smoking' regimen to avoid confusion between it and the existing ISO/FTC regimen.

The selection of the modified intense smoking regimen was based on several criteria. First, the larger quantity of smoke generated by this regimen reduces the coefficient of variation of replicate measurements for TSNA, which are the initial set of toxicants recommended for regulatory consideration. Figure 3.4 presents the mean coefficient of variation for four TSNA (*N'*-nitrosoanabasine, *N'*-nitrosoanatabine, NNN and NNK) in each of the international brands of cigarettes measured by Counts et al. (2005), with the results for all three machine testing regimens presented in the same figure and plotted against the tar yield for each brand measured with the machine testing method.

Figure 3.4

Mean of coefficients of variation of replicate measurements of four nitrosamines plotted by the tar level in individual brands measured by each of three machine testing protocols

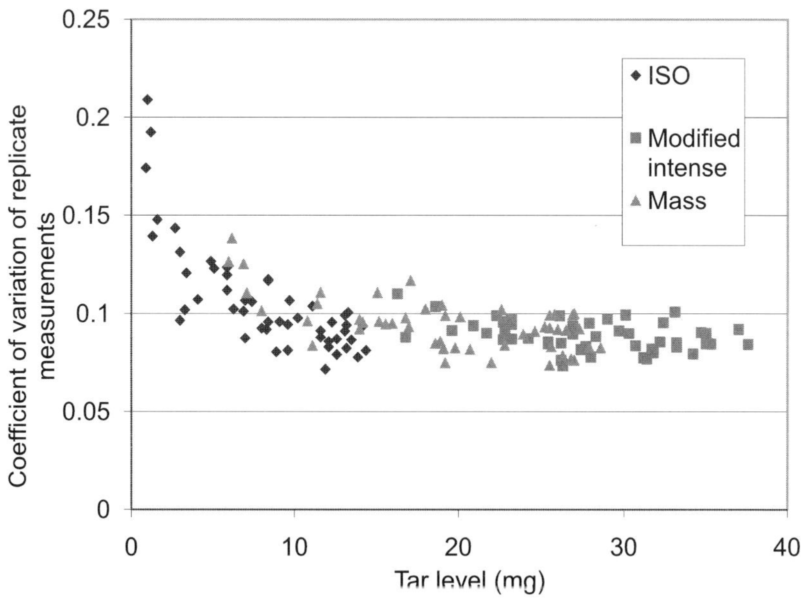

It is evident from the graph that the variation in replicate measurements of the TSNA increases when the testing regimen generates less than approximately 10 mg of tar. The measurements of both the ISO and the Massachusetts regimen include substantial numbers of international brands that have less than 10 mg of tar and correspondingly show larger variation in replicate measurements. Only the modified intense smoking regimen yielded a stable variation in replicate measurements across brands with different tar levels.

A second reason for selecting the modified intense smoking regimen was that with certain design features the more intense machine parameters may yield levels of individual smoke toxicants substantially above those that would result when ISO smoking conditions are used, even when standardized by reporting them per milligram of nicotine. Higher yields are generated under machine conditions that correspond to a more intense human smoking profile and therefore may better reflect how the product performs under these intense conditions.

Third, in selecting a machine testing regimen, TobReg considered it important to select a regimen that could accurately characterize cigarette design changes, other than filter ventilation, as correction of toxicant yields by expressing them per milligram of nicotine alone was not sufficient to characterize the yields produced under conditions of more intense puffing.

The use of charcoal in cigarette filters is an example of a design change with an impact that is not well characterized by normalization to nicotine. Use of the ISO smoking regimen (35-ml puff, 60-s puff interval, 2-s puff, no vent blocking) to test the delivery of volatile (e.g. benzene, 1,3-butadiene, acrylonitrile) components in smoke from cigarettes with charcoal filters showed that the levels of these compounds are significantly lower than those of other smoke toxicants, including nicotine.

As long as enough charcoal is included in the filter, these reductions are present even when an intense puffing regimen like the modified intense smoking regimen (55-ml puff, 30-s puff interval, 2-s puff, 100% vent blocking) is used. The newly introduced Marlboro UltraSmooth that is being marketed in Salt Lake City, Utah, USA, has an example of a filter in which sufficient charcoal is present to maintain reductions in yields of volatile compounds even under the modified intense smoking regimen. The Marlboro UltraSmooth cigarette marketed in Atlanta, Georgia, USA, and the modified charcoal filtered Marlboro Ultralight marketed in North Dakota, USA, have less charcoal, however, and there is breakthrough of the volatiles with more intense puffing regimens, resulting in higher yields. For these two products, smoking with the ISO regimen indicates that the levels of smoke volatiles are significantly lower than in other cigarettes with similar delivery that are not charcoal-filtered, and the difference persists even when presented per milligram of nicotine. When these products are smoked with the modified intense smoking regimen, however, the proportionate increase in the levels of volatile components is much greater than the increase in nicotine. Normalization per milligram of nicotine with data from the ISO smoking regimen would not correct for the increased smoke toxicant yields of these intermediate level charcoal filter brands that results from more intense smoking patterns.

Regulatory authorities need correct information about the products for sale in their jurisdictions, and the regulatory smoking regimen selected should be able to characterize design changes that result in significantly higher smoke toxicant delivery relative to nicotine delivery with more intense smoking. While no one machine smoking regimen perfectly characterizes cigarette toxicant yields, TobReg concluded that the modified intense smoking regimen offers significant advantages over the other two regimens.

When cigarettes are tested with different smoking regimens and the smoke deliveries are normalized for nicotine, significant differences remain in the relative nicotine-normalized deliveries under different smoking conditions. Table 3.2 shows data taken from Counts and colleagues (2005) on the delivery of three smoke toxicants of concern (acrolein, benzo[*a*]pyrene and NNN) measured with three different smoking regimens (ISO/FTC, Massachusetts Department of Health, modified intense), normalized for nicotine delivery determined under the same smoking conditions for five types of cigarettes (two full flavour, two light and one ultralight).

The two full-flavour cigarettes (E5 and E7) showed little change in the relative delivery of all three toxicants in the three puffing regimens. Nicotine-normalized acrolein in the two 'light' cigarettes (E17 and E24) and the 'ultra-light' cigarette (E33) increased significantly as the puff parameters became more intense and ventilation holes were blocked. Nicotine-normalized benzo[*a*]pyrene in the two 'light' cigarettes and the 'ultra-light' cigarette showed virtually no change as the puff parameters became more intense and ventilation holes were blocked. Nicotine-normalized NNN in the two 'light' cigarettes showed an inconsistent pattern, but a small decrease was seen as the puff parameters became more intense and ventilation holes were blocked. For the 'ultra-light' cigarette, the nicotine- normalized NNN decreased substantially as the puff parameters became more intense and ventilation holes were blocked.

These results show that the puffing regimen affects not only differences in the dilution of smoke but also in the cigarette burning properties that alter the relative delivery of toxicants. This affects the relative levels of toxicants measured in smoke with different smoking regimens. These results are in agreement with TobReg Recommendation 1 (WHO, 2004), which suggested

Table 3.2
Delivery of specified toxicants under different machine smoking conditions

Lot	Manufacturer and type	Acrolein (µg/mg nicotine)		
		ISO/FTC	Massachusetts State	Modified intense
E5	Marlboro KS F SP/US	54.31	54.10	58.13
E7	L&M KS F HP/EU	71.11	66.04	74.73
E17	L&M KS F Lt/EU	61.38	69.17	84.93
E24	Marlboro KS F HP Lt/UK	56.79	63.93	78.86
E33	Marlboro KS F HP Ult/EU	40.69	53.02	69.32

Lot	Manufacturer and type	Benzo[*a*]pyrene (ng/mg nicotine)		
		ISO/FTC	Massachusetts State	Modified intense
E5	Marlboro KS F SP/US	11.7	9.0	9.9
E7	L&M KS F HP/EU	12.9	11.6	10.0
E17	L&M KS F Lt/EU	12.8	11.6	9.6
E24	Marlboro KS F HP Lt/UK	11.1	9.5	10.0
E33	Marlboro KS F HP Ult/EU	8.1	7.4	7.7

Lot	Manufacturer and type	NNN (ng/mg nicotine)		
		ISO/FTC	Massachusetts State	Modified intense
E5	Marlboro KS F SP/US	154	145	151
E7	L&M KS F HP/EU	96	84	93
E17	L&M KS F Lt/EU	101	84	95
E24	Marlboro KS F HP Lt/UK	85	77	64
E33	Marlboro KS F HP Ult/EU	116	91	74

ISO, International Organization for Standardization; FTC, Federal Trade Commission; KS, king size; F, filter; SP, soft pack; US, United States; L&M, Liggett & Meyers; HP, hard pack; EU, European Union; Lt, light; UK, United Kingdom; Ult, ultra-light; NNN, *N*′-nitrosonornicotine
From Counts et al. (2005)

that, when the resources are available, a second set of puffing parameters should be used to test cigarettes under more intense smoking conditions in addition to the ISO/FTC regimen. Where possible, measurements should be taken over a range of puffing parameters to understand the delivery of toxicants in smoke emissions.

3.5.3 *Sources of data on toxicants*

Comprehensive lists of toxicants measured in a consistent manner with the modified intense smoking regimen are available from three sources: a publication by Counts and colleagues (2005) comparing a set of international brands manufactured by Philip Morris, a set of Canadian brands (Health Canada, 2004) reported by law to Health Canada for the year 2004, and a set of Australian brands (Australian Department of Health and Aging, 2001). The data from these three sources are listed in Annex 3.1. The data comparisons are for measurements made with the modified intense smoking regimen with all ventilation holes blocked.

The Canadian data were modified slightly to remove those brands that are either US-style blended cigarettes or French-manufactured Gauloise brands. This modification was made to eliminate those high-TSNA brands (NNN levels > 100 ng/mg of nicotine) which might distort the averages for brands of more traditional Canadian style (Figure 3.1). In addition, the values for toluene and styrene for the brands Vantage Rich 12 king size and Vantage Max 15 king size were deleted from the analyses because they appeared to have been transposed and, as a result, substantially distorted the maximum and minimum values of all brands reported for the same toxicants when they were included.

3.5.4 *Criteria for selecting toxicants for mandatory lowering regulation*

The toxicants considered were those on the list reported to Health Canada (2004) and measured by Counts and colleagues (2005). The list was selected by Health Canada to represent those constituents of smoke that contribute the most to its toxicity.

Priorities on the list were based on the known animal and human toxicity of the compounds, toxicity indices based on the concentration of the constituent multiplied by its toxic potency, the variation in the toxicant across brands, the potential for the toxicant to be lowered in cigarette smoke with existing methods and the need to have constituents that represent the different phases of smoke (gas and particulate), different chemical families and toxicities that reflect heart and lung disease as well as cancer. The most important criterion for selecting compounds for regulation was the evidence on toxicity.

In addition, the yield per milligram of nicotine of a toxicant has to vary substantially across the brands on the market, or little will be gained by removing those with higher yields. The variation in toxicant yields across brands should be substantially greater than the variation in repeated measurement in a single brand. Otherwise, more measurements would be required for each toxicant in each brand to have a precise estimate of the mean value, and the cost of testing would increase proportionally.

The availability of technology or other approaches to reduce the level of a specific toxicant per milligram of nicotine in smoke is also a consideration. When readily available alterations in tobacco processing or cigarette design and manufacture are known to reduce the level of certain toxicants in smoke, it is feasible to set limits on these toxicants, which are therefore of higher priority. Toxicants are generated in smoke in at least three ways, which may influence the ability to reduce their levels. The levels of toxicants such as TSNA that are generated mainly by the way in which the tobacco plant is treated (cured) can be lowered by changing the production process. For toxicants derived mainly during the combustion of organic material, such as polycyclic aromatic hydrocarbons (PAHs such as benzo[*a*]pyrene) and CO, changes in design characteristics, tobacco blends and manufacturing processes (e.g. catalysts) might be needed to substantially lower their levels. Other toxicants are generated by combustion from substances added to a product for various reasons (e.g. processing aids, sugars and flavours); these include aldehydes and other volatile organic compounds, such as acetaldehyde, formaldehyde, acrolein and acrylonitrile, which contribute substantially to the toxicity of smoke. The levels of these toxicants could be reduced by lowering or removing sugars as additives from the products.

A final consideration is the existence of a market for brands low in a particular toxicant (such as Canadian brands low in TSNA). For these markets, mandated limits might be set on toxicants to prevent the introduction of brands from other markets that have substantially higher levels of that toxicant than the native brands.

A list of toxicants with all these characteristics would be very long, and the larger the number of toxicants regulated, the more distortion there will be in the existing market and the more complex will be regulatory oversight. Therefore, TobReg examined the list of reported toxicants in order to identify a smaller number of compounds that would balance the concerns identified with the practical reality of a regulatory structure.

Examination of evidence for toxicity

A principal consideration in selecting compounds for regulation is their known toxicity. A review of the toxicity of all the compounds in smoke is beyond the scope of this report, but the evidence for the toxicity of those compounds recommended for regulation or for reporting was reviewed.

Examination of toxicant levels and quantitative data on toxicity

Characterizing the hazards of chemical products and their emissions generally involves estimating the levels of individual components, describing the inherent properties of those components to cause adverse effects (toxicity) and relating this to their inherent strength to cause adverse effects (potency). A comprehensive hazard characterization of smoked tobacco products and their emissions would be very complex, in view of the very many components of smoke (more than 4000), limited toxicological information on many of these compounds and the possibility for interaction between the various toxicants. Fowles and Dybing (2003) presented a simplified system for characterizing the hazards of the components of cigarette smoke by calculating cancer risk and non-cancer risk indices. This system involves multiplying the yields of individual smoke toxicants derived with the standard ISO machine smoking method by cancer and non-cancer potency factors.

The method devised by Fowles and Dybing (2003) is expanded in this report, in that yields of toxicologically important constituents of smoke were taken from published data based on the modified intense smoking regime and normalized per milligram of nicotine. The amount of smoke collected under the modified intense regimen is greater than under ISO machine conditions, and the smoke is generated under more intense conditions of tobacco combustion. Normalizing levels of toxicants per milligram of nicotine has been identified as a means for reducing the misleading differences between levels of toxicants expressed per cigarette (WHO, 2004).

Cancer potency factors: The T25 cancer potency estimation method of Dybing et al. (1997) was used. The T25 value is the long-term daily dose that will produce tumours in 25% of animals above the background rate at a specific tissue site. The T25 is determined by linear extrapolation from the lowest dose that results in a statistically significant increase in tumours. The pertinent data from the cancer bioassays underlying calculation of the T25 values are presented in Annex 3.2. For the present calculations, the T25 values were converted into cancer potency factors per milligram (1/T25).

Non-cancer potency factors: Long-term reference exposure levels published by the Office of Environmental Health Hazard Assessment, California Environmental Protection Agency, in February 2005 were used (http://www.oehha.ca.gov/air/chronic_rels/AllChrels.html). This level is an airborne level of a chemical at or below which no adverse health effects are anticipated for individuals with long-term exposure to that level. Reference exposure levels were derived from both human and animal toxicological data and presented for the target system for each substance. For the present calculations, a reference exposure level is viewed as the inverse of the respective toxicant's non-cancer potency factor, and the term 'tolerable level' is used in this report instead of 'reference exposure level'.

Toxicant animal carcinogenicity and toxicant non-cancer response indices: A toxicant animal carcinogenicity index is the numerical value of the amount of an individual component in cigarette smoke, normalized per milligram of nicotine and multiplied by its cancer potency factor (1/T25). A toxicant non-cancer response index is the numerical value of the amount of an individual component in cigarette smoke, normalized per milligram of nicotine and multiplied by its non-cancer potency factor (or divided by its tolerable level).

The toxicant animal carcinogenicity and the toxicant non-cancer response indices are calculated from the mean level of the individual toxicant per milligram of nicotine in all brands in the data set and are presented in Annex 3.3 Tables A3.1–A3.3. The indices are estimated from data sets of machine-generated smoke yields obtained by the modified intense smoking regimen for international Philip Morris brands (Counts et al., 2005), Canadian brands (Health Canada, 2004) and Australian brands (Australian Department of Health and Aging, 2001). The indices were calculated from the reported levels in the three data sets and are presented as means, 90th percentiles and maxima per milligram of nicotine per cigarette. The data sets include yield levels for up to 43 individual toxicants; some elements, such as arsenic, chromium and selenium, were not reported or quantified in some of the data sets. Information on methyl ethyl ketone was not reported in the Canadian data.

Absolute T25 values and T25 per milligram of carcinogen per milligram of nicotine are also presented in Annex 3.3 Tables A3.1–A3.3 for the 14 carcinogens measured in tobacco smoke when such values could be calculated (see Annex 3.2 for the basis used to calculate T25 values). Toxicant animal carcinogenicity indices are calculated by multiplying the yield per milligram of nicotine by the unit milligram T25 value. Toxicant non-cancer response indices are calculated by multiplying the yield per milligram of nicotine by the inverse tolerable level (or divided by the tolerable level).

Tables 3.3 and 3.4 list the mean toxicant animal carcinogenicity and toxicant non-cancer response indices from the three data sets. A similar picture is seen in the ranking of toxicants with respect to both cancer and non-cancer responses. With respect to cancer hazards, 1,3-butadiene, acetaldehyde, isoprene, NNK, benzene and cadmium ranked highest. As the experimental data on 4-aminobiphenyl did not allow proper estimation of a T25 value, a toxicant animal carcinogenicity index value for this human carcinogen could not be calculated. With respect to toxicant non-cancer responses, the index was much higher for acrolein (targets: respiratory system, eyes) than for the other toxicants; acetaldehyde (target: respiratory system), formaldehyde (targets: respiratory system, eyes) and hydrogen cyanide (targets: cardiovascular system, nervous system, endocrine system) followed in ranking order.

Table 3.3

Ranking of toxicants in smoke with respect to toxicant animal carcinogenicity indices

Toxicant	Mean			
	Counts et al. (2005)	**Canadian data**	**Australian data**	**All**
1,3-Butadiene	11.4	8.9	9.5	9.9
Acetaldehyde	7.0	5.7	5.5	6.1
Isoprene	4.6	2.9	3.6	3.7
NNK	4.7	3.8	1.8	3.4
Benzene	2.7	2.8	2.4	2.6
Cadmium	1.6	2.4	1.2	1.7
Acrylonitrile	1.7	1.4	1.2	1.4
Hydroquinone	1.1	1.3	1.2	1.2
Catechol	0.49	0.75	0.50	0.58
NNN	0.55	0.22	0.10	0.29
Benzo[*a*]pyrene	0.0082	0.0096	0.0081	0.0086
2-Aminonaphthalene	0.00081	0.00077	0.00047	0.00068
1-Aminonaphthalene	0.00049	0.00032	0.00028	0.000363
Lead	0.00	0.00	0.00	0.00

NNK, 4-(*N*-nitrosomethylamino)-1-(3-pyridyl)-1-butanone

Table 3.4

Ranking of toxicants in smoke with respect to toxicant non-cancer response indices

Toxicant	Mean			
	Counts et al. (2005)	**Canadian data**	**Australian data**	**Mean**
Acrolein	1127	1188	983	1099
Acetaldehyde	77.2	62.9	61.1	67.1
Formaldehyde	13.7	25.8	20.0	19.8
Hydrogen cyanide	22.7	15.9	13.0	17.2
Nitrogen oxides	5.0	2.2	2.1	3.1
Cadmium	2.4	3.6	1.8	2.6
1,3-Butadiene	2.7	2.1	2.3	2.4
Acrylonitrile	2.5	2.0	1.8	2.1
Carbon monoxide	1.5	1.2	1.1	1.3
Benzene	0.66	0.68	0.57	0.64
Toluene	0.24	0.24	0.18	0.22
Arsenic	0.16	–	–	0.16
Methyl ethyl ketone	0.09	–	0.07	0.08
Ammonia	0.11	0.06	0.05	0.07
Phenol	0.06	0.09	0.06	0.07
Mercury	0.04	0.03	0.00	0.02
Styrene	0.02	0.01	–	0.02
m- and *p*-Cresol	0.01	0.02	0.01	0.01
o-Cresol	0.01	0.01	0.00	0.01

This ranking of measured carcinogens and non-carcinogens in cigarette smoke is based on integration of machine smoking yield data normalized per milligram of nicotine with information on the toxic potency of the measured toxicants. One approach to quantifying the potential independent contribution of individual toxicants to the toxicity of the products examined in the three data sets is to compare the hazard indices. Generally, the same ranking order was achieved, whether the hazard indices were calculated per mean, 90th percentile or maximum levels of toxicants. Another finding was that the relative ranking order, with respect to both carcinogenicity and non-carcinogenicity, was similar across the three data sets, although they covered brands with different tobacco blends. This suggests that the similar basic designs of the products and the general characteristics of the combustion process contribute relatively uniformly to the hazard of the products, and that the priority of compounds for regulatory consideration is similar for the brands in all three data sets.

There are obvious limitations to the method used here for ranking cigarette smoke toxicants. As each measured toxicant is treated individually, the possibility of chemical interactions that either enhance or reduce the hazardous properties of the smoke is not taken into account. Further, these calculations were possible only for those toxicants for which T25 and tolerable level values had been estimated, and not for the remaining some 4000 constituents of cigarette smoke (IARC, 2004). In addition, potency factors were not available for many of the measured compounds, tolerable levels were lacking for 21 of the 43 compounds, and proper carcinogenicity bioassays have been carried out for only some of the toxicants. As many of the potency factors were derived from animal experiments, the limitations in extrapolating from animal models to the human situation also apply. These limitations preclude use of these indices as quantitative estimates of the likely harm or risk of exposure to these toxicants or of the risk or harm of different cigarette brands. They do, however, provide a useful set of metrics that can be considered in selecting which toxicants to regulate.

Variation in toxicants levels by brand

The variation in the level of toxicant per milligram of nicotine across different brands of cigarettes is a second criterion that can be used to identify toxicants for which mandated reductions are likely to have the greatest impact on lowering the mean levels per milligram of nicotine. The primary criteria remain those related to toxicity; however, little reduction in the average level of a toxicant will be achieved if the values for different brands are clustered tightly around the mean value. Correspondingly, mandated lowering of toxicants with the broadest variation around the mid-point value will result in the largest lowering of the levels in brands containing levels above the mean value.

Measurement of variation among brands

A substantial proportion of the variation across cigarette brands in level of toxicants produced by machine smoking is due to dilution of the smoke produced by ventilation holes in the filter. Normalizing the yields per milligram of nicotine and blocking all the filter vents in the testing regimen are intended to reduce the effect of ventilation on the values recommended as regulatory levels.

The variation in levels of different toxicants can be expressed as the coefficient of variation, which is the standard deviation of the measurement across brands divided by the mean value for all the brands. The coefficient of variation is then stated as the percentage variation for each toxicant around the mean value, allowing direct comparison of the extent to which different toxicants vary across brands. The coefficients of variation for individual toxicants in brands on the market are presented in Annex 3.4 for each of the data sets examined.

An issue of practical concern is the variation in repeated measurements of a given toxicant in a given brand. The reproducibility of testing can vary substantially for different toxicants and with different testing methods. Repeated measurements are used to estimate the mean (true) value for a brand, and the variation of the repeated measurements defines the confidence interval around that mean (true) value. When the variation of repeated measurements is high, more measurements are needed to estimate the mean within a specified confidence interval than when there is little variation. As a practical matter, a regulatory authority will be obliged to validate some of the values for toxicants reported by tobacco companies, by comparing the reported and validated mean values for the toxicant in order to determine whether the value reported by the tobacco company is outside the standard error of the estimate of the mean of the measurements made by the independent laboratory. If the variation of the replicate measurements is high, either larger numbers of replicate measurements will be needed or a wide confidence interval around that mean will result, making regulatory oversight of tobacco industry toxicant testing and reporting difficult and expensive.

Variation among brands and the variation of replicate measurements can be combined into a single measure for the purpose of examining different toxicants. The coefficient of variation across brands for the brand-specific mean values of a toxicant per milligram of nicotine can be presented as a ratio by dividing it by the mean of the coefficients of variation reported for the replicate measurements of that toxicant per milligram of nicotine by brand (the coefficient of variation among brands over the replicate coefficient of variation). This measure provides an estimate of the magnitude of the variation across brands relative to the reproducibility of the measurement, and potentially identifies those toxicants for which the brand variation is sufficiently large to support mandated reduction regulation and for which the burden of regulatory validation of tobacco industry smoke toxicant reporting will be modest.

Table 3.5 presents the ratios of the coefficients of variation for Philip Morris international brands, Canadian brands and Australian brands. The shaded cells of the table represent toxicants for which animal carcinogenicity and non-cancer response indices have been calculated. Examination of the values for the ratios and the ranking of the toxicants in each of the three data sets shows that there are substantial differences in the variation of toxicants in cigarette brands in the three markets. For example, benzo[*a*]pyrene, which ranks high in the Canadian brands, is much lower in the Philip Morris international brands. In contrast, some toxicants such as phenol and CO rank high in each of the three data sets.

The values of the ratios for individual toxicants found in the Philip Morris international brands and the Canadian brands suggest that there is sufficient variation across brands in most of the toxicant levels that mandated reductions would have a substantial effect on the levels in the brands remaining on the market.

A second approach to examining variation across brands is presented in Figures 3.5–3.7, which present the maximum and minimum values for each toxicant in the brand data set, expressed as a ratio of the median value for that toxicant. The value for the 90th percentile value is also presented, as is the line for 125% of the median value. This format allows direct examination of the range of toxicant values across brands without any adjustment for variation in replicate measurement for that toxicant. The 90% value is presented to identify those toxicants for which a single brand or a few brands are outliers on the high side of the median value, and correspondingly for which only a few brands have a high level per milligram of nicotine. The figures indicate that the Philip Morris international brands and the Canadian brands show more variation than the Australian brands, which may be due partly to the small number of brands (15) reported to the Australian Government. Furthermore, in each data set, the variation for some toxicants is proportionally larger than for other toxicants, suggesting that they may be toxicants for which setting mandated limits would have a relatively greater effect. For some toxicants, the maximum value is substantially higher than the 90th percentile value, indicating that relatively few brands in the data set have disproportionately high levels of these toxicants.

Table 3.5
Ratio of coefficient of variation in toxicant levels per milligram of nicotine among brands to the mean of replicate coefficients of variation

Philip Morris brands		Canadian brands (excluding French and US brands)		Australian brands	
Toxicant	**Ratio**	**Toxicant**	**Ratio**	**Toxicant**	**Ratio**
NNN	4.89	Benzo[*a*]pyrene	4.90	Resorcinol	2.75
Carbon monoxide	4.83	Phenol	4.90	Phenol	2.71
N′-Nitrosoanatabine	4.72	Isoprene	4.87	*o*-Cresol	2.57
Cadmium	4.19	*m*- and *p*-Cresol	4.27	4-Aminobiphenyl	2.48
Phenol	3.93	Carbon monoxide	4.22	Cadmium	2.41
Nitric oxide	3.84	NNK	4.12	NNN	2.39
Nitrogen oxides	3.74	2-Aminonaphthalene	3.81	Carbon monoxide	2.27
m- and *p*-Cresol	3.65	*o*-Cresol	3.78	3-Aminobiphenyl	2.27
Total hydrogen cyanide	3.55	4-Aminobiphenyl	3.75	*N′*-Nitrosoanatabine	2.07
Hydroquinone	3.5	Toluene	3.58	Mercury	1.96
Ammonia	3.41	Hydrogen cyanide	3.39	*m*- and *p*-Cresol	1.95
Lead	3.05	Butyraldehyde	3.33	Benzo[*a*]pyrene	1.94
Impinger hydrogen cyanide	3.03	Cadmium	3.31	2-Aminonaphthalene	1.90
Quinoline	3.01	Acetone	3.28	Quinoline	1.88
Styrene	2.98	Benzene	3.27	Styrene	1.78
Formaldehyde	2.97	Formaldehyde	3.24	Hydrogen cyanide	1.75
Pad hydrogen cyanide	2.93	Lead	3.22	1,3-Butadiene	1.67
o-Cresol	2.88	Acetaldehyde	3.21	Benzene	1.61
NNK	2.86	Acrolein	3.10	Butyraldehyde	1.60
N′-Nitrosoanabasine	2.86	*N′*-Nitrosoanatabine	3.09	NNK	1.60
4-Aminobiphenyl	2.62	Quinoline	2.89	Isoprene	1.55

Propionaldehyde	2.53	1,3-Butadiene	2.88	*N´*-Nitrosoanabasine	1.55
Acetaldehyde	2.52	Nitrogen oxides	2.78	1-Aminonaphthalene	1.53
Acrolein	2.51	Propionaldeyde	2.78	Ammonia	1.53
Acetone	2.5	Crotonaldehyde	2.74	Acetaldehyde	1.49
Butyraldehyde	2.49	NNN	2.72	Nitric oxide	1.45
Isoprene	2.47	Hydroquinone	2.71	Methyl ethyl ketone	1.44
Catechol	2.44	Nitric oxide	2.56	Nitrogen oxides	1.43
Pyridine	2.36	Pyridine	2.44	Propionaldehyde	1.43
3-Aminobiphenyl	2.08	Acrylonitrile	2.40	Acrolein	1.42
Acrylonitrite	2.05	Catechol	2.38	Pyridine	1.42
Crotonaldehyde	2	Ammonia	2.36	Toluene	1.41
1,3-Butadiene	1.92	*N´*-Nitrosoanabasine	2.14	Acrylonitrile	1.28
Resorcinol	1.9	Styrene	1.93	Acetone	1.28
Benzo[*a*]pyrene	1.89	1-Aminonaphthalene	1.75	Catechol	1.11
Methyl ethyl ketone	1.88	3-Aminobiphenyl	1.74	Hydroquinone	0.99
2-Aminonaphthalene	1.73	Resorcinol	1.72	Formaldehyde	0.98
Toluene	1.72	Mercury	1.59	Crotonaldehyde	0.92
Mercury	1.62			Lead	0.43
Benzene	1.55				
1-Aminonaphthalene	1.53				
Arsenic	0.88				

NNN, *N´*-nitrosonornicotine; NNK, 4-(*N*-nitrosomethylamino)-1-(3-pyridyl)-1-butanone

Figure 3.5

Maximum, minimum and 90% values as ratios of the median of each constituent per milligram of nicotine for international Philip Morris brands, modified intense regimen

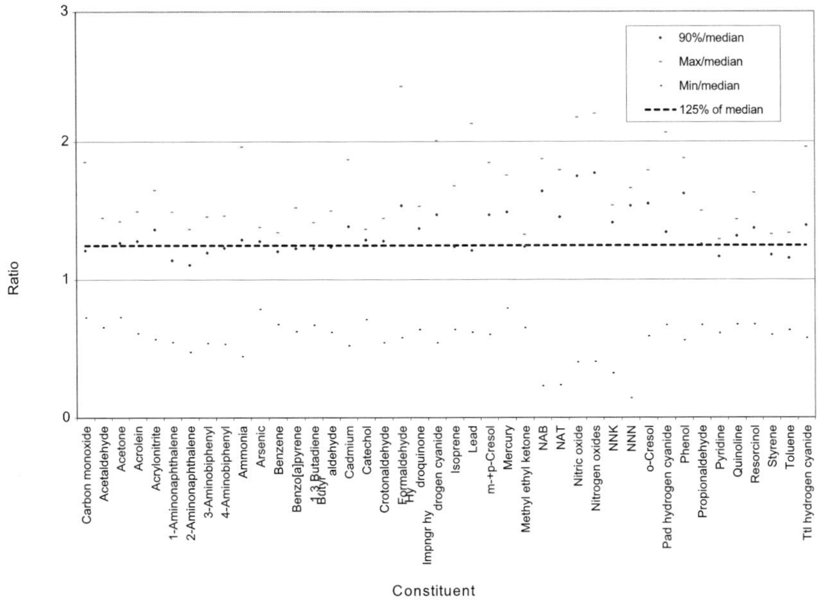

Figure 3.6

Maximum, minimum and 90% values as ratios of the median of each constituent per milligram of nicotine for Canadian brands, minus French and US brands, modified intense regimen

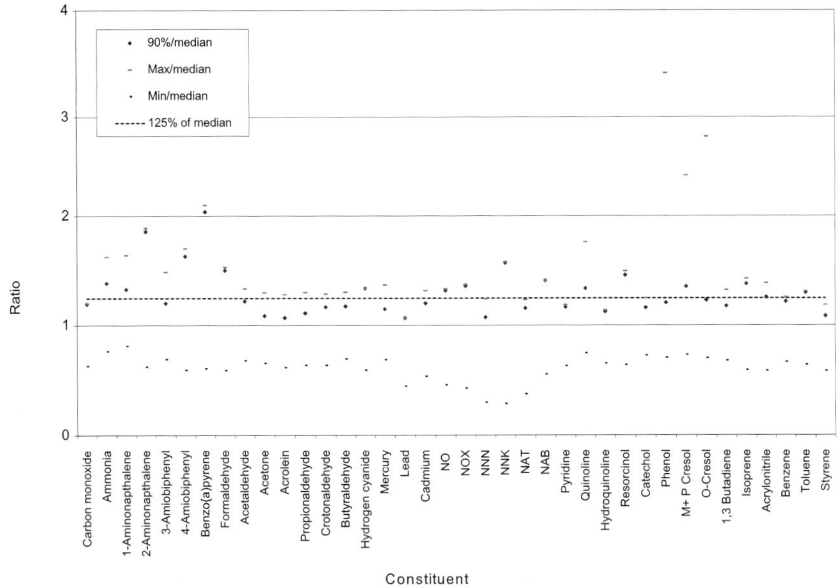

Figure 3.7

Maximum, minimum and 90% values as ratios of the median of each constituent per milligram of nicotine for Australian brands, modified intense regimen

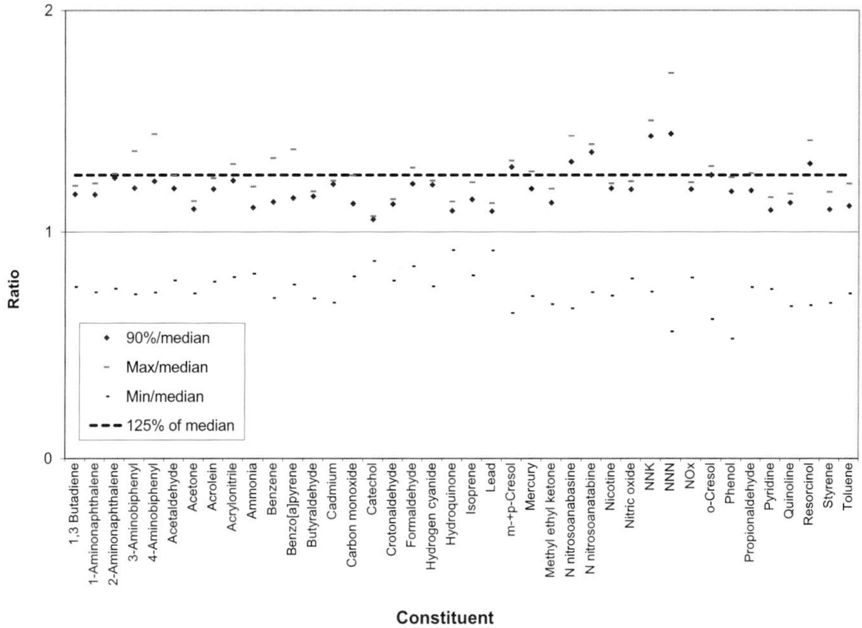

It is also worth noting that, even when the French and US brands are excluded, the Canadian data set showed substantial variation in the levels of TSNA per milligram of nicotine, suggesting that setting national levels for these compounds might be reasonable for countries that do not have a high fraction of blended cigarettes on their market.

Variation across data sets

A further useful formulation of the variation in toxicant levels is a comparison of the mean levels of toxicants in different data sets. This defines differences in yield from the modified intense smoking regimen that result from differences in the design of cigarettes offered for sale in different markets. These differences may allow identification of toxicants that can be lowered by changing cigarette design or blends. If the mean level of toxicant per milligram of nicotine in brands sold in one market, or by one manufacturer, differs substantially from that in other markets or from other manufacturers, it is clearly possible to manufacture cigarettes that yield lower levels of that toxicant. This kind of evidence can be used to define targets for toxicant levels per milligram of nicotine that might be set by regulators as mandatory goals, as it defines the levels that can be achieved by different cigarette designs more broadly than with a single market or a single manufacturer.

Figure 3.8 presents the mean levels of each toxicant per milligram of nicotine across brands for the Canadian data, the Canadian data minus French and US brands and the Australian data. The means are presented as the ratio of the mean value for the toxicant per milligram of nicotine in the specified data set to the mean levels reported by Counts et al. (2005) for the international Philip Morris brands. The variation in toxicant levels between the data sets is as large as, and sometimes exceeds, the variation in levels across brands within a data set. The differences between the Philip Morris international brands and the Canadian and Australian brands are not limited to the commonly recognized differences in TSNA levels, and the magnitude of the variations suggests that examination of differences in toxicant yields from brands sold in different markets could provide better understanding of the levels of individual toxicants that could be achieved by changing cigarette design and manufacturing practices.

Figure 3.8
Ratios of means for constituents of brands in Australian and two Canadian samples to the mean found in the sample of Counts et al. (2005)

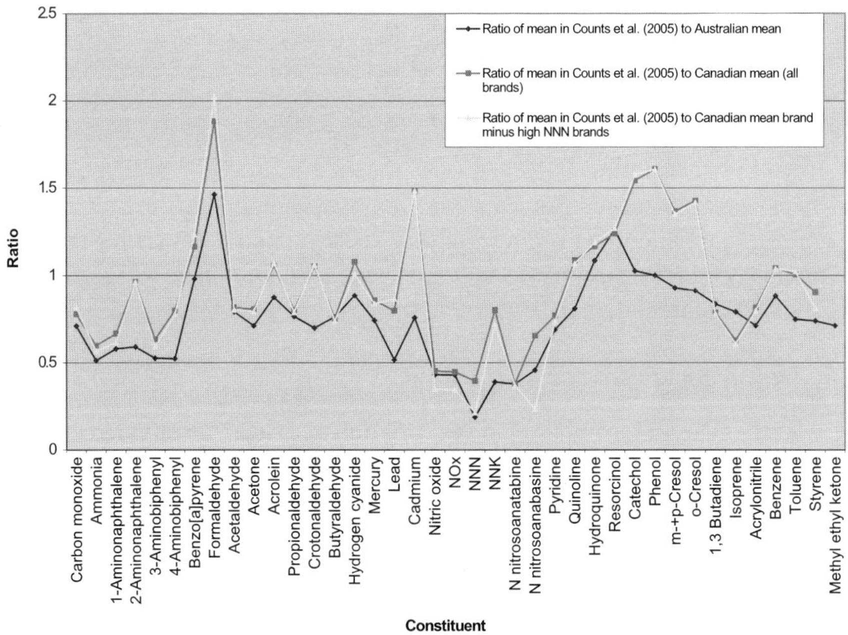

NNN, *N*′-nitrosonornicotine

3.6 Recommended toxicants for reporting and regulation

A list of toxicants with high priority for consideration was identified on the basis of the criteria described above (Table 3.6). Benzo[*a*]pyrene was included despite its low toxicant animal carcinogenicity index because it is a proxy for a family of PAHs found in smoke and because there is a wealth of evidence establishing the carcinogenicity of many of these PAHs. The toxicant 4- aminobiphenyl was added because it is a human carcinogen, although experimental data did not allow a proper T25 calculation. Isoprene was omitted because of its structural similarity to 1,3-butadiene and its lower toxicant animal carcinogenicity index. NNK and NNN were included as they had already been identified in the first report (WHO, 2007) on mandating reductions in toxicant yields. Crotonaldehyde was included because of its reactive α,β-unsaturated aldehyde structure, although a tolerable level value was lacking. CO was also included even though it has a relatively low toxicant non-cancer response index, as it is thought to be mechanistically related to cardiovascular disease.

Table 3.6
Initial list of priority toxicants

Toxicant	Comments
Acetaldehyde	TACI 6.1, TNCRI 67.1
Acrolein	TNCRI 1099
Acrylonitrile	TACI 1.4, TNCRI 2.1
4-Aminobiphenhyl	Human carcinogen, but no experimental data for T25 calculation
2-Aminonaphthalene	TACI 0.68
Benzene	TACI 2.6
Benzo[*a*]pyrene	TACI 0.01
1,3-Butadiene	TACI 9.9, TNCRI 2.6, Group 1, Human carcinogen
Cadmium	TACI 1.7, TNCRI 2.6
Carbon monoxide	Relatively low TNCRI, but mechanistically related to endothelial dysfunction in cardiovascular disease
Catechol	TACI 0.58
Crotonaldehyde	Aldehyde with reactive alkene structure, no threshold limit value, inadequate evidence for carcinogenicity
Formaldehyde	TNCRI 19.8
Hydrogen cyanide	TNCRI 17.2
Hydroquinone	TACI 1.2
Nitrogen oxides	TNCRI 3.1
NNN	Identified by WHO (2007)
NNK	Identified by WHO (2007)

TACI, toxicant animal carcinogenicity index; TNCRI, toxicant non-cancer response index; NNN, *N*′-nitrosonornicotine; NNK, 4-(*N*-nitrosomethylamino)-1-(3-pyridyl)-1-butanone

The working group also considered other measured toxicants for which no T25 or tolerable level values were available. There are several metals in cigarette smoke (arsenic, cadmium, chromium, nickel, lead, mercury, selenium) that occur either at low levels or could not be quantified in the three data sets. Although these metals are quite toxic, only cadmium was found to present at levels that contribute appreciably to the toxicant animal carcinogenicity and toxicant non-cancer response indices, and so was included.

The preliminary list of 16 toxicants in Table 3.6 satisfied the criteria for sufficient evidence of carcinogenicity or known respiratory or cardiac toxicity, variation in levels in different brands in different countries, being readily measurable and with possibilities for lowering yields in a product.

This initial list of 16 priority toxicants plus NNN and NNK was then discussed by the group at length to reduce it to a number that would be considered to be manageable by regulators. As an overall expert assessment, it was concluded that seven (in addition to NNN and NNK) compounds are the most hazardous toxicants in cigarette smoke for which there is potential for reduction in cigarette smoke emissions, which represent different chemical families of toxicants and different phases of smoke and which show lung and cardiovascular toxicity as well as carcinogenicity. The seven toxicants are:

- acetaldehyde
- acrolein
- benzene
- benzo[a]pyrene
- 1,3-butadiene
- carbon monoxide and
- formaldehyde.

The remaining toxicants in the initial list of 16 should be measured and reported.

3.6.1 *Toxicity of the selected constituents*

Compounds proposed for regulation

Acetaldehyde: The concentrations of acetaldehyde in mainstream cigarette smoke are similar to those of nicotine, more than 1000 times that of total carcinogenic TSNA and about 100 000 times the concentration of benzo[*a*]pyrene, although acetaldehyde is a weaker carcinogen. Acetaldehyde is found widely in the diet and the environment and is the major metabolite of ethanol. It is also implicated as an enhancer of behavioural, endocrine and neuronal responses to nicotine in rats (Cao et al., 2007). Feron et al. (1991) demonstrated the carcinogenicity of acetaldehyde administered by inhalation to rats and hamsters (IARC, 1999a). Acetaldehyde is widely considered to be a major cause of head-and-neck cancers related to alcohol consumption (IARC, 1999a; Brennan et al., 2004; Baan et al., 2007). The genetic effects of acetaldehyde have been summarized (IARC, 1999a). Positive responses have been obtained in a variety of asays for genotoxicity in eukaryotes. DNA adducts of acetaldehyde have been detected in leukocytes of smokers, which decrease upon smoking cessation (Chen et al., 2006). There is inadequate evidence for the carcinogenicity of acetaldehyde in humans (IARC, 1999a). Acetaldehyde has been evaluated as 'possibly carcinogenic to humans' (Group 2B) by an IARC working group (IARC, 1999a) and as 'reasonably anticipated to be a human carcinogen' by the US Department of Health and Human Services (2004b).

Acrolein: Acrolein is a commonly occurring combustion product to which there is occupational and environmental exposure via inhalation (IARC, 1995a). It is an intense irritant, and displays a range of toxic effects including ciliotoxicity (IARC, 1995a; Kensler, Battista, 1963). It causes eye and respiratory irritation in humans, andepeated inhalation results in changes in the upper and lower respiratory tract. In dogs, acute congestion, changes in bronchiolar epithelial cells and emphysema were found after inhalation of acrolein (IARC, 1995a). Acrolein potentiates the contractile response of passively sensitized human bronchi to specific antigen stimulation (Roux et al., 1999). Acrolein has been identified as a hazardous air pollutant that is of particular concern for people with asthma (Leikauf, 2002). With the exception of one study in which bladder tumours were produced in an initiation–promotion protocol in rats treated with acrolein (by intraperitoneal injection) followed by dietary uracil, no carcinogenic effects of acrolein were reported (Cohen et al., 1992). Acrolein as a metabolite is widely considered to be responsible for the bladder toxicity of the chemotherapeutic agent cyclophosphamide. Acrolein–DNA adducts have been identified in a variety of human tissues, and their levels are higher in oral tissue from smokers than from non-smokers (Chung, Chen, Nath, 1996; Nath et al., 1998). The pattern of mutations in the *P53* tumour suppressor gene in lung tumours from smokers is similar to the pattern of DNA damage caused by acrolein (Feng et al., 2006). An IARC working group concluded that acrolein was not classifiable with respect to its carcinogenicity to humans (Group 3) (IARC, 1995a).

Benzene: Humans are exposed to benzene mainly through inhalation of ambient air. Sources of benzene include automobile engine exhaust, industrial emissions and evaporation from fuel during gasoline self-service. There are also small amounts in food. Cigarette smoke is a major source of benzene, both for smokers and for non-smokers exposed to second-hand smoke (Department of Health and Human Services 2004b). Benzene induces chromosomal aberrations, micronuclei and sister chromatid exchanges in bone-marrow cells of mice (IARC, 1987). Benzene causes multiple types of tumours in both rats and mice exposed by various routes, including oral administration, inhalation, injection and dermal application (IARC, 1987; Department of Health and Human Services, 2004b). Cohort epidemiological studies studies of occupational exposure demonstrate that benzene causes acute and chronic myelogenic leukaemias (IARC, 1987; Department of Health and Human Services, 2004b). Benzene is classified as carcinogenic to humans by both IARC (Group 1) (IARC, 1987) and the US Department of Health and Human Services (2004b) and is probably a cause of leukaemia in smokers (IARC, 2004).

*Benzo[*a*]pyrene*: Benzo[*a*]pyrene is a prototypic representative of the PAH class of carcinogens, which are products of the incomplete combustion of organic matter and occur in cigarette smoke and the general environment as a mixture. Benzo[*a*]pyrene is always a component of this mixture and is considered a surrogate for carcinogenic PAHs. Considerable evidence supports an important role for PAHs as causes of lung cancer and other cancers in smokers (Hecht, 1999; Pfeifer et al., 2002; Hecht, 2003). Carcinogenic PAHs in cigarette smoke include benzo[*a*]pyrene, benz[*a*]anthracene, methylchrysenes, benzofluoranthenes, indeno[1,2,3-*cd*]pyrene and dibenz [*a,h*]anthracene, with total concentrations at least 5–10 times that of benzo [*a*]pyrene (IARC, 2004). Certain PAHs, including some of those in cigarette smoke, are potent locally acting carcinogens that induce lung and tracheal tumours in rodents and skin tumours in mice. Fractions of cigarette smoke condensate enriched in PAHs are carcinogenic on mouse skin (Hecht, 1999). The uptake of PAHs by smokers has been clearly demonstrated, and there is solid evidence for the presence of DNA adducts derived from benzo[*a*]pyrene in lung tissue from some smokers (Hecht, 2002; Boysen, Hecht, 2003; Beland et al., 2005). The pattern of mutations in the *P53* tumour suppressor gene in lung tumours from smokers is similar to the pattern of DNA damage caused in vitro by diol epoxide metabolites of PAHs and by benzo[*a*]pyrene in cell culture (Denissenko et al., 1996; Smith et al., 2000; Pfeifer et al., 2002; Tretyakova et al. 2002). The pattern of *KRAS* oncogene mutations observed in lung tumours from smokers is also similar to that found in lung tumours from animals treated with PAHs such as benzo[*a*]pyrene (Westra et al., 1993; Mills et al., 1995; Nesnow et al., 1998; Ahrendt et al., 2001). Collectively, these observations strongly support the role of PAHs as causes of lung cancer and perhaps other cancers in smokers. An IARC working group classified benzo[*a*]pyrene as carcinogenic to humans (Group 1) (Straif et al., 2005).

1,3-Butadiene: Other than through cigarette smoking, exposure to 1,3-butadiene occurs mainly in occupational settings and predominantly by inhalation (IARC, 1999c; Department of Health and Human Services 2004f). It is used as an intermediate in the manufacture of polymers and copolymers and in synthetic rubber production. 1,3-Butadiene is a multi-organ carcinogen in mice and rats. The sites of tumour induction in mice include the haematopoietic system, heart, lung, forestomach, Harderian gland, preputial gland, liver, mammary gland, ovary and kidney, while in rats tumours have been observed in pancreas, testis, thyroid gland, mammary gland, uterus and Zymbal gland (IARC, 1999a; Department of Health and Human Services 2004a). *Hprt* mutations have been observed in lymphocytes isolated from mice exposed to 1,3-butadiene or its epoxide metabolites, and in workers exposed occupationally (Department of Health and Human Services, 2004b). Epoxide metabolites of 1,3-butadiene form DNA adducts, including cross-links (Park, Tretyakova, 2004). These metabolites are formed in rodents and humans (Department of Health and Human Services, 2004b). The US Department of Health and Human Services (2004b) ranks 1,3-butadiene as a 'known human carcinogen', and an IARC working group declared it a Group 1 human carcinogen (IARC, in press).

Carbon monoxide: Half of the carbon monoxide produced is due to incomplete combustion of organic material, automobile exhaust being a major source. CO is formed endogenously from catabolic degradation of haem, the carboxyhaemoglobin level being about 0.7%. CO competes with oxygen for binding to haemoglobin with an affinity that is 250 times greater than that of oxygen. CO impairs the release of oxygen from haemoglobin, resulting in tissue hypoxia. CO has neurotoxic effects that may be related to the release of nitric oxide. Exposure to CO at a level of 2000 mg/l of air for 3–4 h results in 70% carboxyhaemoglobin and death. Acute CO-related symptoms are unlikely to occur in smokers, who usually have carboxyhaemoglobin levels of about 5–6% (Scherer, 2006). CO in smokers is believed to reduce oxygen delivery, cause endothelial dysfunction and promote the progression of atherosclerosis and other cardiovascular diseases (Department of Health and Human Services, 2004a; Ludvig, Miner, Eisenberg, 2005; Scherer, 2006).

Formaldehyde: Exposure to formaldehyde occurs through endogenous metabolism and in a variety of occupational and environmental settings in addition to cigarette smoke. Formaldehyde is genotoxic in multiple in vitro systems and in exposed humans and laboratory animals. Inhalation exposure to formaldehyde induces squamous cell carcinomas of the nasal cavities in rats, while studies in mice and hamsters by inhalation and by other routes of administration produced mixed results. Epidemiological studies of the relation of occupational exposure to formaldehyde and cancer at various sites provide, according to an IARC working group (IARC, 2006), sufficient evidence that formaldehyde causes nasopharyngeal cancer in humans, strong but not sufficient evidence for a causal association between leukaemia and occupational exposure to formaldehyde, and limited epidemiological evidence that formaldehyde causes sinonasal cancer in humans. Taking all the evidence together, the IARC working group concluded that formaldehyde is carcinogenic to humans (Group 1) (IARC, 2006). The US Department of Health and Human Services (2004b) rates formaldehyde as 'reasonably anticipated to be a human carcinogen'.

Compounds proposed for reporting

Acrylonitrile: Acrylonitrile is an important industrial chemical used in the manufacture of synthetic fibres, resins, plastics, elastomers and rubber (Department of Health and Human Services, 2004b). Inhalation and dermal exposure in occupational settings constitute the primary exposure circumstances, in addition to cigarette smoke. Acrylonitrile induces tumours at multiple sites, including the forestomach, central nervous system, mammary gland and Zymbal gland, in rats when administered orally or by inhalation. Increases in cancer frequency have not been found consistently in epidemiological studies of workers exposed to acrylonitrile (IARC, 1999a; Department of Health and Human Services, 2004b). Acrylonitrile is mutagenic in some genotoxicity assays (IARC, 1999a). It readily forms adducts with proteins, presumably through its epoxide metabolite, and acrylonitrile–haemoglobin adducts are found at higher levels in smokers than non-smokers (IARC, 1999a; Fennell et al., 2000). An IARC working group concluded that acrylonitrile is possibly carcinogenic to humans (Group 2B) (IARC, 1999a), while the US Department of Health and Human Services (2004b) concluded that it is 'reasonably anticipated to be a human carcinogen'.

4-Aminobiphenyl: Commercial use and production of 4-aminobiphenyl have been widely discontinued, and cigarette smoking is presently probably the major source of human exposure. 4- Aminobiphenyl induced bladder papillomas and carcinomas in rabbits and dogs after oral administration and caused neoplasms at various sites in mice, including angiosarcoma, hepatocellular tumours and bladder carcinomas. Subcutaneous administration to rats produced tumours of the mammary gland and intestine. 4-Aminobiphenyl was genotoxic in short-term mutagenicity assays and formed DNA adducts in the bladder epithelium of dogs (IARC, 1987). 4-Aminobiphenyl– haemoglobin adducts have been quantified in smokers (Skipper, Tannenbaum, 1990) at levels higher than in non-smokers, related to dose and decreasing upon smoking cessation (Maclure et al., 1990; Skipper, Tannenbaum, 1990; Castelao et al., 2001). Epidemiological studies conclusively demonstrate that 4-aminobiphenyl causes bladder cancer in humans (IARC, 1987; Department of Health and Human Services, 2004b). Both IARC and the US Department of

Health and Human Services classify 4-aminobiphenyl as carcinogenic to humans (IARC Group 1) and as a probable cause of bladder cancer in smokers (IARC, 1987, 2004; Department of Health and Human Services, 2004b).

Cadmium: Exposure to cadmium can occur by inhalation of cadmium-containing particles in the ambient air or by consumption of food or drinking-water. Occupational and consumer exposure also occurs. The carcinogenicity of cadmium salts has been demonstrated in multiple studies in rats and other species (IARC, 1999b; Department of Health and Human Services, 2004b). Inhalation of a variety of cadmium compounds caused lung tumours in rats, with a positive dose–response relation. Lung tumours were also induced by intratracheal administration of cadmium compounds to rats. When given orally to rats, cadmium chloride caused dose-related increases in leukaemia and testicular tumours. Cadmium induced DNA and chromosomal damage in several mammalian systems in vitro. Several epidemiological studies of occupationally exposed workers indicate that cadmium exposure is a cause of lung cancer. Cadmium is classified as carcinogenic to humans by both IARC (Group 1) (IARC, 1999b) and the US Department of Health and Human Services (2004b).

Catechol: Catechol occurs in various natural dietary items, such as fruits and vegetables. It may be released into the environment during chemical manufacture, but it is not a common environmental pollutant. Catechol has not been shown to induce tumours in mice but caused adenocarcinomas of the glandular stomach after oral administration to several strains of rat. It has considerable co- carcinogenic activity on mouse skin (with benzo[*a*]pyrene) and in rat tongue, oesophagus and stomach. Catechol caused gene mutations in mammalian cells in vitro. There are no available epidemiological data. An IARC working group concluded that catechol is possibly carcinogenic to humans (Group 2B) (IARC, 1999a).

Crotonaldehyde: Crotonaldehyde is a toxicant in gasoline and diesel engine exhaust and occurs in various foods (IARC, 1995b). It is also formed endogenously by lipid peroxidation (Chung, Chen, Nath, 1996). Crotonaldehyde induces neoplastic nodules of the liver after oral administration to rats, and it is mutagenic in various genotoxicity assays (IARC, 1995b). Crotonaldehyde–DNA adducts have been detected in human tissues, including the oral mucosa and lungs of smokers (Chung et al., 1999; Zhang et al., 2006). These adducts can also be formed from acetaldehyde. An IARC working group concluded that crotonaldehyde was not classifiable as to its carcinogenicity to humans (Group 3) (IARC, 1995b).

Hydrogen cyanide: Cyanides occur as glycosides in various food products such as nuts and beans. Hydrogen cyanide and other cyanides are converted metabolically to thiocyanate, which occurs in cruciferous vegetables.

Hydrogen cyanide is very toxic, causing immediate death in humans after on oral dose of 0.5–3.5 mg/kg body weight (bw) or inhalation of 270 mg/l of air for a few minutes. It acts by inhibiting cytochrome oxidase in the respiratory chain. Cigarette smoke can reduce detoxification of hydrogen cyanide, which normally occurs via formation of thiocyanate, leading to chronic hydrogen cyanide exposure of smokers and consequent amblyopy, retrobulbar neuritis and sterility (Scherer, 2006). Hydrogen cyanide could be involved in impaired wound healing in smokers (Silverstein, 1992).

Hydroquinone: Hydroquinone occurs as a conjugate in the leaves, bark and fruit of various plants and in some occupational settings, such as in photography. It is also used in the treatment of skin hyperpigmentation. Hydroquinone is a metabolite of benzene and may be involved in leukaemia induction by benzene. Hydroquinone was modestly carcinogenic in mice, inducing hepatocellular adenomas in females in one study and in males in another. It caused renal tubule adenomas in male rats; it was devoid of tumour-promoting activity in most assays. There are no convincing epidemiological data implicating hydroquinone as a carcinogen. It is mutagenic in a variety of in vitro systems. Hydroquinone causes nephropathy in rats as well as aplastic anaemia, liver cord-cell atrophy and ulceration of the gastric mucosa. An IARC working group concluded that hydroquinone is not classifiable as to its carcinogenicity to humans (Group 3) (IARC, 1999a). Hydroquionone is classified in the European Union as a Category 3 carcinogen ('limited evidence of a carcinogenic effect') (http://ecb.jrc.it/classification-labelling/).

2-Naphthylamine: Commercial use and production of 2-naphthylamine is banned in several countries, and there is probably little exposure other than from cigarette smoke (Department of Health and Human Services, 2004b). 2-Naphthylamine is carcinogenic in many animal species. After oral administration, it caused bladder neoplasms in hamsters, dogs and nonhuman primates and liver tumours in mice. Bladder carcinomas have been observed in rats, and it gave positive results in the strain A/J mouse lung adenoma bioassay. 2-Naphthylamine increased the incidence of sister chromatid exchanges in mice and rabbits and was positive in a variety of other short-term assays for genotoxicity. It formed DNA adducts in bladder and liver cells of dogs in vivo. Epidemiological studies conclusively demonstrate that 2-naphthylamine causes bladder cancer in humans (IARC, 1987). Both IARC (1987) and the US Department of Health and Human Services (2004b) rank 2- naphthylamine as carcinogenic to humans (IARC Group 1), and it is probably a cause of bladder cancer in smokers (IARC, 2004).

Nitrogen oxides: Tobacco smoke contains nitric oxide, nitrogen dioxide and nitrous oxide, although freshly generated smoke contains almost exclusively nitric oxide, while nitrogen dioxide is rapidly formed upon 'ageing' of the smoke. The nitrate content of the tobacco determines the nitrogen oxide yields in smoke (IARC, 1986). Nitric oxide induces vasodilation and has been used as a targeted pulmonary vasodilator in newborns (Weinberger et al., 2001). In aqueous solution, nitric oxide can decay to nitrite and nitrogen trioxide, which can nitrosate glutathione and amines. Nitrosation of amines can lead to the formation of carcinogenic nitrosamines. Such in vivo nitrosation has been demonstrated in some studies of smokers (Hecht, 2002). Nitric oxide also causes DNA strand breaks and base alterations, possibly leading directly to mutagenesis and carcinogenesis. It reacts with superoxide to form peroxynitrite, an oxidant that can cause lipid peroxidation, may be involved in DNA damage and could interfere with surfactant functioning (Weinberger et al., 2001). Nitric oxide may contribute to nicotine addiction by increasing nicotine absorption, reducing symptoms of stress and increasing post-synaptic dopamine levels (Vleeming, Rambali, Opperhuizen, 2002). Nitric oxide is readily oxidized to nitrogen dioxide, a pulmonary irritant. The WHO 1-h mean guideline value for nitrogen dioxide is 200 $\mu g/m^3$, and the annual mean guideline value is 40 $\mu g/m^3$ (http://www.who.euro.int/document/E87950.pdf).

3.6.2 *Methods for measuring the toxicants*

Sampling and reporting

The results of testing for toxicants should be reported yearly for each product for regulation and reporting. Temporal and geographical differences, which are important sources of product variability, should be included in any examination of dissimilarities within and across products. Samples should be collected by the standard method described in ISO 8243. Cigarettes should be obtained as part of a series of samplings at different times. The period for reporting (1 year) should be divided into at least five sub-periods. For each brand, 200 cigarettes (10 packs of 20 cigarettes per pack or equivalent) should be taken in each sub-period. Each sample should be drawn from different sampling points. Cigarettes for each analytical method should be assigned equally from each sub-period. Additional samples should be used if repeated testing is required due to any analytical problems. The results of the analyses of these samples should be combined for reporting purposes.

Samples can be taken from manufacturers or importers at their premises or from retail locations. Taking samples at business location allows easier access to samples but presents other concerns. If the date of the visit is known, the products may be altered or chosen to ensure that they meet regulatory limits. If sampling at a business location is used, samples must be collected without prior notification, by independent investigators. Under no circumstances should regulators allow samples to be delivered by the regulated business for analysis. Obtaining samples at retail locations requires additional resources, but this approach ensures that the products will be those that are directly available to smokers. Purchasing from multiple retail locations can be particularly challenging if the country is large, has limited transport infrastructure or comprises multiple islands or geographical regions that could have different products that are difficult to access. In this case, regulatory authorities may determine that broader sampling is required to obtain a representative sample. Decisions about where to obtain samples are best taken by government officials in each country.

In order to reduce variation in a product due to storage conditions, samples should be conditioned for at least 24 h before machine smoking according to the ISO 3402 standard.

Analytical methods

Cigarettes should be analysed by the machine smoking method commonly known as the Canadian intense method, with a 55-ml puff volume, 2.0-s puff duration, 30-s puff interval and 100% vent blocking. The butt length is 23 mm for non-filter cigarettes or the length of filter paper plus 3 mm for filter brands. Smoke is collected on Cambridge filter pads in most cases. Alternative situations are described below.

Individual measurements are made for each pad, and the number of pads analysed, the mean, the standard deviation and the minimum and maximum are reported for each brand. The dates and locations where each sample was taken are reported with the final results.

Nicotine and carbon monoxide: Nicotine and CO are measured by ISO methods 10315 and 8454, respectively, which have been well validated and are in use in many laboratories worldwide. Cigarettes are smoked with the Canadian intense smoking regimen in standard commercial smoking machines, which are generally equipped with an automated CO analyser as an option. In linear smoking machines, three cigarettes are smoked on each of 20 Cambridge filter pads. In rotary smoking machines, 10 cigarettes are smoked on each of five pads. Care must be taken that breakthrough of the pads does not occur. Nicotine is measured in the cigarette smoke particulate matter that is collected on Cambridge filter pads, and CO is measured in the gas phase, collected in a vapour phase collection bag. The gas phase is automatically passed through a non-dispersive infra-red analyser, and the percentage CO is determined by comparison with known standard CO gas concentrations. The Cambridge filter pad is extracted with isopropanol containing anethole as the internal standard. The extract is analysed for nicotine by packed column gas chromatography with flame ionization detection. The gas chromatography response is compared with that of known standard solutions to determine the amount of nicotine in each pad. Details of this official Health Canada method can be found at http://www.qp.gov.bc.ca/stat_reg/regs/health/oic_94.pdf (p. 165; accessed 21 December 2006). The official ISO method can be obtained at http://www.iso.ch/iso/en/cataloguelistpage.cataloguelist?commid=3350&scopelist=all.

Tobacco-specific nitrosamines: There is currently no ISO-validated method for measuring TSNA in mainstream tobacco smoke, but an ISO method is being developed. A method that has been in use in many tobacco testing laboratories and is widely used to measure these compounds is gas chromatography with thermal energy analysis. This technique is selective for nitroso-containing compounds and has been successfully used for many years for measuring TSNA in tobacco smoke. In linear smoking machines, five cigarettes are smoked on each of 20 Cambridge filter pads. In rotary smoking machines, 20 cigarettes are smoked on each of five pads. TSNA are measured in the mainstream cigarette smoke particulate that is captured on Cambridge filter pads and are concentrated by extraction with dichloromethane, followed by column chromatography onto basic alumina. The fraction containing the TSNA is eluted and analysed by gas chromatography–thermal energy analysis. A description of this official Health Canada method can be found at http://www.qp.gov.bc.ca/stat_reg/ regs/health/oic_94.pdf (p. 119; accessed 21 December 2006). Alternative methods, including liquid chromatography with tandem mass spectrometry (http://www.aristalabs.com/pdf/mainstreamanalysis.pdf (accessed 26 April 2006) or that described by Wu, Ashley and Watson (2003), have also been used, but any alternative technique used must be shown to be as accurate and reproducible as gas chromatography–thermal energy analysis before use. *N′*-Nitrosoanatabine and *N′*-nitrosoanabasine can also be determined with this method at minimal additional cost.

Carbonyls (formaldehyde, acetaldehyde, acrolein, crotonaldehyde): There is currently no ISO- validated method for measuring carbonyls in mainstream tobacco smoke, but a method has been used successfully in many laboratories to measure these compounds. Two cigarettes are smoked in each of 25 smoking runs. The unfiltered mainstream cigarette smoke is bubbled through impingers containing 2,4-dinitrophenylhydrazine in acidified acetonitrile. An aliquot of the extract is filtered, diluted and subjected to reversed-phase gradient liquid chromatography with ultraviolet detection. Levels are quantified by external standard procedures. Care must be taken that breakthrough of the impinger solution does not occur; if this occurs, the number of cigarettes tested must be decreased. Retention times and analysis of pure compounds are used to verify the identification of peaks of interest. Details of this official Health Canada method can be found at http://www.qp.gov.bc.ca/stat_reg/regs/health/oic_94.pdf (p. 41; accessed 21 December 2006). Acetone, propionaldehyde and butyraldehyde can also be determined with this method at minimal additional cost.

Volatiles (1,3-butadiene, acrylonitrile, benzene): There is currently no ISO-validated method for measuring volatiles in mainstream tobacco smoke, but a method has been used successfully in many laboratories to measure these compounds. The unfiltered mainstream cigarette smoke is bubbled through cryogenic traps containing purge-and-trap grade methanol, with benzene-D_6 as an internal standard. Five cigarettes are smoked through each of 10 traps. An aliquot of the solution is injected into a gas chromatograph–mass spectrometer for analysis. Quantification is carried out by comparing relative peak areas to those of standard solutions of known concentrations of the analytes of interest. Retention times and analysis of pure compounds are used to verify the identification of peaks of interest. Details of this official Health Canada method can be found at http://www.qp.gov.bc.ca/stat_reg/regs/health/oic_94.pdf (p. 173; accessed 21 December 2006). Isoprene, toluene and styrene can also be determined with this method at minimal additional cost.

*Benzo[*a*]pyrene*: There is currently no ISO-validated method for measuring benzo[*a*]pyrene in mainstream tobacco smoke, but an ISO method is being developed. A method has nevertheless been used successfully in many laboratories to measure this compound. In linear smoking machines, two cigarettes are smoked on each of 25 Cambridge filter pads. In rotary smoking machines, 10 cigarettes are smoked on each of five pads. The mainstream cigarette smoke particulate is captured on Cambridge filter pads, but care must be taken that breakthrough of the pad does not occur. Particulate matter is extracted from the pad with cyclohexane. A portion of this extract is passed through silica and NH_2 (amino) cartridges. Benzo[*a*]pyrene is eluted from the cartridge with hexane, blown down to dryness and reconstituted in acetonitrile. The sample is subjected to reverse-phase liquid chromatography and quantified by fluorescence detection. A description of this official Health Canada method can be found at http://www.qp.gov.bc.ca/stat_reg/regs/health/oic_94.pdf (p. 27; accessed 21 December 2006). Alternative methods, including gas chromatography–mass spectrometry http://www.aristalabs.com/pdf/mainstreamanalysis.pdf (accessed 26 April 2006) or that described by Ding and colleagues (2005), have also been used. An ISO method being developed by ISO involving gas chromatography–mass spectrometry can be purchased (http://www.iso.ch/iso/en/cataloguelistpage.cataloguelist?commid=3350&scopelist=all). These gas chromatography–mass spectrometry methods can also be used to measure a series of PAHs other than benzo[*a*]pyrene.

Aromatic amines (2-aminonaphthalene, 4-aminobiphenyl): There is currently no ISO-validated method for measuring aromatic amines in mainstream tobacco smoke, but a method has been used successfully in many laboratories. In linear smoking machines, five cigarettes are smoked on each of 20 Cambridge filter pads. In rotary smoking machines, 20 cigarettes are smoked on each of five pads. Care must be taken that breakthrough of the Cambridge filter pad does not occur. The pad is extracted with 100 ml of 5% hydrochloric acid solution. The internal standard (D_9-aminobiphenyl) is spiked into the solution. The extract is washed with basic dichloromethane and extracted with hexane. Sodium sulfate is used to dry the extracts, and the aromatic amines are derivitized with pentafluoropropionic acid anhydride and trimethylamine. The resulting material is passed through a Florisil column. Aromatic amines are quantified by gas chromatography–mass spectrometry. A description of this official Health Canada method can be found at http://www.qp.gov.bc.ca/stat_reg/regs/health/oic_94.pdf (p. 16; accessed 21 December 2006). 1-Aminonaphthalene and 3-aminobiphenyl can also be determined with this method at minimal additional cost.

Hydrogen cyanide: There is currently no ISO-validated method for measuring hydrogen cyanide in mainstream tobacco smoke, but a method has been used successfully in many laboratories. While two cigarettes are smoked, the particulate is collected on a Cambridge filter pad, and the gas phase is trapped in an impinger containing 0.1N sodium hydroxide directly behind the pad. Twenty-five smoke sampling runs are carried out. The Cambridge filter pad is extracted with 0.1N sodium hydroxide. Both the pad extract and the impinger solution are analysed by continuous flow colorimetric analysis. The analysis step involves conversion of cyanide to cyanogen chloride and reaction with a pyrazolone reagent. Quantification is accomplished by comparison with the response of known standards. Details of this official Health Canada method can be found at http://www.qp.gov.bc.ca/stat_reg/regs/health/oic_94.pdf (p. 63; accessed 21 December 2006).

Cadmium: There is currently no ISO-validated method for measuring cadmium in mainstream tobacco smoke, but methods have been used successfully in many laboratories. The most challenging aspect of the analysis of heavy metals is collecting the sample without contamination. The Cambridge filter pads used in the usual mainstream smoke collection methods can be significantly contaminated, invalidating the measurement. Scientists have turned to alternative means of collecting smoke. Once the smoke has been collected, a number of equally valid analytical instruments can be used for quantification. Ten cigarettes are smoked for each determination, and the particulate is collected by electrostatic precipitation to avoid contamination. Ten separate smoking runs are carried out. The total particulate matter in the precipitator is removed by washing with methanol. The methanol is removed by gentle heating and blow-down. The remaining material is microwave-digested with hydrochloric acid, nitric acid and hydrogen peroxide. The resulting solution is analysed by atomic absorption spectroscopy, inductively coupled argon plasma–atomic emission spectroscopy or inductively coupled argon plasma–mass spectrometry. Quantification is accomplished by comparison with the response of known standards. Details of this official Health Canada method can be found at http://www.qp.gov.bc.ca/stat_reg/regs/health/oic_94.pdf (p. 85; accessed 21 December 2006). Other heavy metals, such as nickel, lead, chromium, arsenic and selenium, can also be determined with this method. A similar method can be found at http://www.aristalabs.com/pdf/mainstreamanalysis.pdf (accessed 26 April 2006). An alternative means of collecting smoke particulate has been described by Pappas et al. (2006). While requiring specially prepared filters, it does allow the use of normal particulate collection procedures instead of an electrostatic analyser.

Nitrogen oxides: There is no ISO-validated method for measuring oxides of nitrogen in mainstream tobacco smoke, but a method has been used successfully in many laboratories. One cigarette is smoked in the Canadian intense smoking regimen, with 25 smoke sampling runs. The unfiltered smoke is allowed to mix in a smoke-mixing chamber and is then pulled, at regular intervals, into a chemiluminescence nitrogen oxide analyser for measurement of total nitrogen oxides. By reacting the smoke with ozone before determination, the amount of nitric oxide can be determined. The difference in levels of nitrogen oxides and nitric oxide is calculated as nitrogen dioxide. Quantification is accomplished by comparison with the response of known standards. Details of this official Health Canada method can be found at http://www.qp.gov.bc.ca/stat_reg/regs/health/oic_94.pdf (p. 103; accessed 21 December 2006).

Phenols (catechol, hydroquinone): There is currently no ISO-validated method for measuring phenols in mainstream tobacco smoke, but a method has been used successfully in many laboratories. In linear smoking machines, two cigarettes are smoked on each of 25 Cambridge filter pads. In rotary smoking machines, 10 cigarettes are smoked on each of five pads. The mainstream cigarette smoke particulate is captured on Cambridge filter pads; care must be taken that breakthrough of the pad does not occur. The pad is extracted with 40 ml of 1% acetic acid. An aliquot of the extract is filtered and subjected to reverse-phase gradient liquid chromatography with selective fluorescence detection. Phenols are quantified by gas chromatography–mass spectrometry. A description of this official Health Canada method can be found at http://www.qp.gov.bc.ca/stat_reg/regs/health/oic_94.pdf (p. 153; accessed 21 December 2006). Resorcinol, phenol, *m*-cresol, *o*-cresol and *p*-cresol can also be determined with this method at minimal additional cost.

3.6.3 *Existing techniques to reduce specific toxicant emissions in cigarette smoke*

An additional consideration in setting levels of toxicants per milligram of nicotine is the ability of the tobacco industry to modify their products to comply with lower toxicant levels. Examining the published literature and publicly available tobacco industry documents and patents can help determine the extent to which existing technology can be used to reduce the emissions of the specified toxicants in cigarette smoke. An important caveat is that there may be additional evidence of industry capacity to reduce toxicant levels that is not yet publicly available.

Most of the data cited in publicly available reports and documents were obtained by machine smoking with the ISO regimen rather than with the modified intense smoking regimen recommended by TobReg. Nevertheless, the ISO data may provide some insight into the general design changes that would be required. Where possible, attempts have been made to standardize reductions per milligram of tar or nicotine or per unit volume. Most of the data are presented as emissions per stick, but it is important to note that comparisons of per-stick emissions can be highly misleading unless identical products are being compared.

NNN and NNK: The evidence for differences in TSNA levels in different countries was reviewed above. Different approaches have been reported in the literature for reducing the TSNA levels in mainstream smoke. These fall into three broad categories: changing agricultural practices, curing and tobacco blending.

The existing evidence indicates that reducing the use of nitrate fertilizers would reduce TSNA in all types of tobacco cured by any method.

Changing the heating source for flue-curing from propane appears to have reduced TSNA in tobacco cured in this way. Air curing in well-ventilated structures can also lower TSNA in these types of tobacco. In general, cooler temperature and lower relative humidity at the time of curing favour the production of air-cured tobaccos with low leaf TSNA concentrations (1.5–3.5 μg/g), provided that the variety has a low nornicotine content, nitrogen fertilization is moderate, curing is performed in a well-ventilated environment, the tobacco is taken down and stripped as soon as it is cured, and the bales are stored as briefly as possible before the leaves are threshed and stabilized.

Using tobaccos with low TSNA contents would be effective for reducing the content of TSNA in mainstream smoke. The simplest way of reducing TSNA emissions would be to use blends that consist primarily of bright, flue-cured tobacco, as is the tradition in Australia and Canada, where the levels are up to 10-fold lower than those in US blended cigarettes, which contain air-cured burley and other tobaccos. As new curing and other techniques reduce preformed (i.e. in the blend) TSNA, however, formation by pyrosynthesis will become the predominant source. Nitrosation of nicotine, a tertiary amine, during smoking occurs at a much slower rate than that of nornicotine, a secondary amine. This will favour formation of NNN, *N′*-nitrosoanatabine and *N′*-nitrosoanabasine rather than NNK during smoking.

There is little evidence that specialized filters, additives, paper type or porosity or other physical parameters significantly affect TSNA in mainstream smoke, apart from their general effects on overall smoke concentration. Therefore, no engineering changes to products were identified that would specifically affect TSNA concentration. Irwin (1990), in an internal review for British American Tobacco, reported that filtration efficiency for NNN and NNK varied closely with total particulate matter and nicotine, suggesting no selectivity.

Carbonyl compounds (acetaldehyde, acrolein, formaldehyde): These compounds are grouped as they share similar molecular structures and properties. In theory, therefore, the methods for their reduction in smoke should be similar or related.

Acetaldehyde appears to derive from combustion of polysaccharides, including cellulose and added sugars. A number of options have been explored by the tobacco industry to reduce acetaldehyde emissions.

Reducing the concentration of sugars added to tobacco or using blends that contain fewer sugars should reduce acetaldehyde levels. Norman (1999) summarized research on tobacco type, reconstituted sheet and expanded tobacco. On the basis of amount per gram of tobacco burnt, burley tobacco delivered more than bright; reconstituted tobacco was not significantly different from strip tobacco; and expanded tobacco delivered slightly more acetaldehyde. This would suggest that reducing the amount of burley and expanded tobacco in a blend could reduce acetaldehyde yields. Rodgman (1977) noted that increasing the amount of G13 expanded tobacco in a blend yielded less acetaldehyde per cigarette but slightly increased the acetaldehyde per puff.

Because acetaldehyde is a component of the vapour phase that has a low relative molecular mass, it does not affect cellulose acetate fibres or other mechanical filtration devices. Despite a relatively short contact time (< 100 ms), certain volatile components in cigarette smoke are selectively removed by activated charcoal, which has a porous structure and a high surface area (e.g. Tiggelbeck 1967, 1976). In mainstream smoke deliveries, charcoal-filtered cigarettes have been shown to significantly reduce many volatile components, including acetaldehyde (e.g. Xue, Thomas, Koller,

2002). The amount of volatile compounds removed varies directly with the amount of charcoal present in the filter (Norman, 1999). Polzin et al. (2008) reported on three charcoal filtered brands with different levels of charcoal (0, 45, 120 and 180 mg) but similar FTC tar delivery (5–6 mg) and other design parameters. When normalized for nicotine and smoked under Health Canada intense conditions, the filter with the highest carbon content resulted in a greater reduction in acetaldehyde than the non-charcoal brand (brand 1 in Figure 3.9). The trend in the Canadian intense smoking data shows little difference in levels until brand 5, which may suggest that substantial amounts of charcoal (180 mg) are required to reduce acetaldehyde significantly. The large difference between the ISO and Health Canada levels for the 120-mg carbon filter (brand 4) suggests that, at least for acetaldehyde, the higher puffing intensity or vent blocking may overwhelm even 120 mg of charcoal on a filter. These data suggest that a filter containing at least 180 mg of charcoal could reduce the acetaldehyde concentration of smoke by approximately 45% under intense smoking conditions.

Figure 3.9
Acetaldehyde per milligram of nicotine in different brands machine smoked in the ISO and Health Canada intense regimens

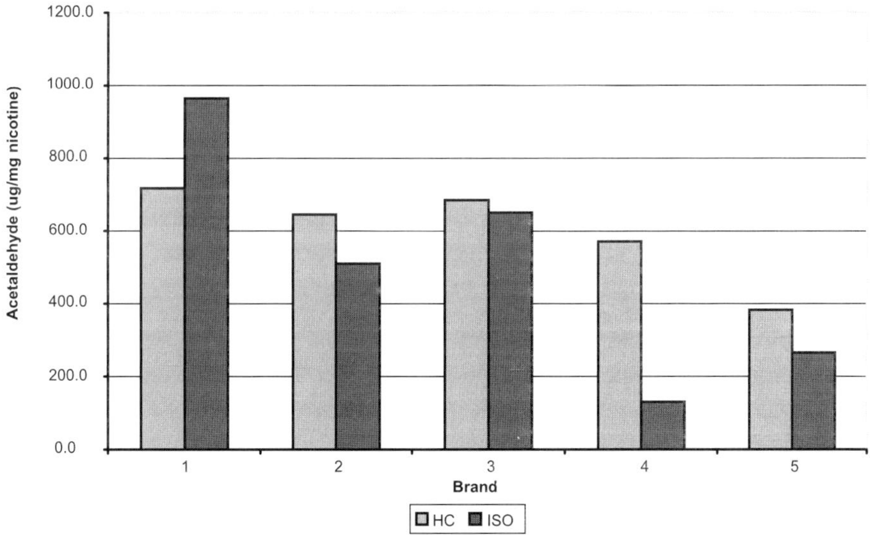

Rodgman (1977) reported the results of an RJ Reynolds study showing that a combination of charcoal and bauxites removed up to 30% of acetaldehyde from smoke. As noted in this internal memo, however, "Charcoal-filtered cigarettes with substantially reduced aldehydes (as well as other gas-phase components) have generally not fared well in the [US] marketplace. Generally, charcoal filtration does not affect FTC 'tar' yield". Laugeson and Fowles

(2005) reported no difference in acetaldehyde levels from two Mild Seven versions containing charcoal and from a similar brand without carbon under Canadian intense conditions. In fact, when normalized for nicotine, the Mild Seven Light actually showed the highest level of acetaldehyde.

Philip Morris USA holds a patent (Rainer, Feins, 1980) for a filter claimed to remove aldehydes selectively from mainstream smoke "comprising a granular carrier containing concentrated hydrogen peroxide, water, and a hydrophilic stabilizer for said hydrogen peroxide." A filter constructed in this manner with silica gel granules was claimed to reduce the acetaldehyde level by 78% as compared with a standard cellulose acetate filter and by approximately 50% as compared with an activated charcoal filter.

Brown & Williamson made commercial use of Duolite in filters, particularly on its Fact 'low-gas' cigarette introduced in the USA in the 1970s. An employee's hand-drawing of the resin's structure is shown in Figure 3.10 (Litzinger, 1972). Duolite is a "porous granular resin ... reacts with hydrogen cyanide and aldehydes removing them from smoke. The resin, partially combined with acetic acid to catalyze the removal of adlehydes was made to Brown & Williamson specifications by Diamond Shamrock. ... Unlike charcoal, which is indiscriminate in that it also removes flavor compounds, Duolite filters smoke selectively" (Brown & Williamson Tobacco, 1977). Duolite resin contains primary, secondary and tertiary amine groups, and acetaldehyde is removed from smoke by addition to primary and secondary amines; subsequent to capture, it may undergo further reactions. The authors of the report on the effectiveness of Duolite noted that the efficiency of filtration depended on smoke pH, regardless of the amount of Duolite used. Brown & Williamson did extensive research on the resin's properties, filtration effectiveness and particle release during manufacture, packaging and smoking (including inhalation and pyrolisis).

In 2002, Brown & Williamson introduced Advance Lights, featuring a 'Trionic' filter, which comprised an ion-exchange resin, charcoal and cellulose acetate at the mouth end and claimed to provide "All of the taste ... Less of the toxins." Little information is available about this product; however, it is described in some detail in the comments of Brown & Williamson in response to petitions from the Campaign for Tobacco Free Kids and the Society for Research on Nicotine and Tobacco for advance regulation by the US Food and Drug Administration (Brown & Williamson, 2002):

> "Smoke released from the burning tobacco first moves through the filter segment containing the Ion Exchange Resin. This material interacts primarily with the semi-volatile constituents of tobacco smoke, particularly ... aldehydes (including formaldehyde) and others like hydrogen cyanide. Some of these materials are trapped within the first segment, reducing their levels as the smoke continues through the filer.

Figure 3.10
Brown & Williamson employee's hand drawing of Duolite structure

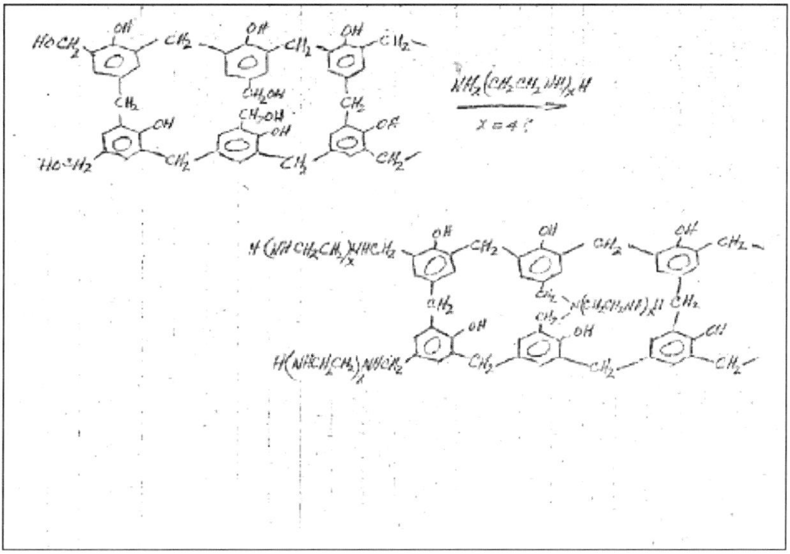

> "Smoke next moves into the filter segment containing specialty carbon. This material adsorbs both semi-volatile constituents and gases. It continues to adsorb the aldehydes from the smoke, as well as trapping other constituents like benzene and acrolein. ... The result of smoke passing through the three-stage Trionic filter is a significant reduction in many of the toxins, as compared to the levels found in smoke delivered by the leading lights cigarette brands."

The acetaldehyde concentration, normalized for tar, does not appear to vary by cigarette circumference (Seeman, Dixon, Haussmann, 2002). Therefore, reducing the circumference of cigarettes would not appear to be an effective reduction strategy. More permeable papers reduce volatile phase constituents generally, but the reduction is less than 10% per cigarette across the range of 20–100 CORESTA [Cooperation Centre for Scientific Research Relative to Tobacco] units (Owens, 1978). Perforated cigarette papers would reduce vapour phase constituents by up to 25% per cigarette across the range of 20–200 CORESTA units, with the greatest drop between 20 and 100 units. Rodgman (1977) noted that "increased porosity paper, perforations in the tobacco rod wrapper, and/or perforations in the filter wrapper" can decrease aldehydes generally, including acetaldehyde. This makes sense, given that it is a gas-phase constituent; thus, increasing the paper porosity would allow more vapour constituents to leave the burning rod. No data could be found on the effects of paper additives on the acetaldehyde concentration, although the 1977 memo notes that slower-burning papers yield more acetaldehyde per cigarette, probably as a consequence of a higher puff count.

Acrolein is an aldehyde and is part of the gas phase of cigarette smoke. Therefore, design changes that would reduce acetaldehyde, as outlined in the previous section, would also tend to reduce acrolein. Indeed, a chart in the RJ Reynolds memo (Rodgman, 1977) shows that, for increasing total air dilution, reductions in acrolein parallel the reduction in acetaldehyde. This includes filter ventilation effects, which would not be effective under Canadian intense smoking conditions, in which the filter vents are blocked. Reducing the use of humectants such as glycerol might also lower emissions of acrolein.

Charcoal filters are known to reduce acrolein levels through adsorption. Polzin et al. (2008) show that acrolein can be reduced by as much as 69% under Canadian intense conditions (normalized for nicotine) when a high-carbon filter (120–180 mg charcoal) is used. Laugeson and Fowles (2005) reported a difference of approximately 15% in acrolein levels in Mild Seven varieties (which contain far less charcoal than the varieties tested by Polzin et al.) and a non-charcoal brand under Canadian intense condition. This held true whether emissions were normalized for nicotine or not. In the 1970s, Lorillard explored an alternative means for reducing acrolein, by addition of various reactive compounds to the filter or tobacco rod, including hydrazines, amines with high relative molecular mass, ammonium phosphate and ammonium carbonate (Ihrig, 1972). By 1976, they had identified some additives that worked to reduce acrolein selectively, but none were patentable (Ihrig, 1976) and the work appears to have been abandoned.

Figure 3.11 shows the levels of acrolein per milligram of nicotine in different brands machine smoked in the ISO and Health Canada intense regimens.

Formaldehyde is known to be generated by both natural and added sugars (Baker, 2006). Therefore, reducing or eliminating exogenous sugars from tobacco processing (e.g. casings) should reduce the formaldehyde yields of cigarettes. Carbon filters have been shown to have some efficacy against formaldehyde in smoke, like other gas-phase constituents. Laugeson and Fowles (2005) reported an approximately 33% reduction in formaldehyde from Mild Seven cigarettes when compared with a non-charcoal-filter comparison brand under intense smoking conditions (normalized for nicotine). They reported a reduction of 75% in formaldehyde from a 180-mg charcoal market brand (Marlboro Ultrasmooth) compared to Marlboro regular when not normalized for nicotine, but the reduction was only 51% when adjusted for nicotine.

It has been shown that the presence of ammonium compounds and amino acids inhibits the generation of formaldehyde from sugars (Baker, 2006). RJ Reynolds explored the reduction in formaldehyde in mainstream smoke by reactions with ammonia. In a memo, Furin and Gentry (1990) described

Figure 3.11

Acrolein per milligram of nicotine in different brands machine smoked in the ISO and Health Canada intense regimens

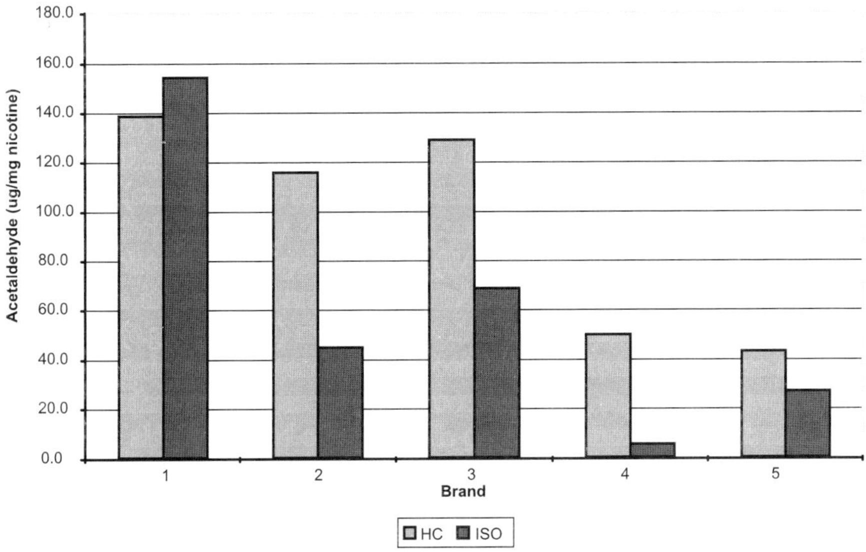

the results of a study of the effects of including ammonia sources (urea and glycine) in the tobacco rod on mainstream yields of various carbonyl compounds. Reductions of 70–98% were found, depending on the level of urea or glycine added. They proposed that formaldehyde is reduced by reaction with ammonia to form hexamethylenetetramine. The authors noted potential tradeoffs between urea and glycine as sources of ammonia, as urea has 2.5 times more ammonia, yet the reductions were similar to those obtained with glycine at equal applications.

A memo from Philip Morris (1998) described the use of silica gels to remove formaldehyde from gas streams. γ-Aminopropylsilane–silica gels are reported to filter formaldehyde from cigarette smoke selectively. In a model system in which formaldehyde-laden gas was puffed through a smoking machine under FTC conditions, the ability of various configurations of silica gels, γ-aminopropylsilane–silica gels and traditional cellulose acetate filters to remove formaldehyde were compared. Correlation analysis of the physical properties of 15 silica gels showed that pore diameter and pore volume were most strongly correlated (values of 0.63 and 0.59, respectively) with the percentage formaldehyde reduction, while particle size showed a negative or no correlation (–0.17 to 0.09). Philip Morris holds at least one patent for γ-aminopropylsilane–silica gels in cigarette filters (Koller et al., 2005).

Benzene is a volatile component of the gas phase with multiple rod precursors (see Ferguson, 2000). Therefore, charcoal filters have been proposed for reducing benzene levels in smoke. G.M. Polzin and colleagues (2008) reported that, under intense smoking conditions and normalization for nicotine, a filter containing at least 120 mg of carbon can reduce benzene emissions by nearly 85%. This observation of machine-generated smoke parallels data on human exposure: Scherer and colleagues (2006) reported that smoking carbon-filter cigarettes resulted in statistically significant reductions in biomarkers of exposure to benzene (e.g. *S*-phenyl mercapturic acid in urine), although the mass-market charcoal-filter cigarettes studied would probably contain far less than 120 mg charcoal. Searches of tobacco documents and patents failed to reveal other methods tested for the reduction of benzene in mainstream smoke.

*Benzo[*a*]pyrene* is the prototypic PAH. Methods to reduce PAH levels in mainstream smoke have been investigated ever since these compounds were identified as significant components of smoke. In the 1950s and early 1960s, several patents were issued for processes for extracting precursor components from tobacco. Rodgman and colleagues at RJ Reynolds (reviewed by Rodgman and Perfetti, 2006) showed that extracting saturated aliphatic hydrocarbons, phytosterols and terpenoids such as solanesol from tobacco decreased the PAH levels in the mainstream smoke of cigarettes made from extracted tobaccos. A study by Tennessee Eastman (1959) examined the effect of extraction on benzo[*a*]pyrene levels. Extracting these components also increased the per-unit-weight content of carbohydrates (including cellulose) in the tobacco, which, as discussed earlier, are precursors of aldehydes. By the 1960s, it was shown that higher levels of nitrates in tobacco led to lower PAH levels in smoke, probably due to the ability of nitrate to interfere with the free-radical processes that generate PAHs.

Wynder and Hoffman (1967) postulated that the observed drops in benzo[*a*]pyrene yields over time might be due to the introduction of reconstituted tobacco, particularly that made from stems (with relatively high nitrate levels), in cigarette design. As nitrates are precursors of the TSNA in smoke, however, this may have increased the TSNA content while lowering the PAH content, in essence trading one class of carcinogen for another. Similarly, given differences in benzo[*a*]pyrene yield between flue-cured and burley tobaccos, a blend containing more burley would be expected to have less benzo[*a*]pyrene. Burley is, however, known to produce more TSNA.

Norman (1999) showed that different types of reconstituted and expanded tobacco have different yields of benzo[*a*]pyrene (and other constituents), depending on how they are processed. Paper process reconstituted tobacco has less benzo[*a*]pyrene than slurry process reconstituted tobacco (0.52 vs. 0.85 μg/g) but more formaldehyde (56.8 vs. 40.5 μg/g) (Halter, Ito, 1978). Similarly, different types of expanded tobacco had different levels of benzo[*a*]pyrene: a standard blend had 0.71 μg/g, an RJ Reynolds puffed tobacco cigarette had 0.76 μg/g, a Philip Morris expanded cigarette had 0.45 μg/g, and a freeze-dried tobacco cigarette had 0.57 μg/g (Halter, Ito, 1978). Rodgman (2001) summarized the changes in cigarettes at various stages of production that had been investigated in order to reduce PAH yields in smoke, as shown in Table 3.7.

Table 3.7
Changes to cigarettes at various stages of production explored to reduce PAH yields in smoke

Changes to plants	Changes to tobacco rod	Changes to design
Tobacco type	Combustion modifiers	Paper porosity
Stalk position	Casing materials	Paper additives
Nitrate content	Flavours	Paper coatings
Nicotine content	Tobacco weight	Filter efficiency or selectivity
Curing	Reconstituted sheet	Filter additives
Grading	Stem inclusion	Filter ventilation
Fermentation	Expanded lamina	
Extraction	Moisture content	
Denicotinization	Dilutants (e.g. Cytrel)	
Ammoniation		
Pesticides		
Agricultural chemicals		

Adapted from Rodgman (2001), Table 5
PAH, polycyclic aromatic hydrocarbon

The Cippilone case, one of the early cigarette product liability cases in the USA, brought to light the existence of the 'XA' cigarette, in which the tobacco had been treated with nitrate salts containing a palladium catalyst to reduce the biological activity of smoke. In the 1977 patent issued to Liggett for the palladium additive (Norman, Bryant, 1977), it is mentioned that the additive reduces PAHs in smoke. An 'Attorney Work Product' (1992) provides a good summary of the testimony given at the trial. Liggett never marketed a cigarette with the palladium technology, however, allegedly because the company feared this would be tantamount to admitting that their other cigarettes caused cancer, and because their claims of reduced biological activity would be based on tests (e.g. mouse painting) that they had in other instances derided. The palladium technology was resurrected in the Omni cigarette sold by Vector Tobacco in the early 2000s. Vector claimed 2–42% lower PAH emissions (depending on the measurement method) than conventional cigarettes. Human studies showed, however, that people who switched to Omni did not have reduced PAH exposure, as measured by urinary 1-hydroxypyrene (Hatsukami et al., 2004; Hughes et al., 2004).

More recent attempts to reduce PAHs in mainstream smoke include the idea of 'free-radical traps' to inhibit their formation during pyrolosis or selective filtration of PAHs. Fillagent patented a porphyrin additive for filters that purports to trap PAHs (Lesser & Von Borstel, 2003), and this appears to have been introduced into a new Fact cigarette (no relation to the Brown & Williamson product described earlier) being test-marketed in the USA.

Lodovici et al. (2007) reported that a DNA-based solution (extracted from salmon sperm: Maillard, Hada, 2005) could be added to a cellulose acetate filter to bind with PAHs, including benzo[*a*]pyrene, as smoke passed through the filter. The solution added approximately 10 mg of DNA per cigarette to the filter. They reported that the smoking machine yield of benzo[*a*]pyrene was 40% lower in treated than in control cigarettes. It is not clear whether this level of reduction is reproducible, however, given that most PAHs do not react with DNA until reduced to epoxides (which is not known to occur in smoke). It is also not known whether 10 mg of DNA would be sufficient to reduce PAHs to the reported level.

1,3-Butadiene, like most gas phase constituents, has been proposed to be removed selectively from smoke by activated charcoal, but little information is available. RJ Reynolds explored a 'carbon scrubber' filter technique, involving a 17.8-cm piece of wood-pulp paper impregnated with 40-μm particles of carbon placed to provide channels of 0.2–0.7 mm (RJ Reynolds, 1994; Stiles et al., 1994). The technique was supposed to reduce gas-phase constituents, including butadiene, acrolein and formaldehyde. An internal report (Rogers, 1993a) noted that the level of butadiene per milligram wet particulate matter was 24% lower in a modified Camel Light with the carbon scrubber in conjuction with higher filter ventilation. Adding potassium carbonate to the blend increased the percentage reduction to approximately 48%. Another analysis with 'straight-grade' cigarettes showed no significant difference in butadiene content (Rogers, Bluhm, 1993b). The research on carbon scrubber filters went as far as human studies (Rogers, Bluhm, 1993b; Smith et al., 1994a,b). The product evolved into a disposable filter attachment (i.e. an aftermarket accessory) rather than a filter used in manufacture (RJ Reynolds, 1995).

Another option is to remove potential precursors in tobacco; however, Ferguson (2000) noted that there are many possible precursors in tobacco, and butadiene is probably formed through a number of competing pathways. Thus, lowering one set of precursors in the rod might not necessarily reduce the butadiene yield in smoke.

Carbon monoxide has been a target for emission reduction for some time. As it is a gas-phase component, selective filtration has been considered as a strategy; however, most studies show that activated charcoal is ineffective in significantly reducing CO in mainstream smoke (e.g. Tigglebeck, 1967), probably because the gas is so abundant. British American Tobacco noted that CO "is present in smoke at substantially greater concentrations than other smoke components considered in this review. Hence substantial quantities of substances which combine chemically with it will be required to effect filtration." (Irwin, 1990). Polzin et al. (2008) showed that even 120 mg or more of charcoal, while effective in lowering other gas-phase volatiles (see earlier sections), had no significant effect on CO.

Tolman (1970) summarized a number of possible techniques for removing CO from smoke and British American Tobacco's work to date in the area of selective CO filtration:

- chemisorption in a microporous subtrate (molecular sieve), physical adsorption,
- chemical complex formation,
- absorption in a liquid in which CO is soluble,
- oxidation to CO_2,
- catalytic oxidation in which oxygen is consumed,
- disproportionation to carbon and CO_2 and
- reduction to carbon.

British American Tobacco appears to have done substantial work on selective filtration of CO in the early 1970s, led by Tolman (1970, 1971, 1973). In particular, they explored manganese dioxide and other catalysts for converting CO to CO_2 in smoke. In summarizing this work, Irwin (1990) noted that effective catalysts were obtained by depositing manganese dioxide in the pores of activated carbon, but that the exothermic CO to CO_2 conversion catalysed by manganese oxide heated the charcoal to the point that it glowed red (probably from oxidation of accumulated particulates) and the filter almost disintegrated. Irwin found that there was "little evidence of effectiveness" of complexing agents and concluded that the best route for future research was molecular sieves.

RJ Reynolds developed an internal 'reactor system' for rapid assessment of filter additives for reducing CO, relying on tests of the substance's ability to remove CO from a gas stream (Townsend, 1978). They also performed extensive research in the 1980s on paper porosity and filter dilution to reduce

CO. One internal memo mentioned the possibility of building a 'catalytic converter' into the filter to remove CO by converting it to CO_2 with hydrogen peroxide in some form (Maselli, 1986). In the 1990s, they explored a grooved filter that was claimed to reduce CO by up to 50%, although this relied mainly on filter dilution.

In 1997, a Greek cigarette manufacturer began marketing cigarettes featuring a 'bio-filter', claiming that haemoglobin embedded in the filter sequestered CO (Deliconstantinos, Villiotou, Stavridis, 1994; Valavanidis, Haralambous, 2001). Given the strong affinity of haemoglobin for CO, this seems to be a plausible strategy; however, a Lorillard memo (Robinson, 1998) reported that in-house attempts to reproduce the findings reported by Deliconstantinos, Villiotou and Stavridis (1994) had been unsuccessful. The author speculated that "failure of the proteins to alter the delivery of the measured components may have resulted from the incorporation of a smaller than adequate amount of each protein. A larger amount of each protein could not be incorporated using the Deliconstantinos method since the protein solutions used were at the saturation limit." Valavanidis and Haralambous (2001) reported less CO removal than achieved in the original paper (30–35% vs. 90%). Tolman (1971) calculated that 10–20 g of haemoglobin would be required on a filter to remove 15–20 mg of CO from smoke. Philip Morris also explored haemoglobin filters over the years (Philip Morris, 1997). Patents exist for haemoglobin and other absorbent additives to filters (Scheinberg, 1974; Charalambous, Bullin Haines, Morgan, 1987; Kubrina et al., 1989; Stavridis, Deliconstaninos, 1999), but no or only small changes to CO yields are claimed, suggesting that they are insufficient to remove the large amounts of CO present.

RJ Reynolds explored palladium salts as a method for reducing CO in smoke (Riggs, 1989). Lewis, Norman and Robinson (1990) summarized their investigations of addition of palladium and copper catalysts to the filter and showed that they could reduce CO in smoke by as much as 20%. Concern about cost, availability of sufficient materials and toxicology appear to have caused them to abandon the work.

3.6.4 *Considerations in applying mandatory lowering to multiple toxicants*

In considering a recommendation to expand the list of toxicants for mandated lowering of their levels in cigarette smoke, TobReg examined the effects of correlating the different toxicants across brands, the effects of various levels of reduction of these toxicants on the number of brands remaining on the market, and methods for examining and tracking the net effect on toxicant yields of the proposed regulatory strategy. These analyses were conducted without considering the effect of brand reduction due to the previously recommended mandated limits for NNN and NNK, as TobReg considered that changes in curing and manufacturing processes would probably allow most if not all brands to meet those limits.

The lower the regulatory level set for a given toxicant, the greater will be the reduction in the level of that toxicant in the brands remaining on the market, because more brands will either be reformulated to comply with new toxicant limits or be banned from sale.

A possible effect of setting levels for multiple toxicants is the elimination of most brands on the market if the level is set at the median value for several toxicants (Figure 3.12). It is impossible to know which brands would have to be removed from the market rather than simply undergoing product re-design in order to remain on the market, because TobReg does not know the full extent of the industry's reformulation capacity. Higher mandated limits allow more brands to remain on the market unchanged and more toxicants to be regulated simultaneously, but result in higher levels of toxicants in the machine-generated smoke from the remaining brands. The result is a complicated trade-off between the number of toxicants regulated, the magnitude of the reductions in toxicant levels and the number of brands removed from the market. TobReg examined a number of considerations relative to these trade-offs in arriving at the recommended set of toxicants and their maximum levels.

Figure 3.12
Proportion of brands remaining after constituents removed, by percentile in order of their cancer index; international brands, modified intense regimen

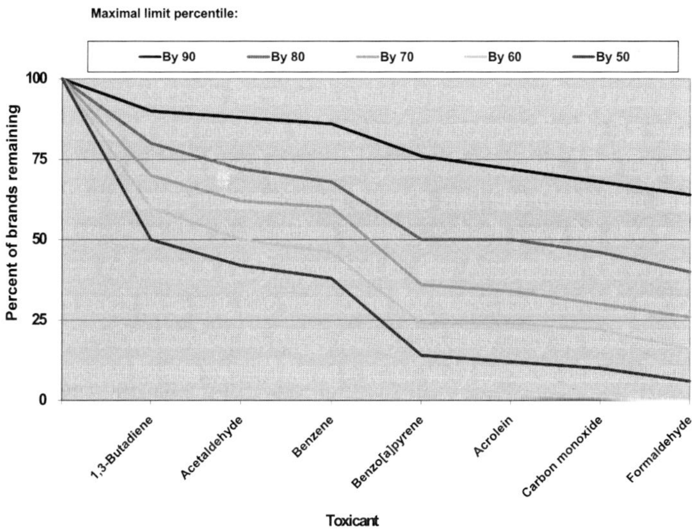

The analyses presented give the maximum number of brands that would be eliminated on the basis of existing data, on the unlikely assumption that no modifications would be made to existing products with the introduction of mandated lowering regulations. As described elsewhere in this report, a specific anticipated outcome of the proposed product regulation strategy is a change in the manufacture of individual brands to reduce the toxicant yields measured under standardized machine smoking conditions. It is expected that the setting of mandated limits will spur further advances in methods to lower toxicant yields. As a result, TobReg assumed the most draconian potential impact on existing brands. In reality, it is anticipated that far fewer brands would actually be restricted from sale if the mandated limits for toxicants were implemented.

Correlations among levels of different toxicants

One consideration in examining the list of toxicants is the extent to which the levels of one toxicant in a brand are correlated with those of other toxicants in the same brand. This association can be quantified statistically as a correlation coefficient. The correlation coefficients for the toxicants under consideration, plus NNN and NNK, are presented in Tables 3.8 and 3.9 for the sample of international Philip Morris brands and for the Canadian data minus those brands high in NNN. The plots of the actual data from which the correlations are derived are presented in Figures A4.1 and A4.2 in Annex 3.4, with the r^2, which is the correlation coefficient for each toxicant with all of the other toxicants on the list recommended for mandated reduction. Also included in Annex 3.4 is the correlation matrix for all the toxicants reported to Health Canada and measured by Counts and colleagues (2005). Some toxicants are highly correlated, others show little correlation, and a few are negatively correlated.

A positive correlation suggests that removing brands with high levels of one toxicant by mandating lower levels will also lower the level of the correlated toxicant, which is high in the same brands. This might mean that the levels of one toxicant could serve as a proxy for several other toxicants in a regulatory strategy. Caution should be exercised in relying on this assumption, as a strong correlation does not mean that the toxicants are generated by the same mechanism in the smoke. For example, toxicants might be derived from different flavouring agents in tobacco and therefore subject to independent manipulation, but they may be correlated because some brands contain multiple flavouring agents and other brands only a few.

Table 3.8

Correlation coefficients for levels of toxicants in the same brand, international brands, modified intense regimen

	(1)	(2)	(3)	(4)	(5)	(6)	(7)	(8)	(9)
(1) Acetaldehyde	1.000								
(2) Acrolein	0.949	1.000							
(3) Benzene	0.760	0.764	1.000						
(4) Benzo[*a*]pyrene	–0.272	–0.208	–0.266	1.000					
(5) 1,3 Butadiene	0.852	0.855	0.874	–0.401	1.000				
(6) Carbon monoxide	0.830	0.761	0.673	–0.369	0.807	1.000			
(7) Formaldehyde	0.156	0.244	0.081	0.340	0.094	–0.111	1.000		
(8) NNK	0.010	–0.111	0.002	–0.393	–0.051	0.214	–0.639	1.000	
(9) NNN	0.103	–0.014	0.042	–0.476	0.062	0.252	–0.717	0.853	1.000

NNK, 4-(*N*-nitrosomethylamino)-1-(3-pyridyl)-1-butanone; NNN, *N*′-nitrosonornicotine

Table 3.9

Correlation coefficients for levels of toxicants in the same brand, Canadian brands (NNN limited), modified intense regimen

	(1)	(2)	(3)	(4)	(5)	(6)	(7)	(8)	(9)
(1) Acetaldehyde	1.000								
(2) Acrolein	0.792	1.000							
(3) Benzene	0.957	0.779	1.000						
(4) Benzo[*a*]pyrene	0.810	0.474	0.859	1.000					
(5) 1,3-Butadiene	0.953	0.836	0.944	0.765	1.000				
(6) Carbon monoxide	0.949	0.848	0.972	0.810	0.949	1.000			
(7) Formaldehyde	0.844	0.568	0.867	0.912	0.827	0.810	1.000		
(8) NNK	0.707	0.426	0.762	0.817	0.627	0.744	0.710	1.000	
(9) NNN	0.454	0.128	0.462	0.464	0.376	0.447	0.347	0.774	1.000

NNK, 4-(*N*-nitrosomethylamino)-1-(3-pyridyl)-1-butanone; NNN, *N*′-nitrosonornicotine

A negative correlation suggests that brands with a high level of one toxicant have a relatively low level of the other. Mandatory lowering of the levels of two toxicants with negative correlation coefficients will result in more brands being eliminated from the market than when two brands have strong positive correlation coefficients. The effect on the levels in the remaining brands is less clear, as the regulatory level set for each toxicant might also result in elimination of the brands that are low in the second toxicant, with the result that the toxicity indices for the brands remaining on the market might change less than would be expected from the number of brands eliminated.

The uncertain nature of cigarette manufacturers' responses and the complexity of predicting the effect of mandated reductions on toxicant yields under standardized conditions on the brands remaining on the market make a strong case for continued monitoring of the toxicant yields of cigarettes after implementation of regulations to mandate lower levels. After discussion, TobReg considered that regulating a larger number of toxicants is the more appropriate strategy, rather than allowing closely correlated toxicants to serve as proxies for one another. This approach was considered to offer the greatest protection against uncertainties about the manufacturing changes likely to be implemented in response to the proposed regulatory strategy and their consequences for toxicant yields.

Effect on number of brands affected by limits

In the absence of a change in cigarette manufacture, the number of brands potentially eliminated from the market by the proposed regulatory approach will depend on the level set and the number of toxicants regulated. Figure 3.12 presents the percentage reduction in number of brands on the market with the regulated levels set at different percentiles of the distribution of the toxicant per milligram of nicotine for the brands on that market, and with the sequential addition of the toxicants being considered. The number of brands potentially eliminated as each toxicant is regulated depends on the order in which the toxicants are added to the analyses. In Figure 3.12, the toxicants are entered in the order of their animal carcinogenicity index from Table 3.3. Data for the sample of international Philip Morris brands demonstrate that if all the brands with values for the seven toxicants above the median were eliminated, almost all the brands would be eliminated from the market. There is clearly a need to balance the number of toxicants regulated against the levels mandated in order to avoid substantial market disruption.

Monitoring for unintended increases in toxicant yields

Mandating a reduction in the levels of some toxicants does not guarantee that the levels of other, non- regulated toxicants will also be reduced. It is therefore possible that removal from the market of brands high in levels of the regulated toxicants will leave brands with high levels of unregulated toxicants. In addition, changes in cigarette design and manufacture implemented to lower the regulated toxicants might have the effect of increasing the levels of unregulated toxicants. TobReg recognized the potential for these unintended consequences of mandating the reduction of specific toxicants and considered how monitoring might be put in place to detect them.

One approach would be to track the yields, or the percentage change in median yields, of the entire list of toxicants measured by Health Canada. Different toxicants have different potencies as toxicants, however, and the range of toxicant per milligram of nicotine (defining the reduction possible with the proposed regulatory approach) is different. As a result, the net effect of a mandated reduction of some toxicants on total toxicant yields from the brands remaining will depend on the toxicant selected and the levels set.

On the basis of these considerations, TobReg recommends using the sum of the individual toxicant animal carcinogenicity indices of the brands remaining on the market to examine the potential unintended consequences of regulation on net toxicant yields. TobReg chose this approach as a means of integrating data on animal toxicity and data on the levels of toxicants in smoke generated under standardized conditions for the purpose of monitoring the effects of implementing the proposed regulatory approach on net toxicant yields. The sum of the toxicant animal carcinogenicity indices generated and changes in that index are mathematical constructs of toxicant yields and are based mainly on animal toxicological evidence. They do not account for potential interactions between toxicants or the effects of toxicants for which no animal carcinogenicity index has been generated. They are not quantitative estimates of the human toxicity of the smoke from different brands, of the risk for cancer or other diseases due to smoking different brands, and should not be applied in a quantitative way for estimating the risk of smoking or the actual toxicity of the smoke generated. They are recommended solely for use as a monitoring tool for regulators.

Figure 3.13 presents the sum of the toxicant animal carcinogenicity indices for the brands remaining on the market with mandated limits set at different percentiles of the distribution of the toxicant per milligram of nicotine for the brands on that market. The effect of sequentially adding toxicant mandated limits at the same percentile is presented, with the toxicants added in order of their toxicant animal carcinogenicity index. The sum is calculated for all the toxicants listed in Annex 3.3 Table A3.1 for which there are toxicant animal carcinogenicity indices, with the exception of NNN and NNK. The sum of the indices is not limited to the indices of the seven toxicants under consideration. The value presented is the brand-specific arithmetic sum of the hazard indices for all toxicants for which there are cancer indices, expressed as the mean of the brands remaining on the market. The dashed line represents the sum for the brand with the lowest value and therefore represents the lowest value that can be achieved with mandated lowering based on the distribution of toxicants in the brands reported by Counts and colleagues (2005). Further lowering would require modification of the existing products by the manufacturers.

Figure 3.13

Means of sums of animal carcinogenicity indices for brands remaining as additional toxicants are regulated; international brands, modified intense regimen

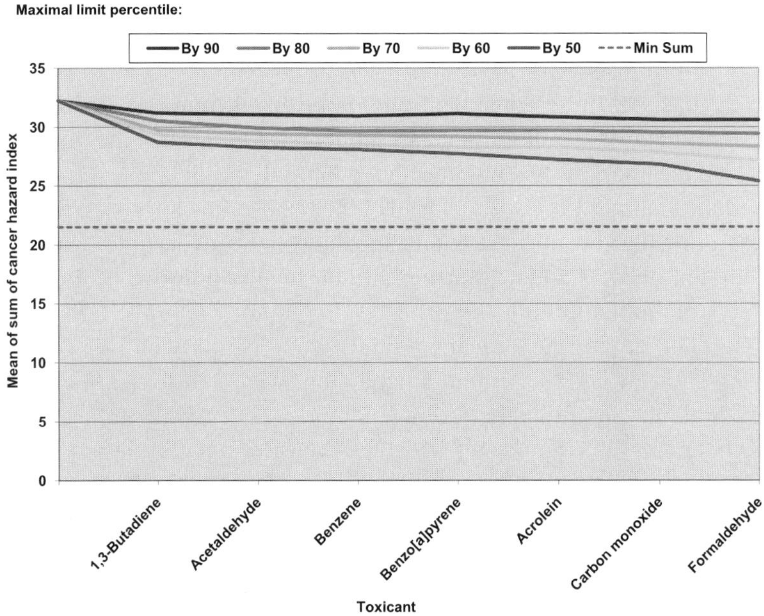

The result of this analysis suggests that the net toxicant yield of the brands remaining on the market will decrease (at least by this measure), and no net increase in toxicant yield will result from the proposed regulatory strategy. Ongoing monitoring would be needed to ensure that changes in cigarette manufacture in response to the proposed mandated lowering do not increase the yields of other toxicants.

Almost the entire range of values for the existing market is contained in the top one third of the sum of the toxicant animal carcinogenicity indices, limiting the effect of any regulatory strategy on this summary measure of toxicant yields. It is important to note, however, that this range is based on existing brands and existing technology, and a regulatory strategy that encourages innovation in lowering the levels of toxicants in smoke might substantially reduce the minimum values for modified brands. This reality supports TobReg's recommendation that market variation in yields be used only for setting the initial mandated lowering levels and that targets based on what can be achieved with advancing technology be examined as a second phase of the mandated lowering approach.

The range of the summary measure presented in Figure 3.13 supports the position that all brands of cigarettes generate smoke with substantial toxicity and that, while it may be possible to lower the toxicity of smoke generated under standardized conditions, it is unlikely that large reductions in toxicity are achievable for conventional cigarettes without substantial advances in cigarette design.

Neither the metric used (the sum of the toxicant animal carcinogenicity indices) nor changes in this metric are measures of human toxicity or risk, and they should not be used as such in estimating changes in human risk with use of different brands or resulting from the regulatory strategy. The data in Figure 3.13 are presented simply to show the effect of regulating some toxicants on the net toxicant yields of the brands remaining on the market. The reader should resist the temptation to view these changes as quantitative estimates of the risk reduction benefit of product regulation, for several reasons. The hazard indices are constructed from potency estimates obtained from the available animal data, and such data are not available for all the known toxicants. The sensitivity of animals and humans to the different toxicants may differ. The effect of exposure to the multiple toxic compounds in smoke has not been established as additive. These realities limit the use of these measures as estimates of even total animal toxicity and obviate their direct extrapolation to humans. The regulatory strategy proposed focuses on lowering levels of known toxicants in the cigarettes on the market as good manufacturing practice. The strategy is not based on a provable or certain reduction in human toxicity resulting from the use of those products, the toxicant animal carcinogenicity index is not a quantitative estimate of human cancer risk, and a regulatory standard that can reliably quantify a reduction in human risk is beyond current scientific capability.

3.7 Recommended toxicants and recommended mandated limits

The toxicants currently recommended for mandated reductions by TobReg are NNN and NNK, acetaldehyde, acrolein, benzene, benzo[*a*]pyrene, 1,3-butadiene, CO and formaldehyde. The levels recommended in this report represent TobReg's judgement on the most practical trade-offs, considering the need to regulate a range of toxicants, to mandate lowering of those toxicants to the greatest extent and yet not to eliminate most brands, in their current form, from the market.

As stated in the first report of TobReg on this regulatory approach (WHO, 2007), the median values for NNN and NNK are used as recommended levels because there is strong evidence that existing technology can dramatically lower the amounts of these toxicants in tobacco smoke. An initial level of 125% of the median value is recommended for the other toxicants. The higher level for the other toxicants reflects the somewhat greater uncertainty about the extent to which these toxicants can be reduced with existing approaches. Substantially lower levels should be the ultimate goal of this regulatory strategy.

An examination of the variation in these toxicants by brand in the data sets available (see Annex 3.5) demonstrates that the levels in most brands fall below 125% of the median per milligram of nicotine of all the brands in the data set. The median level of all brands is likely to be a relatively stable value on which to base the initial regulatory level. It was also viewed as preferable to base the recommended levels on a specific value rather than on a specified percentile of the distribution of brands. TobReg therefore recommends that the levels for the proposed regulation of constituents other than NNN and NNK be set at 125% of the median value of the brands reported. This choice reflects a judgement that incorporates the previously described, conflicting goals of: regulating a number of agents, reducing the levels of toxicants in brands on the market to the greatest extent and maintaining enough brands requiring minimal modification on the market to satisfy consumer demand.

Regulators may of course select different levels that are more appropriate for their own circumstances and are encouraged to base levels on the yields of the brands sold in their own markets, using the principles set out in this report. Table 3.10 presents the recommended levels, based on the data available on the international brands (Counts et al., 2005) and the Canadian brands (Health Canada, 2004) tested with the modified intense machine-smoking regimen.

Table 3.10
Toxicants recommended for mandated lowering

Toxicant	**Level in µg/mg nicotine**		**Value**
	International brands[a]	**Canadian brands**[b]	
NNK	0.072	0.047	Median of data set
NNN	0.114	0.027	Median of data set
Acetaldehyde	860	670	125% of median of data set
Acrolein	83	97	125% of median of data set
Benzene	48	50	125% of median of data set
Benzo[*a*]pyrene	0.011	0.011	125% of median of data set
1,3-Butadiene	67	53	125% of median of data set
Carbon monoxide	18400	15400	125% of median of data set
Formaldehyde	47	97	125% of median of data set

NNK, 4-(*N*-nitrosomethylamino)-1-(3-pyridyl)-1-butanone; NNN, *N*´-nitrosonornicotine

[a] Based on data from Counts et al., 2005

[b] Based on the data reported to Health Canada minus brands with levels of NNN per mg nicotine > 0.1 ng, which eliminates most US and Gauloise brands. (http://www.hc-sc.gc.ca/hl-vs/tobac-tabac/legislation/reg/indust/constitu_e.html)

The levels in Table 3.1 in the column labelled 'international brands' are derived from data on brands in an international sample (Counts at al., 2005), which are US-style cigarettes containing a blend of tobaccos. The column labelled 'Canadian brands' is based on a set reported to Health Canada, which represent unblended cigarettes containing predominantly flue-cured (bright) tobacco. Regulators should use data reported for their own markets to set levels, if they are available, or select the values derived from the data set that conforms most closely to the cigarettes available on the market being regulated. The differences in the reported levels in individual brands are particularly large for the TSNA (NNN, NNK).

In smaller countries, where the style of cigarettes on the market is not readily definable, it is recommended that the mandated limits be based on the international sample initially and that alternative standards be considered as more information on local brands becomes available.

Regulation of brands for toxicants other than NNN and NNK at the levels proposed in Table 3.10 would result in 60% of the brands remaining on the market without modification of the product for the international set of brands and 59% of the brands remaining on the Canadian market.

Given the existing technology for lowering NNN and NNK levels in tobacco, it is expected that most brands will be able to comply with the recommended mandated limits for these compounds. The higher levels present in the international sample of US blend cigarettes than in those from Canada suggest that countries should establish mandated limits for these toxicants that are based on measurements made for the brands on their own markets. The extent to which each of the other toxicants listed in Table 3.10 can be lowered with existing technology is less clear, but, given the variation in levels in the brands currently being sold, it is expected that the manufacturers of many brands with high levels of toxicants on initial reporting would be able to lower those levels in order to continue marketing them.

Success in lowering the levels of individual toxicants can indicate to regulatory authority the potential of existing technology for achieving further lowering of toxicant yields and can help in deciding to set goals for toxicant yields to further lower existing mandated limits for individual toxicants. Over time, it is envisioned that there would be a progressive lowering of the mandated limits, both in response to advances in technology and to the development of new approaches to lowering toxicant yields.

3.8 Implementing mandatory reductions in toxicant yields

The data presented in this report reflect a limited set of brands in a few markets, whereas there are substantial differences in the levels of toxicants in brands in different markets. This suggests that a regulatory strategy should be phased, with a period of required reporting of toxicant levels by cigarette manufacturers, followed by an announcement of the maximum levels for toxicants, and finally enforcement of those mandated limits. For countries without cigarette manufacturing facilities or with limited laboratory capacity, the values presented in Tables 3.1 and 3.10 represent reasonable initial regulatory levels.

The first phase of the proposed regulatory strategy for mandating reductions in toxicant yields would be to require reporting of the levels of constituents present in cigarette smoke from those brands being regulated. It is expected that the tobacco industry would be responsible for the cost of this testing and reporting, either directly or through taxation or licensing. The initial reporting should cover all the toxicants currently reported to Health Canada. This defined list can be used to assess whether there are differences between the toxicant levels generated by brands on the market to be regulated and those reported here. Of particular concern are some of the metals, the levels of which can vary substantially with the source of the tobacco used to manufacture cigarettes. After the initial reporting, a more limited list of toxicants, presented in Table 3.6, is recommended for annual reporting, with the more complete list reported every 5 years.

The levels of the smoke constituents listed in Table 3.6 would be reported annually by brand for 2–3 years to allow analysis of variation in constituent yields of brands on the market. Initial mandated limits for toxicants other than NNN and NNK would be set on the basis of the level of the toxicant per milligram of nicotine representing 125% of the median value for the reported brands. The levels for NNN and NNK would be set at the median value for the reported brands. Mandated limits for NNN, NNK, acetaldehyde, acrolein, benzene, benzo[*a*]pyrene, 1,3-butadiene, CO and formaldehyde would then be established and announced to cigarette manufacturers and importers at the end of the reporting period. Beginning 2 years after announcement of the mandated limits, brands with toxicant yields per milligram of nicotine exceeding the set levels would be excluded from import or sale. Data on the levels of toxicant yields for the toxicants in Table 3.6 would continue to be reported annually.

3.8.1 *Considerations for modified cigarettes and potential reduced exposure products*

The recommendations in this report are intended to apply to traditional manufactured cigarettes in which tobacco is burnt; they should not be applied to cigarettes in which tobacco is heated or in which techniques other than combustion are used to deliver nicotine. Assessments of these unconventional tobacco products and other potential reduced exposure products were discussed in a previous report (Scientific Advisory Committee on Tobacco Product Regulation, 2003).

It is possible to alter the level of a toxicant per milligram of nicotine in cigarette smoke by changing the nicotine yield of the cigarette, as well as by altering the level of the toxicant. The yield of nicotine in cigarette smoke can be increased by adding nicotine to the tobacco or the filter or by using high-nicotine varieties of tobacco. While these approaches may theoretically have independent use in decreasing exposure to tobacco toxicants, their potential to do so remains uncertain. The usefulness of increased nicotine yields as a method of lowering the level of toxicant per milligram of nicotine to a level below the mandated limit value is therefore also unproven for reducing the toxicity of smoke. Regulatory authorities should neither encourage nor allow increased nicotine yields to be used as a method for complying with the mandated values regulation.

Detection of increasing nicotine yields in brands can be facilitated by tracking machine-delivered nicotine yields per cigarette over time and by examining the distribution of tar to nicotine ratios for the brands in a given market. For those brands with increasing nicotine yields over time and those brands with tar to nicotine ratios in the bottom one third of the brands on the market, regulators may choose to require that the brand have below a mandated limit value per milligram of tar as well as per milligram of nicotine.

Some brands of cigarettes may be offered with reduced nicotine in the tobacco used to make the cigarette. Nicotine can be removed from the tobacco leaf, and genetically altered tobacco is available with a very low nicotine content. Cigarettes made with these tobaccos have low nicotine deliveries under any testing method and correspondingly may have very high levels of toxicants per milligram of nicotine. Regulators may want to evaluate separately brands from manufacturers that appear to be intentionally lowering nicotine in the tobacco. Once the regulatory authority is satisfied that the manufacturer is actually using low-nicotine tobacco in the product, the authority may want to use a mandated limit value per milligram of tar instead of per milligram of nicotine.

3.8.2 *Communication of regulatory values and testing results to the public*

Mandated reduction of toxicant levels recommended in this report constitutes a first step towards improved tobacco product regulation. TobReg recognizes the limitations of machine measurements and of setting levels per milligram of nicotine. Existing science does not allow a definitive conclusion that reduction of the level of nitrosamines, or any other toxicants in cigarette smoke, will reduce cancer incidence or the rate of any other tobacco-related disease in smokers who use cigarettes with lower levels of these toxicants. Science has also not demonstrated that the specified changes in regulatory values will result overall in a meaningful change in the actual exposure of consumers, although that is an anticipated outcome. Mandating levels and banning brands with higher levels from the market does not equate to a statement that the remaining brands are safe or less hazardous than the brands removed. It also does not represent government recognition of the safety of the products that remain on the market. The proposed strategy for lowering toxicant yields is based on sound precautionary approaches similar to those used for other consumer products.

Given the limitations of existing science, regulatory authorities have an obligation to ensure that the public is not misled by the results of the recommended machine testing and mandated lowering regulatory strategy, in the way that the public was misled by the use of machine testing for tar and nicotine yields. TobReg noted that labelling of cigarettes with tar, nicotine and CO levels measured with the ISO regimen persists and continues to be harmful to the public. TobReg recommends that any regulatory approach prohibit the use of the results of the proposed testing in marketing or other communications with consumers, including product labelling. It is also recommended that manufacturers be prohibited from making statements such as that a brand has met government regulatory standards and also from publicizing the relative ranking of brands by testing level. Because information is often transmitted to smokers through the kinds of news stories that accompany new regulation implementation, it is the responsibility of the regulatory structure to monitor:

- the accuracy of news reports,
- tobacco industry marketing,
- smokers' understanding of the new regulations,
- how smokers interpret the new regulations relative to the hazard of the products remaining on the market and
- whether understanding about the hazard of the remaining products is influencing initiation or cessation rates.

Regulators should then pursue whatever corrective action is necessary to prevent consumers from being misled. These monitoring and surveillance concerns are described in more detail in the WHO report on evaluation of new or modified tobacco products (Scientific Advisory Committee on Tobacco Product Regulation, 2003).

3.9 Issues for regulators mandating lower levels of toxicants

In proposing mandated reductions in toxicant yields, TobReg considered some of the ramifications of its recommendations on existing markets and on the people who control them. It is not TobReg's obligation to tell the industry how to achieve the changes, as the expertise for this is within the domain of the companies, and there are a number of ways for them to meet the limits.

It is, however, obvious, that implementing TobReg's proposed regulatory strategy over time will change the market substantially. Tobacco may be sourced differently, tobacco-growing is likely to change, manufacturing techniques will change, the number of additives is likely to be reduced and ultimately the number of brands is likely to be reduced. Manufacturers will bear an analytical burden, which will be part of routine quality control; this ought not to be regarded as an imposition. Regulators will have to validate a random sample of the tobacco industry analyses for monitoring and quality assurance, and this will require resources. Taxation or licensing fees for each brand to be marketed could provide a source of funds for this activity.

As explained elsewhere, the setting of mandated limits is proposed as a precautionary approach and is not an excuse for 'health' or advertising claims. There is no reason why any of the changes proposed so far should require public information campaigns, as the cigarettes will remain carcinogenic and toxic despite reductions in toxicant levels. Thus, there is no reason why countries that have banned advertising should re-introduce it. Similarly, there is no reason for allowing advertisements promoting changes as a result of regulation, as the outcomes of the changes will be uncertain until many years of observation have passed.

A number of issues for regulators arise from mandated lowering of toxicant yields. In those countries with no tobacco manufacturing industry, the limits should pose few difficulties, as the governments will merely place import prohibitions on products that do not meet the regulations. Companies that manufacture regulation-compliant products will benefit, while those that do not will be eradicated from the market.

Those countries which are home to manufacturing companies and a growing industry can expect to encounter objections from both manufacturers and growers, as both groups will be affected by regulation. Although some international companies have already embraced the principle of regulation (Philip Morris, 2002), the introduction of mandated limits will require a reasonable time. Some changes, such as reduction of nitrosamine levels, are relatively straightforward and are already occurring (Gray, Boyle, 2004). Others may require different agricultural and manufacturing practices, and they may take longer. There are, however, few excuses for continuing to manufacture excessively toxic or carcinogenic products for any longer than necessary, and an urgent approach is justified.

It is important to consider how the effects of the proposed regulation might be assessed over time. As this is an attempt to reduce toxicant and carcinogen yields, the most direct evaluation would be to measure a change in the mean yield of the toxicant per milligram of nicotine in the brands on the market before and after the regulatory mandate is implemented. This can be accomplished by comparing the data on yields reported by tobacco manufacturers in the initial reporting phase of the programme to the yields reported for the first year after the ban on brands that are over the mandated limit. Comparison of the means of toxicant per milligram of nicotine for all brands on the market before and after the regulation is the recommended comparison. TobReg considered sales weighting the brands on the market for the comparison but decided that this would be less appropriate because of the difficulty in obtaining validated sales data by brand and because the present approach is directed at changing the toxicity yields of most or all the brands on the market. Sales weighting the brands would suggest that the toxicant yields might be used as a measure of human exposure or risk, a use that TobReg strongly rejects.

A second concern in the evaluation of regulations mandating lowering of toxicant yields is the possibility that removing brands with lower levels of one toxicant would leave on the market brands with higher levels of other toxicants, resulting in an increase in the net toxicant yield of the brands remaining on the market. This issue is discussed earlier in this report, where regular calculation of the toxicant animal carcinogenicity and toxicant non-cancer response indices is recommended for the brands remaining on the market, with the trend of their sum over time.

A principal reason for regulating cigarettes is the harm they cause. It is therefore tempting to suggest that the best method for evaluating the effect of regulation would be to evaluate the harm caused by cigarettes with epidemiological approaches and disease end-points. Epidemiology can be expected to provide at best only a partial evaluation. Cigarette composition, and hence emissions, have changed over time, but many of the design changes have remained industry secrets. If regulations are introduced progressively and regulatory levels are lowered over time, cigarette design and composition can be expected to continue to change. It has not been possible to conduct a cohort study based on detailed, progressive information on brands because of tobacco industry secrecy about changes in manufacturing practices. As there have been changes in brands over time, even studies in which the brand smoked is recorded have limited ability to assess differences in the risks of using cigarettes with different designs. The proposed regulatory approach is intended to result in continued, progressive brand changes, in this case in the direction of lower toxicity. The changes in disease risks that will result from these changes will manifest over several decades, and the risks that result will probably be a product of cumulative exposure over time. The complexity of the brand changes, the complexity of the behavioural responses to brand changes that influence exposure, and the switching among brands that characterizes smokers' tobacco use suggest that cohort studies by brand with disease end-points are unlikely to be informative for regulatory monitoring in the future.

For specific toxicants, such as NNK, it may be possible to monitor levels of exposure in the population of smokers before and after mandated lowering of yields is implemented in order to examine the effect of product regulation on population exposure to that toxicant. Population exposure measures are not direct evaluations of the regulatory approach but are research approaches to examine the effect of changes in cigarette yields of specific toxicants on the actual exposure of smokers to those toxicants. Obviously, tobacco-associated disease rates are and will continue to be routinely monitored.

It will be useful to monitor industry compliance and published emission levels together with regular surveys of smoking topography by brand and levels of exposure biomarkers by brand. Such periodic evaluation of human exposure might allow an estimate of trends in exposure resulting from the design changes implemented to comply with the mandated reduction regulation.

3.10 Recommendations for follow-up and future work

3.10.1 *Toxicants in tobacco smoke*

Tobacco smoke is a complex mixture of chemicals. No or limited toxicological data are available for most chemicals, and the concentrations of the compounds in smoke are generally not known by brand. As a result, the hazardous effects of tobacco smoke on humans are not well explained by the usual toxicological paradigm of dose multiplied by toxic potency (Fowles, Dybing, 2003) for those toxicants. The present report recommends reductions in priority toxicants for which data are available as a first step, focusing on a few well-known toxicants that have been quantified in smoke and can be influenced by modifying the design of cigarettes.

There is substantially more documentation of the carcinogenic effects than of the respiratory, cardiovascular or reproductive effects of the toxicants in smoke. Regulatory actions to reduce the risk of cigarette smoke will therefore require substantial work to define the toxicity of individual toxicants other than cancer, and also to expand the understanding of cancer.

Ongoing research will probably provide new insights into the quantitative effects of other smoke constituents, which may be candidates for product regulation. The list of chemicals for regulation should be revised periodically in order to reflect this expansion of knowledge. In addition, the mandated limit for each toxicant might have to be revised periodically. Toxicological evidence and better understanding of the determinants of smoke chemistry might allow the setting of reduction goals on the basis of what can be achieved rather than on the levels in existing products.

By setting and mandating reductions in toxicant yields from tobacco products, governments accept their responsibility to the public for regulating tobacco products as consumer products, albeit extremely hazardous ones. This regulatory responsibility will be discharged by reducing known toxicant yields, rather than the approach used for food and other consumer products (usually based on the no-effect level concept) or medical drugs (based on a risk–benefit concept). For tobacco products, the basis for regulating is the 'best available technology', in combination with a precautionary approach, while acknowledging existing harmful effects due to ongoing use.

TobReg recommends that the list of toxicants recommended for regulation and the levels recommended be reviewed and potentially revised every 2 years; the new recommendations from this review should be presented to the Conference of Parties to the WHO Framework Convention on Tobacco Control and the WHO Tobacco Free Initiative. As the hazardous effects of tobacco smoke are still not completely understood, new paradigms for describing the toxicity of tobacco smoke may arise in the near future and may add to the scientific foundation for tobacco regulation.

The concept of mandated lowering of toxicant yields in smoke could be extended to other products, including additives to tobacco products. Such regulatory efforts might work in tandem. For example, regulation of sugars as additives could influence the levels of acetaldehyde, while acrolein levels might be influenced by the levels of humectants added.

Enforcement of product regulation will require capacity-building for regulatory agencies interested in regulation, which could be facilitated through TobLabNet, an international cooperative effort of non-tobacco industry tobacco laboratories. Capacity-building should include investment in testing and control facilities as well as data-handling capacity and expertise, and resources to support these tasks should be included in national tobacco legislation.

TobReg and TobLabNet, which are scientific advisory bodies to the WHO Tobacco Free Initiative, can provide advice about which toxicants are high priorities for product regulation and suggest the levels to be used by legal bodies as regulatory levels. TobReg will provide advice mainly about the nature of the chemicals and the mandated limits. TobLabNet will provide advice about the required methods for control and implementation. Periodically, ideally every 2 years, the recommendations of TobReg and TobLabNet will be reviewed and potentially revised.

3.10.2 *Smokeless tobacco products*

Smokeless tobacco products are used widely in North America, parts of Europe, Asia (particularly South-East Asia) and Africa. The marketing of moist snuff was prohibited in the European Union in 1992, but Sweden was granted derogation from the ban on its entry into the Union in 1994.

Smokeless tobacco is consumed without burning the product at the time of use. It can be used orally or nasally. Oral smokeless tobacco products are placed in the mouth, cheek or lip and sucked ('dipped') or chewed. Tobacco pastes and powders are used in a similar manner and placed on the gums and teeth. Fine tobacco mixtures may also be inhaled and absorbed into the nasal passages.

Globally, smokeless tobacco products vary widely with respect to their composition and toxicant content. Many of the Asian products contain the psychoactive substance arecoline from the areca nut mixed with tobacco. In addition, the products contain other flavourings, such as sugars, menthol and licorice. *Toombak* is used primarily in Sudan and consists of tobacco and sodium bicarbonate.

Products on the market in the USA also vary with respect to their content of nicotine (Table 3.11). Widely different levels of unprotonated (non-ionized, free-base) nicotine are available for absorption because of differences in the pH of the products in solution.

The levels of TSNA also vary considerably in products sold in different parts of the world. Generally, moist snuff products sold in Europe and the USA contain less TSNA than products on the Indian market or imported from South Asia to the United Kingdom (Tables 3.12–3.14). The levels of NNN and NNK in Sudanese *toombak* are extremely high, with concentrations of NNN reported to be 141–3085 μg/g tobacco and of NNK 188–7870 μg/g tobacco (Idris et al., 1991, 1995; Prokopczyk et al., 1995). This product also has a very high pH (8.0–11), resulting in a high concentration of non-ionized (unprotonated) nicotine.

Smokeless tobacco products may contain PAHs when flue-cured (fire-cured) tobacco is used. The levels of benzo[*a*]pyrene were 0.11–19.3 ng/g in a study by McNeill et al. (2006; Table 3.12), which also showed low levels of metals in the products tested. To date, 31 carcinogens have been identified in smokeless tobacco; the 14 for which there is sufficient evidence of carcinogenicity in humans or animals are listed in Table 3.15 (IARC, in press).

There are no standardized methods for measuring toxicants or emissions from smokeless tobacco products. In the methods reported in the scientific literature for analysing TSNA, samples are prepared in aqueous buffer or methanol and then extracted either directly with ethyl acetate or after purification by

Table 3.11
Chemical composition of the five leading brands of smokeless tobacco purchased at various locations in the USA

Toxicant	Skoal Bandit Straight (2% of market)	Hawken Wintergreen (1% of market)	Skoal Original Fine Cut Wintergreen (39% of market)	Copenhagen Snuff (42% of market)	Kodiak (11% of market)
pH	5.37 ± 0.12	5.71 ±0.1	7.46 ±0.14	8.00 ± 0.31	8.19 ± 0.11
Nicotine (% dry weight)	2.29 ± 0.46	0.46 ± 0.02	2.81 ± 0.34	2.91 ± 0.18	2.5 ± 0.22
Nicotine (mg/g)	10.1 ± 0.8	3.2 ± 0.2	11.9 ± 1.3	12.0 ± 0.7	10.9 ± 0.8
Unprotonated nicotine (%)[a]	0.23 ± 0.05	0.5 ± 0.11	22.0 ± 5.73	49.0 ± 16.7	59.7 ± 6.01

From Djordjevic et al. (1995)
[a] The percentage of unprotonated nicotine, which depends on pH, was calculated according to the Henderson-Hasselbach equation and by using a pKa value of 8.02 for nicotine (Henningfield, Radzius, Cone, 1995)

solid-phase extraction (Österdahl et al., 2004; Stepanov et al., 2006). Analytical identification and quantification of TSNA have been undertaken with liquid chromatography–triple mass spectrometry (Österdahl, Jannson, Paccou, 2004) or gas chromatography–thermal energy analyser instrumentation (Stepanov et al., 2006).

In principle, smokeless tobacco products could initially be regulated as in the interim step described above for cigarettes. This would entail examination of the toxicity of the products as a function of the concentration of the examined toxicant and its potency, normalized for the non-ionized (unprotonated) concentration of nicotine. So far, the database on toxic constituents in smokeless tobacco products is much more limited than that on toxicants in cigarettes and cigarette smoke. It is therefore more difficult to characterize the hazard of emissions from smokeless tobacco products. Also, smokeless tobacco products vary much more in their form and composition than industrially produced cigarettes. The available published data, however, allow characterization of the hazard of NNN and NNK, and some products contain very high levels of these carcinogens. For the same product type sold within a country (e.g. moist snuff, chewing tobacco), it should be possible to set mandated limits on the basis of measured variations within that product type and prohibit the marketing of those products that cannot meet the limit. Such regulation would, however, require the availability of standard methods for analytical quantification.

Table 3.12

Toxicants in smokeless tobacco products available in the United Kingdom and internationally

Brand	TSNA[a] (µg/g)	Benzo[*a*]pyrene (ng/g)	NDMA (µg/g)	Chromium (ng/g)	Nickel (ng/g)	Arsenic (ng/g)	Lead (ng/g)	Nicotine (mg/g)	Average pH	Free nicotine (mg/g)
Products purchased in the United Kingdom										
Guthka products										
Manikchard	0.289	0.40	ND	0.26	1.22	0.04	0.15	3.1	9.19	3.0
Tulsi mix	1.436	1.28	ND	0.33	1.43	0.06	0.19	8.2	9.52	8.0
Zarda products										
Hakim pury	29.705	0.32	ND	2.15	5.35	0.29	1.36	42.7	6.00	0.4
Dalal misti Zarda	1.574	8.89	ND	0.87	2.09	0.11	1.14	8.6	6.15	0.1
Baba zarda (GP)	0.716	2.04	ND	2.34	5.88	0.24	1.18	48.4	5.32	0.1
Tooth-cleaning powder										
A. Quardir Gull	5.117	5.98	7	3.56	5.31	0.46	1.39	64.0	9.94	63.2
Dried tobacco leaves										
Tobacco leaf	0.223	0.11	ND	2.34	4.37	0.20	1.06	83.5	5.52	0.3
Products purchased outside the United Kingdom										
Baba 120 (India)	2.361	2.83	ND	2.08	2.94	0.40	1.56	55.0	4.88	0.04
Snus (Sweden)	0.478	1.99	ND	1.54	2.59	0.30	0.50	15.2	7.86	6.3
Ariva (USA)	ND	0.40	ND	1.40	2.19	0.12	0.28	9.2	7.57	2.4
Copenhagen (USA)	3.509	19.33	ND	1.69	2.64	0.23	0.45	25.8	7.39	4.9

From McNeill et al. (2006)

TSNA, tobacco-specific nitrosamines; NDMA, *N*-nitrosodimethylamine; ND, not detected, detection limit 5 ng/g

[a]Total TSNA: NNK (4-(*N*-nitrosomethylamino)-1-(3-pyridyl)-1-butanone), NNN (*N*′-nitrosonornicotine) and *N*′-nitrosoanabasine

Table 3.13

Chemical composition of smokeless tobacco products used in India

Toxicant	Minimum value	Brand	Maximum value	Brand
pH	5.21	Baba Zarda 120	10.1	Lime Mix–Miraj tobacco
Ammonia (µg/g)	3.8	Goa 1000 Zarda + Supari	5 280	Gai Chhap Zarda
Total carbonate (µg/g)	140	Dabur Red Toothpowder	2 040	Baba Zarda 120
Nicotine (mg/g)	1.2	Khaini	10.16	Dentobac Creamy Snuff
NNN (µg/g)	1.92	Goa 1000 Zarda + Supari	7.36	Baba Zarda 120
NNK (µg/g)	4.38	IPCO Creamy Snuff	11.58	Shimla Jarda + S. Supari
Benzo[*a*]pyrene (µg/g)	< 0.0001	?	0.94	IPCO Creamy Snuff
Cadmium (µg/g)	0.3	Click Eucalyptus	0.5	Baba Zarda 120
Arsenic (µg/g)	0.1	Dabur Red Toothpowder	1.94	Moolchan Super Jarda

From Gupta, 2004 cited in IARC (2007)

NNK, 4-(*N*-nitrosomethylamino)-1-(3-pyridyl)-1-butanone; NNN, *N*′-nitrosonornicotine

Table 3.14

Tobacco-specific nitrosamines in new and conventional smokeless tobacco products

Product	Tobacco-specific nitrosamine (µg/g product wet weight)				
	NNN	NNK	NAT	NAB	Total
Hard snuff Ariva	0.019	0.037	0.12	0.008	0.19
Hard snuff Stonewall	0.056	0.043	0.17	0.007	0.28
Swedish snus General	0.98	0.18	0.79	0.06	2.0
Split-free tobacco Exalt purchased in Sweden	2.3	0.27	0.98	0.13	3.7
Split-free tobacco Exalt purchased in USA	2.1	0.24	0.69	0.05	3.1
Split-free tobacco Revel mint flavoured	0.62	0.033	0.32	0.018	0.99
Split-free tobacco Revel wintergreen flavoured	0.64	0.032	0.31	0.017	1.0
Smokeless tobacco Copenhagen snuff	2.2	0.75	1.8	0.12	4.8
Smokeless tobacco Copenhagen long cut	3.9	1.6	1.9	0.13	7.5
Smokeless tobacco Skoal long cut straight	4.5	0.47	4.1	0.22	9.2
Smokeless Skoal bandits	0.9	0.17	0.24	0.014	1.3
Smokeless Kodiak ice	2.0	0.29	0.72	0.063	3.1
Smokeless Kodiak wintergreen	2.2	0.41	1.8	0.15	4.5

From Stepanov et al. (2006)

NNN, *N*′-nitrosonornicotine; NNK, 4-(*N*-nitrosomethylamino)-1-(3-pyridyl)-1-butanone; NAT, *N*′-nitrosoanatabine; NAB, *N*′-nitrosoanabasine

Table 3.15
Concentrations of classified carcinogenic agents identified in smokeless tobacco products[a]

Agent	Type of product[b]	Concentration range (ng/mg)	IARC classification
Benzo[*a*]pyrene	MS, DS, Z, G	< 0.1–90	2A
Urethane	CT	310–375	2B
Formaldehyde	MS, DS	1600–7400	1
Acetaldehyde	MS, DS	1400–27000	2B
Crotonaldehyde	MS, DS	200–2400	3
N-Nitrosodimethylamine	MS, CT	ND–270	2A
N-Nitrosopyrrolidine	MS, CT	ND–860	2B
N-Nitrosopiperidine	MS, CT	ND–110	2B
N-Nitrosomorpholine	MS, CT	ND–690	2B
N′-Nitrososarcosine	MS	ND–6300	2B
NNN	MS, CT, Z, G	400–58000	1
NNK	MS, CT, Z, G	ND–7800	1
N′-Nitrosoanabasine	MS, CT, Z, G	Present–1190	3
Nickel	MS, G	180–2700	1
Arsenic	Z, G	40–290	1
Chromium	MS, Z, G	260–2340	1

Adapted from IARC (2007)

MS, moist snuff; DS, dry snuff; Z, zarda product; G, gutkha product); CT, chewing tobacco; ND, not detected; NNN, *N*′- nitrosonornicotine; NNK, 4-(*N*-nitrosomethylamino)-1-(3-pyridyl)-1-butanone

[a] In addition, radioactive polonium-210, uranium-235 and -238 are present at picocurie levels in moist snuff.

[b] Not all carcinogens were measured in each product.

References

Ahrendt SA et al. (2001) Cigarette smoking is strongly associated with mutation of the K-ras gene in patients with primary adenocarcinoma of the lung. *Cancer*, 92:1525–1530.

Attorney Work Product (1992) *The 'palladium cigarette' and its role in the Cipollone trial.* Bates No: 2021382482.

Australian Department of Health and Aging (2001) *Cigarette emissions data, 2001.* Available from: http://www.health.gov.au/internet/wcms/publishing.nsf/Content/health-pubhlth-strateg-drugs-tobacco-emis_data.htm.

Baker RR (2006) The generation of formaldehyde in cigarettes—Overview and recent experiments. *Food and Chemical Toxicology*, 44:1799–1822.

Baan R et al. (2007) Carcinogenicity of alcoholic beverages. *Lancet Oncology*, 8:292–293.

Beland FA et al. (2005) High-performance liquid chromatography electrospray ionization tandem mass spectrometry for the detection and quantitation of benzo[a]pyrene–DNA adducts. *Chemical Research in Toxicology*, 18:1306–1315.

Benowitz NL et al. (1983) Smokers of low-yield cigarettes do not consume less nicotine. *New England Journal of Medicine*, 309:139–142.

Boysen G, Hecht SS (2003) Analysis of DNA and protein adducts of benzo[a]pyrene in human tissues using structure-specific methods. *Mutation Research*, 543:17–30.

Brennan P et al. (2004) Pooled analysis of alcohol dehydrogenase genotypes and head and neck cancer: a HuGE review. *American Journal of Epidemiology*, 159:1–16.

Brown & Williamson (1977) *Duolite. Internal communication.* Bates No: 504000094

Brown & Williamson (2002) *Comments of Brown & Williamson Tobacco Corporation on the petitions for regulation of Brown & Williamson 'Advance' cigarettes submitted by Nat'l Center for Tobacco-Free Kids, et al., and the Society for Research on Nicotine and Tobacco.* Dicket Nos: 01P-0571, 02P-0206.

Cao J et al. (2007) Acetaldehyde, a major toxicant of tobacco smoke, enhances behavioral, endocrine, and neuronal responses to nicotine in adolescent and adult rats. *Neuropsychopharmacology*, 32:2025–2035.

Castelao JE et al. (2001) Gender- and smoking-related bladder cancer risk. Journal of the National Cancer Institute, 93:538–545.

Charalambous J, Bullin Haines LI, Morgan JS (1987) *Tobacco smoke filter*. Filtrona Ltd. UK Patent GB 2,150,806.

Chen L et al. (2006) Quantitation of an acetaldehyde adduct in human leukocyte DNA and the effect of smoking cessation. *Chemical Research in Toxicology*, 20:108–113.

Chung FL, Chen HJC, Nath RG (1996) Lipid peroxidation as a potential source for the formation of exocyclic DNA adducts. *Carcinogenesis*, 17:2105–2111.

Chung FL et al. (1999) Endogenous formation and significance of 1,N2-propanodeoxyguanosine adducts. *Mutation Research Fundamental and Molecular Mechanisms of Mutagenesis*, 424:71–81.

Cogliano V et al. (2004) Smokeless tobacco and tobacco related nitrosamines. *Lancet Oncology*, 5:708.

Cohen SM et al. (1992) Acrolein intiates rat urinary bladder carcinogenesis. *Cancer Research*, 52:3577–3581.

Counts ME et al. (2004) Mainstream smoke toxicant yields and predicting relationships from a worldwide market sample of cigarette brands: ISO smoking conditions. *Regulatory Toxicology and Pharmacology*, 39:111–134.

Counts ME et al. (2005) Smoke composition and predicting relationships for international commercial cigarettes smoked with three machine-smoking conditions. *Regulatory Toxicology and Pharmacology*, 41:185–227.

Deliconstantinos G, Villiotou V, Stavrides JC (1994) Scavenging effects of hemoglobin and related heme containing compounds on nitric oxide, reactive oxidants and carcinogenic volatile nitrosocompounds of cigarette smoke. A new method for protection against the dangerous cigarette constituents. *Anticancer Research*, 14:2717–2726.

Denissenko MF et al. (1996) Preferential formation of benzo[a]pyrene adducts at lung cancer mutational hot spots in P53. *Science*, 274:430–432.

Department of Health and Human Services (2004a) *The health consequences of tobacco use: a report of the Surgeon General*. Rockville, Maryland, Public Health Service, Centers for Disease Control and Prevention, National Center for Chronic Disease Prevention and Health Promotion, Office on Smoking and Health.

Department of Health and Human Services (2004b) *Report on carcinogens*, 11th Ed. Research Triangle Park, North Carolina.

Ding YS et al. (2005) Determination of 14 polycyclic aromatic hydrocarbons in mainstream smoke from domestic cigarettes. *Environmental Science and Technology*, 39:471–478.

Djordjevic MV et al. (1995) US commercial brands of moist snuff, 1994. I. Assessment of nicotine, moisture, and pH. *Tobacco Control*, 4:62–66.

Djordjevic MV, Stellman SD, Zang E (2000) Doses of nicotine and lung carcinogens delivered to cigarette smokers. Journal of the National Cancer Institute, 92:106–111.

Dybing E et al. (1997) T25: a simplified carcinogenic potency index. Description of the system and study of correlations between carcinogenic potency and species/site specificity and mutagenicity. *Pharmacology and Toxicology*, 80:272–279.

European Commission (1999) *Guidelines for setting specific concentration limits for carcinogens in Annex 1 of Directive 67/548/EEC. Inclusion of potency considerations*. Brussels, Commission Working Group on the Classification and Labelling of Dangerous Substances.

Feng Z et al. (2006) Acrolein is a major cigarette-related lung cancer agent: preferential binding at p53 mutational hotspots and inhibition of DNA repair. *Proceedings of the National Academy of Sciences of the United States*, 103:15404–15409.

Fennell TR et al. (2000) Hemoglobin adducts from acrylonitrile and ethylene oxide in cigarette smokers: effects of glutathione S-transferase T1-null and M1-null genotypes. *Cancer Epidemiology, Biomarkers and Prevention*, 9:705–712.

Ferguson R (2000) *Reports on filler precursors of selected smoke constituents. Consultant evaluation. 10 October 2000*. Bates No: 2082742847.

Feron VJ et al. (1991) Aldehydes: occurrence, carcinogenic potential, mechanism of action and risk assessment. *Mutation Research*, 259:363–385.

Fowles J, Dybing E (2003) Application of toxicological risk assessment principles to the chemical toxicants of cigarette smoke. *Tobacco Control*, 12:424–430.

Furin OD, Gentry JS (1990) *Confirmation of formaldehyde reduction via reaction with ammonia*. Bates No: 509495561.

Gold LS et al. (1984) A carcinogenic potency database of the standardized results of animal bioassays. *Environmental Health Perspectives*, 58:9–319.

Gray N, Boyle P (2004) The case of the disappearing nitrosamines: a potentially global phenomenon. *Tobacco Control*, 13:13–16.

Halter HM, Ito TI (1978) Effect of tobacco reconstitution and expansion processes on smoke composition. *Recent Advances in Tobacco Science*, 4:113–132.

Hatsukami DK et al. (2004) Evaluation of carcinogen exposure in people who used 'reduced exposure' tobacco products. *Journal of the National Cancer Institute*, 96:844–852.

Health Canada (2000) *Tobacco industry reporting: tobacco reporting regulations*. http://www.hc-sc.gc.ca/hl-vs/pubs/tobac-tabac/tir-rft/emissions_e.html.

Health Canada (2004) *Data for 2004 using the intense smoking protocol*. http://www.hc-sc.gc.ca/hl-vs/tobac-tabac/legislation/reg/indust/constitu_e.html

Hecht SS (1999) Tobacco smoke carcinogens and lung cancer. *Journal of the National Cancer Institute*, 91:1194–1210.

Hecht SS (2002) Human urinary carcinogen metabolites: biomarkers for investigating tobacco and cancer. *Carcinogenesis*, 23:907–922.

Hecht SS (2003) Tobacco carcinogens, their biomarkers, and tobacco-induced cancer. *Nature Reviews Cancer*, 3:733–744.

Henningfield JE, Radzius A, Cone EJ (1995) Estimation of available nicotine content of six smokeless tobacco products. *Tobacco Control*, 4:57–61.

Hughes JR et al. (2004) Smoking behaviour and toxin exposure during six weeks use of a potential reduced exposure product: Omni. *Tobacco Control*, 13:175–180.

IARC (1986) *Tobacco smoking*. Lyon, International Agency for Research on Cancer (IARC Monographs on the Evaluation of Carcinogenic Risk of Chemicals to Humans, Vol. 38) p 95, IARC, Lyon, FR.

IARC (1987) *Overall evaluations of carcinogenicity: an updating of IARC Monographs Volumes 1 to 42*. Lyon, International Agency for Research on Cancer (IARC Monographs on the Evaluation of the Carcinogenic Risk of Chemicals to Humans, Suppl. 7).

IARC (1995a) *Acrolein*. Lyon, International Agency for Research on Cancer (IARC Monographs on the Evaluation of Carcinogenic Risks to Humans, Vol. 63).

IARC (1995b) *Dry cleaning, some chlorinated solvents and other industrial chemicals*. Lyon, International Agency for Research on Cancer (IARC Monographs on the Evaluation of Carcinogenic Risks to Humans, Vol. 63).

IARC (1999a) *Re-evaluation of some organic chemicals, hydrazine and hydrogen peroxide*. Lyon, International Agency for Research on Cancer (IARC Monographs on the Evaluation of Carcinogenic Risks to Humans, Vol. 71).

IARC (1999b) *Beryllium, cadmium, mercury, and exposures in the glass manufacturing industry*. Lyon, International Agency for Research on Cancer (IARC Monographs on the Evaluation of Carcinogenic Risks to Humans, Vol. 58).

IARC (2004) *Tobacco smoke and involuntary smoking*. Lyon, International Agency for Research on Cancer (IARC Monographs on the Evaluation of Carcinogenic Risks to Humans, Vol. 83).

IARC (2006) *Formaldehyde, 2-butoxyethanol and 1-tert-butoxy-2-propanol*. Lyon, International Agency for Research on Cancer (IARC Monographs on the Evaluation of Carcinogenic Risks to Humans, Vol. 88).

IARC (2007) *Smokeless tobacco and some related nitrosamines*. Lyon, International Agency for Research on Cancer (IARC Monographs on the Evaluation of Carcinogenic Risks to Humans, Vol. 89).

IARC (in press) 1,3-Butadiene, ethylene oxide and vinyl halides (vinyl fluoride, vinyl chloride and vinyl bromide). Lyon, International Agency for Research on Cancer (IARC Monographs on the Evaluation of Carcinogenic Risks to Humans, Vol. 97).

Idris AM et al. (1991) Unusually high levels of carcinogenic nitrosamines in Sudan snuff (toombak). *Carcinogenesis*, 12:1115–1118.

Idris AM, Ahmed HM, Malik MO (1995) Toombak dipping and cancer of the oral cavity in the Sudan: a case–control study. *International Journal of Cancer*, 63:477–480.

Ihrig AM (1972) *Lorillard research and development project request: selective removal of acrolein*. Bates No: 80600686.

Ihrig A (1976) *Lorillard monthly management status report: selective removal of acrolein*. Bates No: 01409538.

Irwin WDE (1990) *Filter materials for the reduction of selected minor smoke components: a literature review*. British American Tobacco. Bates No: 570262514.

ISO (2006) *Final report on the work of ISO/TC 126/WG 9. Smoking methods for cigarettes*. Geneva, International Organization for Standardization (ISO/TC 126/WG 9).

Jarvis MJ et al. (2001) Nicotine yield from machine-smoked cigarettes and nicotine intakes in smokers: evidence from a representative population survey. *Journal of the National Cancer Institute*, 93:134–138.

Kensler CJ, Battista SP (1963) Components of cigarette smoke with ciliary-depressant activity. Their selective removal by filters containing activated charcoal granules. *New England Journal of Medicine*, 269:1161–1166.

Koller KB et al. (2005) *Filter for selective removal of a gaseous component*. Philip Morris and Co. US Patent 6,911,189 B1.

Kubrina LN et al. (1989) European Patent application 0,351,252.

Laugesen M, Fowles J (2005) Scope for regulation of cigarette smoke toxicity: the case for including charcoal filters. *New Zealand Medical Journal*, 118:U1402.

Leikauf GD (2002) Hazardous air pollutants and asthma. *Environmental Health Perspectives*, 110 (Suppl. 4):505–526.

Lesser C, Von Borstel RW (2003) *Cigarette filter containing dry water and a porphyrin*. US Patent No. 6530377B1.

Lewis LS, Norman AB, Robinson AL (1990) *The evaluation of palladium/copper catalysts for CO removal*. Bates No: 508537386.

Litzinger EF (1972) *Duolite: properties and effects on smoke*. Bates No: 508006642.

Lodovici M et al. (2007) DNA solution in cigarette filters reduces polycyclic aromatic hydrocarbon (PAH) levels in mainstream tobacco smoke. *Food and Chemical Toxicology*, 45:1752–1756.

Ludvig J, Miner B, Eisenberg MJ (2005) Smoking cessation in patients with coronary artery disease. *American Heart Journal*, 149:565–572.

Maclure M et al. (1990) Decline of the hemoglobin adduct of 4-minobiphenyl during withdrawal from smoking. *Cancer Research*, 50:181–184.

Maillard F, Hada G (2005) *Filtration method and filter consisting of nitrogen-containing cycles of heterocycles such as DNA or RNA*. Sun Zero Co. US Patent 6,866,045.

Maselli JA (1986) *RJ Reynolds internal communication*. Bates No: 505491763.

Melikian AA et al. (2007a) Effect of delivered dosage of cigarette smoke toxins on the levels of urinary biomarkers of exposure. *Cancer Epidemiology, Biomarkers and Prevention*,16:1408–1415.

Melikian AA et al. (2007b) Gender differences relative to smoking behavior and emissions of toxins from mainstream cigarette smoke. *Nicotine and Tobacco Research*, 9:377–387.

McNeill A et al. (2006) Levels of toxins in oral tobacco products in the UK. *Tobacco Control*, 15:64–67.

Mills XE et al. (1995) Increased prevalence of K-ras oncogene mutations in lung adenocarcinma. *Cancer Research*, 55:1444–1447.

Nath RG et al. (1998) 1,N2-Propanodeoxyguanosine adducts: potential new biomarkers of smoking-induced DNA damage in human oral tissue. *Cancer Research*, 58:581–584.

National Cancer Institute (2001) *Risk associated with smoking cigarettes with low machine-measured yields of tar and nicotine*. Bethesda, Maryland, Department of Health and Human Services, Public Health Service, National Institutes of Health (Smoking and Tobacco Control Monograph No. 13) http://news.findlaw.com/hdocs/docs/tobacco/nihnci112701cigstdy.pdf.

Nesnow S et al. (1998) Mechanistic relationships between DNA adducts, oncogene mutations, and lung tumorigenesis in strain A mice. *Experimental Lung Research*, 24:395–405.

Norman A (1999) Cigarette design and materials. In: Davis EL, Nielsen MT, eds. *Tobacco. Production, chemistry and technology*. Oxford, Blackwell Science.

Norman V, Bryant HG Jr (1977) *Tobacco composition*. Liggett and Myers Inc. US Patent 4,055,191.

Österdahl BG, Jannson C, Paccou A (2004) Decreased levels of tobacco-specific N-nitrosamines in moist snuff on the Swedish market. *Journal of Agricultural and Food Chemistry*, 52:5085–5088.

Owens WF Jr (1978) Effect of cigarette paper on smoke yield and composition. *Recent Advances in Tobacco Science*, 4:3–24.

Pappas RS et al. (2006) Cadmium, lead, and thallium in mainstream tobacco smoke particulate. *Food and Chemical Toxicology*, 44:714–723.

Park S, Tretyakova N. (2004) Structural characterization of the major DNA–DNA cross-link of 1,2,3,4-diepoxybutane. *Chemical Research in Toxicology*, 17:129–136.

Peele DM, Riddick MG, Edwards ME (2001) Formation of tobacco-specific nitrosamines in flue cured tobacco. *Recent Advances in Tobacco Science*, 27:3–12.

Pfeifer GP et al. (2002) Tobacco smoke carcinogens, DNA damage and p53 mutations in smoking-associated cancers. *Oncogene*, 21:7435–7451.

Philip Morris (1997) *Internal research on hemoglobin filters from CFile*. Bates No: 2060531188.

Philip Morris (1998) *An evaluation of formaldehyde reduction by various silica gels and γ-aminopropylsilane-silica gels in a flowing gas stream*. Bates No: 2075879330.

Philip Morris (2002) *FDA regulation. Philip Morris USA 2002*. Available from: http://www.philipmorrisusa.com/company_news/fda_news_list.asp.

Polzin GM et al. (2008) Effect of charcoal-containing filters on gas phase volatile organic compounds in mainstream cigarette smoke. *Tobacco Control*, 17 (Suppl.1):i10–i16.

Prokopczyk B et al. (1995) Improved methodology for the quantitative assessment of tobacco-specific N-nitrosamines in tobacco by supercritical fluid extraction. *Journal of Agricultural and Food Chemistry*, 43:916–922.

Rainer NB, Feins IR (1980) *Filter material for selective removal of aldehydes for cigarette smoke*. Philip Morris and Co., US Patent 4,182,743.

Riggs DM (1989) CO reduction in premier fuels by catalyst impregnation. Bates No: 514820423.

RJ Reynolds (1994) *Carbon scrubber*. Bates No: 514723150.

RJ Reynolds (1995) *New product concept: carbon scrubber filter attachment*. Bates No: 510357383.

Robinson EA (1998) *Incorporation of proteins into filters of experimental cigarettes*. Memo to LH Gains. Lorillard Tobacco Co. Bates No: 96555438.

Rodgman A (1977) *RJR inter-office memorandum: aldehydes*. Bates No: 503245386.

Rodgman A (2001) Studies of polycyclic aromatic hydrocarbons in cigarette mainstream smoke: identification, tobacco precursors, control of levels: a review. *Beitraege zur Tobakforschung*, 19:361–379.

Rodgman A, Perfetti TA (2006) The composition of cigarette smoke: a chronology of the studies of four polycyclic aromatic hydrocarbons. *Beitraege zur Tobakforschung*, 22:208–254.

Rogers JC, Bluhm BK (1993a) *Determination of 1,3-butadiene and isoprene concentrations in mainstream cigarette smoke of cigarettes with and without carbon scrubber filters*. Bates No: 510636228.

Rogers JC, Bluhm BK (1993b) *Determination of 1,3-butadiene and isoprene concentrations in mainstream cigarette smoke of straight-grade cigarettes with and without carbon scrubber filters*. Bates No: 508441181.

Roux E et al. (1999) Human isolated airway contraction: interaction between air pollutants and passive sensitization. *American Journal of Respiratory Critical Care Medicine*, 160:439–445.

Scheinberg IH (1974) UK Patent 1,369,067

Scherer G (2006) Carboxyhemoglobin and thiocyanate as biomarkers of exposure to carbon monoxide and hydrogen cyanide in tobacco smoke. *Experimental Toxicology and Pathology,* 58:101–124.

Scherer G et al. (2006) Influence of smoking charcoal filter tipped cigarettes on various biomarkers of exposure. *Inhalation Toxicology*, 18:821–829.

Scientific Advisory Committee on Tobacco Product Regulation (2002) *Conclusions and recommendations on health claims derived from ISO/FTC method to measure cigarette yield*. Geneva, World Health Organization.

Scientific Advisory Committee on Tobacco Product Regulation (2003) *Statement of principles guiding the evaluation of new or modified tobacco products*. Geneva, World Health Organization.

Seeman JI, Dixon M, Haussmann HJ (2002) Acetaldehyde in mainstream tobacco smoke: formation and occurrence in smoke and bioavailability in the smoker. *Chemical Research in Toxicology*, 15:1331–1350.

Silverstein P (1992) Smoking and wound healing. *American Journal of Medicine*, 93:22S–24S.

Skipper PL, Tannenbaum SR (1990) Protein adducts in the molecular dosimetry of chemical carcinogens. *Carcinogenesis*, 11:507–518.

Smith C et al. (1994a) *Comparison study utilizing subject's usual brand cigarette, (3) carbon scrubber prototypes, and (1) grooved filter prototype to determine their effects on human smoker's breath carbon monoxide and % carboxyhemoglobin levels*. Bates No: 510636183.

Smith C et al. (1994b) *HRRC proposal: comparison study utilizing subject's usual brand cigarette, (3) carbon scrubber prototypes, and (1) grooved filter prototype to determine their effects on human smoker's breath carbon monoxide and % carboxyhemoglobin levels*. Bates No: 510641328.

Smith LE et al. (2000) Targeting of lung cancer mutational hotspots by polycyclic aromatic hydrocarbons. *Journal of the National Cancer Institute*, 92:803–811.

Stavridis I, Deliconstantinos G (1999) *Removal of noxious oxidants and carcinogenic volatile nitrosocompounds from cigarette smoke using biological substances*. US Patent 5,909,736.

Stepanov I et al. (2006) Tobacco-specific nitrosamines in new tobacco products. *Nicotine and Tobacco Research*, 8:309–313.

Stiles M et al. (1994) *Human smoking behavior study examining carbon scrubber filter technology*. Bates No: 511823912.

Straif K et al. (2005) Carcinogenicity of polycyclic aromatic hydrocarbons. *Lancet Oncology*, 6:931–932.

Stratton K et al. (2001) *Clearing the smoke. Assessing the science base for tobacco harm reduction*. Washington DC, National Academy Press.

Tennessee Eastman (1959) *Composition of tobacco smoke. III. Effects of the extraction of tobacco on amount of benzo[a]pyrene in cigarette smoke tar*. Kingsport, Tennessee (Tennessee Eastman Corp. Research Report No. 4-1201-3).

Tiggelbeck D (1967) Comments on selective cigarette smoke filtration. In: eds. Wynder EL, Hoffmann D, eds. *Toward a Less Harmful Cigarette.* Bethesda, Maryland, National Cancer Institute (National Cancer Institute Monograph 28:249–258).

Tiggelbeck D (1976) Vapor phase modification. An under-utilized technology. In: Wynder EL, Hoffmann D, Gori GB, eds. *Proceedings of the Third World Conference on Smoking and Health.* Bethesda, Maryland, Department of Health, Education and Welfare, Public Health Service, National Institutes of Health, National Cancer Institute, pp. 507–514 (DHEW Publication No. (NIH) 76-1221).

Tolman TW (1970) *The theoretical and practical aspects of carbon monoxide filtration.* British-American Tobacco Co. Ltd (Report No. RD.687-R). Bates No: 650315732.

Tolman TW (1971) *Further work on the filtration of carbon monoxide and nitric oxide.* British-American Tobacco Co. Ltd. (Report No. RD. 802-R). Bates No: 650316111.

Tolman TW (1973) *The oxidation of carbon monoxide in cigarette smoke catalysed by manganese dioxide.* British-American Tobacco Co. Ltd (Report No. RD.1011-R. 1973). Bates No: 570508384.

Townsend DE (1978) *A reactor system for the rapid initial evaluation of prospective filter additives for carbon monoxide removal from cigarette smoke.* RJ Reynolds Tobacco Co. Bates No: 500607965.

Tretyakova NT et al. (2002) Formation of benzo[a]pyrene diol epoxide-DNA adducts at specific guanines within K-ras and p53 gene sequences: stable isotope-labeling mass spectrometry approach. *Biochemistry*, 41:9535–9544.

Valavanidis A, Haralambous E (2001) A comparative study by electron paramagnetic resonance of free radical species in the mainstream and sidestream smoke of cigarettes with conventional acetate filters and 'bio-filters'. *Redox Report*, 6:161–171.

Vleeming W, Rambali B, Opperhuizen A (2002) The role of nitric oxide in cigarette smoking and nicotine addiction. *Nicotine and Tobacco Research*, 4:341–348.

Weinberger B et al. (2001) The toxicology of inhaled nitric oxide. *Toxicological Science*, 59:5–16.

Westra WH et al. (1993) K-ras oncogene activation in lung adenocarcinomas from former smokers. *Cancer*, 72:432–438.

WHO. *Guiding principles for the development of tobacco product research and testing capacity and proposed protocols for the initiation of tobacco product testing*. Geneva, World Health Organization, Study Group on Tobacco Product Regulation. http://www.who.int/tobacco/global_interaction/tobreg/goa_2003_principles/en/index.html.

WHO (2007) Setting maximal limits for toxic constituents in cigarette smoke. Geneva, World Health Organization, Study Group on Tobacco Product Regulation. http://www.who.int/tobacco/global_interaction/tobreg/tsr/en/index.html.

Wu W, Ashley D, Watson C (2003) Simultaneous determination of 5 tobacco-specific nitrosamines in mainstream cigarette smoke by isotope dilution liquid chromatography/electrospray ionization tandem mass spectrometry. *Analytical Chemistry*, 75:4827–4832.

Wynder EL, Hoffman D (1967) *Tobacco and tobacco smoke: studies in experimental carcinogenesis*. New York, Academic Press.

Xue L, Thomas CE, Koller KB (2002) Mainstream smoke gas phase filtration performance of adsorption materials evaluated with a puff-by-puff multiplex GC-MS method. *Beitraege zur Tabakforschung International*, 20:251–256.

Zhang S et al. (2006) Analysis of crotonaldehyde- and acetaldehyde-derived 1,N2-propanodeoxyguanosine adducts in DNA from human tissues using liquid chromatography-electrosopray ionization-tandem mass spectrometry. *Chemical Research in Toxicology*, 19:1386–1392.

Annex 3.1 Levels of toxicants per milligram of nicotine for international Philip Morris brands, Canadian brands and Australian brands

Table A1.1.

Yields per milligram of nicotine of toxicants reported to Health Canada (2004)

Brand	Nicotine	Carbon monoxide	Ammonia	1-Aminonaphthalene	2-Aminonaphthalene	3-Aminobiphenyl
Export 'A' Ultra Light Regular Size	2.49	9.07	8.54	10.48	6.71	1.60
Vantage Slims Extra Light 4 100's	2.92	9.07	8.50	11.16	7.05	1.64
Export 'A' Medium King Size	2.65	9.66	10.60	8.45	6.19	1.68
Export 'A' Full Flavour King Size	2.79	10.04	11.08	8.42	5.81	1.64
Craven A Extra Light King Size	2.38	11.77	9.12	11.23	6.98	1.70
Export 'A' Medium Regular Size	2.51	10.83	9.03	11.73	7.25	1.72
Export 'A' Extra Light Regular Size	2.48	9.05	8.77	10.09	6.80	1.72
More Regular 120's	2.70	14.07	13.44	12.93	8.04	2.06
Export 'A' Light / Special Light King Size	2.60	9.92	11.08	8.96	6.23	1.65
Export 'A' Light / Special Light Regular Size	2.37	10.89	9.77	12.46	7.73	2.01
More Menthol 120's	2.60	15.65	13.77	12.27	8.04	1.98
Vantage Ultra Light 1 King Size	2.10	11.32	9.02	12.01	7.56	1.79
Export 'A' Extra Light King Size	2.27	10.70	11.10	9.16	6.34	1.68
Export 'A' Mild King Size	2.60	9.77	11.69	7.46	5.38	1.56
Export 'A' Mild Regular Size	2.60	9.77	11.69	7.46	5.38	1.56
Export 'A' Ultra Light King Size	2.57	9.88	11.83	7.55	5.45	1.58
Number 7 King Size	2.60	11.79	9.97	13.84	8.33	2.06
Craven Milds Ultra Mild King Size	1.59	14.88	9.88	13.80	8.93	2.39

Camel Light King Size	1.74	14.54	15.06	15.75	10.75	2.66
Winston Light King Size	1.74	14.54	15.06	15.75	10.75	2.66
Export Plain Regular Size	2.60	8.38	12.42	12.73	7.42	1.62
Rothmans Special Mild King Size	2.56	11.63	9.73	11.92	8.47	2.11
Winston Light 100's	2.19	14.06	15.43	15.75	10.55	2.59
Winston 100's	2.60	11.31	15.38	17.19	10.65	2.57
Gauloises Blondes King Size	2.55	11.58	18.82	12.15	7.45	2.16
Player's Extra Light Regular Size	2.16	10.47	8.99	11.87	7.66	1.82
Camel King Size	2.27	12.51	16.43	16.34	10.22	2.48
Salem King Size	2.27	12.51	16.43	16.34	10.22	2.48
Winston King Size	2.27	12.51	16.43	16.34	10.22	2.48
Export 'A' Full Flavour Regular Size	2.64	10.43	10.65	11.46	7.14	1.82
Du Maurier Extra Light Regular Size	2.25	12.08	9.62	11.43	7.15	1.70
Craven A King Size	2.69	11.75	10.71	10.28	6.26	1.58
Salem Light King Size	2.32	13.15	15.17	13.49	9.31	2.23
Matinee Extra Light King Size	1.76	13.42	9.52	11.33	7.18	1.79
Camel Plain Regular Size	2.45	9.14	18.78	19.63	11.39	2.63
Du Maurier Light King Size	2.55	12.04	9.65	10.98	6.81	1.63
Viscount Extra Mild King Size	1.72	14.62	11.13	12.20	8.19	2.15
Sportsman Plain Regular Size	2.91	7.81	10.33	9.98	5.16	1.14
Vatnage Medium 7 King Size	2.42	11.64	9.97	11.19	7.13	1.74
Benson & Hedges Deluxe Menthol Ultra Lights 100's	2.52	10.93	9.55	9.01	5.71	1.66
Player's Light Regular Size	2.19	10.52	9.69	11.41	7.22	1.87
Vantage Max 15 King Size	3.10	10.45	8.55	9.35	4.77	1.18
Craven Menthol King Size	2.25	13.87	8.84	10.42	6.77	1.72
Matinee Silver Regular Size	1.97	11.22	9.85	10.96	6.14	1.40

Belmont Milds Regular Size	2.35	10.39	9.37	7.67	5.11	1.23
Belmont Milds King Size	2.34	11.31	9.83	9.83	6.41	1.50
Player's Light King Size	2.52	12.35	10.77	12.65	7.90	2.00
Gauloises Blondes Lights King Size	1.97	13.36	18.29	13.72	8.64	2.59
Vantage Rich 12 King Size	2.60	10.81	9.69	11.62	6.04	1.39
Gauloises Blondes Ultra Light King Size	1.68	15.73	19.00	15.44	9.50	2.85
Mark ten Plain King Size	3.21	7.99	10.91	10.28	5.30	1.22
Du Maurier Light Regular Size	1.96	14.09	10.66	15.06	9.24	2.45
Du Maurier King Size	2.49	12.27	9.82	12.69	7.84	1.97
Player's Regular Size	2.46	11.22	10.70	10.31	6.62	1.81
Du Maurier Extra Light King Size	2.14	12.48	9.61	10.89	7.17	1.91
Player's Special Blend King Size	2.63	9.32	11.60	11.94	6.62	1.44
Player's Special Blend Regular Size	2.44	9.63	12.30	12.17	7.01	1.62
Player's Plain Regular Size	2.68	7.87	11.19	12.13	5.75	1.31
Player's Extra Light King Size	2.38	13.60	9.70	12.09	7.62	1.98
Du Maurier Regular Size	2.06	13.28	11.03	11.28	7.04	1.81
Canyon Regular Size	1.87	14.71	15.40	8.34	14.22	1.63
Dakar Regular Size	1.87	14.71	15.40	8.34	14.22	1.63
Discretion Regular Size	1.87	14.71	15.40	8.34	14.22	1.63
Fine Regular Size	1.87	14.71	15.40	8.34	14.22	1.63
Gipsy Regular Size	1.87	14.71	15.40	8.34	14.22	1.63
Selesta Regular Size	1.87	14.71	15.40	8.34	14.22	1.63
Smoking Regular Size	1.87	14.71	15.40	8.34	14.22	1.63
Tremblay Regular Size	1.87	14.71	15.40	8.34	14.22	1.63
Canyon King Size	2.13	14.46	14.13	8.26	14.18	1.61
Dakar King Size	2.13	14.46	14.13	8.26	14.18	1.61

Discretion King Size	2.13	14.46	14.13	8.26	14.18	1.61
Fine King Size	2.13	14.46	14.13	8.26	14.18	1.61
Gipsy King Size	2.13	14.46	14.13	8.26	14.18	1.61
Selesta King Size	2.13	14.46	14.13	8.26	14.18	1.61
Smoking King Size	2.13	14.46	14.13	8.26	14.18	1.61
Tremblay King Size	2.13	14.46	14.13	8.26	14.18	1.61
Dakar Light King Size	2.06	14.85	12.28	8.74	14.47	1.68
Fine Light King Size	2.06	14.85	12.28	8.74	14.47	1.68
Gipsy Light King Size	2.06	14.85	12.28	8.74	14.47	1.68
Rodeo King Size	2.06	14.85	12.28	8.74	14.47	1.68
Selesta Light King Size	2.06	14.85	12.28	8.74	14.47	1.68
Smoking Light King Size	2.06	14.85	12.28	8.74	14.47	1.68
Tremblay Light King Size	2.06	14.85	12.28	8.74	14.47	1.68
Dakar Light Regular Size	1.81	14.64	18.07	8.51	14.14	1.64
Fine Light Regular Size	1.81	14.64	18.07	8.51	14.14	1.64
Gipsy Light Regular Size	1.81	14.64	18.07	8.51	14.14	1.64
Rodeo Regular Size	1.81	14.64	18.07	8.51	14.14	1.64
Selesta Light Regular Size	1.81	14.64	18.07	8.51	14.14	1.64
Smoking Light Regular Size	1.81	14.64	18.07	8.51	14.14	1.64
*** Means ***	2.25	12.54	12.65	10.78	9.69	1.80
*** Standard deviation ***	0.35	2.19	3.03	2.67	3.46	0.36
*** Coefficient of variation ***	0.15	0.17	0.24	0.25	0.36	0.20
Maximum	3.21	15.73	19.00	19.63	14.47	2.85
75th percentile	2.55	14.64	15.38	12.15	14.18	1.97
9th percentile	2.64	14.85	18.07	15.13	14.22	2.48
Median	2.25	12.51	12.28	10.31	8.19	1.68
Minimum	1.59	7.81	8.50	7.46	4.77	1.14

Brand	4-Aminobiphenyl	Benzo[*a*]pyrene	Formaldehyde	Acetaldehyde	Acetone	Acrolein
Export 'A' Ultra Light Regular Size	1.20	5.19	60.76	431.18	231.86	58.40
Vantage Slims Extra Light 4 100's	1.22	5.33	46.20	422.65	237.81	59.09
Export 'A' Medium King Size	1.42	5.74	45.66	443.02	218.11	51.70
Export 'A' Full Flavour King Size	1.36	5.88	50.82	474.91	235.13	55.20
Craven A Extra Light King Size	1.35	5.97	63.96	545.70	277.99	77.79
Export 'A' Medium Regular Size	1.33	6.01	68.02	489.80	255.26	62.90
Export 'A' Extra Light Regular Size	1.34	6.05	57.01	387.72	220.95	57.15
More Regular 120's	1.69	6.07	39.19	619.26	311.11	62.59
Export 'A' Light / Special Light King Size	1.34	6.08	46.62	444.23	223.08	51.92
Export 'A' Light / Special Light Regular Size	1.52	6.11	65.48	500.32	275.34	66.78
More Menthol 120's	1.71	6.23	42.42	660.77	327.31	67.69
Vantage Ultra Light 1 King Size	1.38	6.24	70.17	524.96	284.39	71.70
Export 'A' Extra Light King Size	1.44	6.26	53.30	519.38	248.02	62.56
Export 'A' Mild King Size	1.25	6.38	67.62	472.69	223.46	57.31
Export 'A' Mild Regular Size	1.25	6.38	67.62	472.69	223.46	57.31
Export 'A' Ultra Light King Size	1.26	6.46	68.40	478.21	226.07	57.98
Number 7 King Size	1.57	6.49	61.26	517.57	282.62	78.69
Craven Milds Ultra Mild King Size	1.85	6.58	82.37	716.96	386.06	99.52
Camel Light King Size	2.21	6.72	49.31	686.78	359.77	73.56
Winston Light King Size	2.21	6.72	49.31	686.78	359.77	73.56
Export Plain Regular Size	1.33	6.81	54.23	389.62	196.15	50.38
Rothmans Special Mild King Size	1.61	6.86	67.07	506.07	280.55	80.73

Winston Light 100's	2.11	6.94	39.45	657.99	337.44	68.95
Winston 100's	2.00	6.96	43.65	544.62	282.69	57.31
Gauloises Blondes King Size	1.84	7.06	44.30	548.02	264.99	61.15
Player's Extra Light Regular Size	1.37	7.16	69.21	505.97	279.46	65.88
Camel King Size	2.00	7.18	50.66	586.34	303.96	63.00
Salem King Size	2.00	7.18	50.66	586.34	303.96	63.00
Winston King Size	2.00	7.18	50.66	586.34	303.96	63.00
Export 'A' Full Flavour Regular Size	1.37	7.24	58.97	437.31	238.21	60.75
Du Maurier Extra Light Regular Size	1.25	7.31	60.80	509.90	270.58	76.58
Craven A King Size	1.20	7.39	54.00	463.70	249.95	74.16
Salem Light King Size	1.76	7.41	50.00	607.76	305.17	64.22
Matinee Extra Light King Size	1.34	7.47	81.23	615.55	323.24	86.66
Camel Plain Regular Size	2.00	7.51	52.24	424.90	221.22	46.94
Du Maurier Light King Size	1.23	7.54	58.11	510.09	271.37	76.28
Viscount Extra Mild King Size	1.59	7.55	85.42	641.69	335.48	96.84
Sportsman Plain Regular Size	0.86	7.57	63.33	364.48	194.80	47.84
Vatnage Medium 7 King Size	1.31	7.69	64.68	474.11	277.74	65.65
Benson & Hedges Deluxe Menthol Ultra Lights 100's	1.24	7.70	72.60	506.62	265.77	77.60
Player's Light Regular Size	1.35	7.74	89.83	516.22	289.68	76.73
Vantage Max 15 King Size	0.91	7.77	65.10	430.97	222.58	48.71
Craven Menthol King Size	1.29	7.83	93.58	609.68	313.39	85.97
Matinee Silver Regular Size	1.20	7.87	88.32	598.98	308.12	71.07
Belmont Milds Regular Size	0.94	8.09	68.99	476.54	242.74	57.92
Belmont Milds King Size	1.20	8.12	64.57	535.78	257.84	61.15

Player's Light King Size	1.53	8.13	60.38	528.52	299.86	80.65
Gauloises Blondes Lights King Size	2.29	8.13	44.71	660.03	319.09	72.15
Vantage Rich 12 King Size	1.05	8.27	77.08	479.23	246.92	55.00
Gauloises Blondes Ultra Light King Size	2.61	8.31	43.34	766.50	368.11	81.93
Mark ten Plain King Size	0.87	8.41	71.37	397.37	205.70	53.61
Du Maurier Light Regular Size	1.90	8.53	73.21	595.43	327.51	91.08
Du Maurier King Size	1.41	8.57	77.17	517.59	291.39	83.66
Player's Regular Size	1.29	8.71	74.03	443.81	244.64	70.16
Du Maurier Extra Light King Size	1.45	8.93	72.19	547.00	314.80	81.64
Player's Special Blend King Size	1.23	9.01	59.32	506.46	250.19	54.75
Player's Special Blend Regular Size	1.36	9.14	71.72	523.36	252.87	57.38
Player's Plain Regular Size	1.04	9.18	80.60	406.72	210.07	52.61
Player's Extra Light King Size	1.48	9.25	59.15	531.12	295.11	86.35
Du Maurier Regular Size	1.35	9.59	79.87	531.02	296.55	83.78
Canyon Regular Size	2.34	16.79	116.04	651.87	318.18	78.61
Dakar Regular Size	2.34	16.79	116.04	651.87	318.18	78.61
Discretion Regular Size	2.34	16.79	116.04	651.87	318.18	78.61
Fine Regular Size	2.34	16.79	116.04	651.87	318.18	78.61
Gipsy Regular Size	2.34	16.79	116.04	651.87	318.18	78.61
Se esta Regular Size	2.34	16.79	116.04	651.87	318.18	78.61
Smoking Regular Size	2.34	16.79	116.04	651.87	318.18	78.61
Tremblay Regular Size	2.34	16.79	116.04	651.87	318.18	78.61
Canyon King Size	2.28	16.81	97.65	646.48	319.25	77.46
Dakar King Size	2.28	16.81	97.65	646.48	319.25	77.46
Discretion King Size	2.28	16.81	97.65	646.48	319.25	77.46
Fine King Size	2.28	16.81	97.65	646.48	319.25	77.46

Gipsy King Size	2.28	16.81	97.65	646.48	319.25	77.46
Selesta King Size	2.28	16.81	97.65	646.48	319.25	77.46
Smoking King Size	2.28	16.81	97.65	646.48	319.25	77.46
Tremblay King Size	2.28	16.81	97.65	646.48	319.25	77.46
Dakar Light King Size	2.47	17.38	103.40	657.77	322.33	80.58
Fine Light King Size	2.47	17.38	103.40	657.77	322.33	80.58
Gipsy Light King Size	2.47	17.38	103.40	657.77	322.33	80.58
Rodeo King Size	2.47	17.38	103.40	657.77	322.33	80.58
Selesta Light King Size	2.47	17.38	103.40	657.77	322.33	80.58
Smoking Light King Size	2.47	17.38	103.40	657.77	322.33	80.58
Tremblay Light King Size	2.47	17.38	103.40	657.77	322.33	80.58
Dakar Light Regular Size	2.36	17.90	118.23	644.20	316.57	79.56
Fine Light Regular Size	2.36	17.90	118.23	644.20	316.57	79.56
Gipsy Light Regular Size	2.36	17.90	118.23	644.20	316.57	79.56
Rodeo Regular Size	2.36	17.90	118.23	644.20	316.57	79.56
Selesta Light Regular Size	2.36	17.90	118.23	644.20	316.57	79.56
Smoking Light Regular Size	2.36	17.90	118.23	644.20	316.57	79.56
*** Means ***	1.77	10.52	77.35	566.54	289.06	71.31
*** Standard deviation ***	0.52	4.73	24.84	92.69	42.51	11.71
*** Coefficient of variation ***	0.29	0.45	0.32	0.16	0.15	0.16
Maximum	2.61	17.90	118.23	766.50	386.06	99.52
75th percentile	2.29	16.79	97.65	646.48	319.25	79.56
9th percentile	2.36	17.38	116.04	657.77	322.51	81.70
Median	1.69	8.09	71.37	586.34	303.96	76.73
Minimum	0.86	5.19	39.19	364.48	194.80	46.94

Brand	Propionaldehyde	Crotonaldehyde	Butyraldehyde	Hydrogen cyanide	Mercury	Lead
Export 'A' Ultra Light Regular Size	36.94	25.92	24.55	87.52	2.09	
Vantage Slims Extra Light 4 100's	39.25	24.92	25.45	93.03	1.97	
Export 'A' Medium King Size	37.36	21.85	24.26	112.45	2.54	
Export 'A' Full Flavour King Size	41.18	23.15	26.13	103.23	2.52	
Craven A Extra Light King Size	43.73	31.16	31.62	118.47	2.87	
Export 'A' Medium Regular Size	40.52	29.21	28.03	106.64	2.50	
Export 'A' Extra Light Regular Size	35.67	21.85	22.43	86.07	2.08	
More Regular 120's	53.33	29.00	36.30	219.26	3.10	15.96
Export 'A' Light / Special Light King Size	38.46	21.46	24.54	108.46	2.66	
Export 'A' Light / Special Light Regular Size	45.90	28.76	29.08	115.79	2.64	
More Menthol 120's	58.08	31.42	37.69	230.38	3.07	16.54
Vantage Ultra Light 1 King Size	44.33	29.77	29.56	101.10	2.78	
Export 'A' Extra Light King Size	43.61	24.54	27.71	124.23	2.58	
Export 'A' Mild King Size	41.54	23.15	24.15	109.23	2.56	
Export 'A' Mild Regular Size	41.54	23.15	24.15	109.23	2.56	
Export 'A' Ultra Light King Size	42.02	23.42	24.44	110.51	2.59	
Number 7 King Size	44.97	28.75	30.38	130.39	3.06	
Craven Milds Ultra Mild King Size	63.90	39.62	41.30	160.81	3.93	
Camel Light King Size	57.93	29.89	40.06	211.49	4.05	
Winston Light King Size	57.93	29.89	40.06	211.49	4.05	
Export Plain Regular Size	34.46	23.27	23.38	96.15	2.10	
Rothmans Special Mild King Size	44.89	30.44	30.21	126.96	2.89	

Winston Light 100's	54.79	29.59	38.77	200.00	3.83	12.28
Winston 100's	46.15	25.23	32.19	162.69	2.97	12.54
Gauloises Blondes King Size	46.26	25.87	29.40	157.59	2.43	17.40
Player's Extra Light Regular Size	43.91	30.24	30.05	103.23	2.77	
Camel King Size	49.34	28.63	34.89	196.48	3.33	11.76
Salem King Size	49.34	28.63	34.89	196.48	3.33	11.76
Winston King Size	49.34	28.63	34.89	196.48	3.33	11.76
Export 'A' Full Flavour Regular Size	40.31	24.06	25.32	116.80	2.31	9.76
Du Maurier Extra Light Regular Size	42.67	28.61	29.49	119.06	3.29	
Craven A King Size	39.88	25.07	27.07	123.82	3.17	
Salem Light King Size	52.16	29.78	36.03	200.43	3.32	11.94
Matinee Extra Light King Size	52.53	34.48	35.23	122.18	3.67	
Camel Plain Regular Size	35.92	25.63	26.04	149.80	2.52	12.57
Du Maurier Light King Size	43.00	29.10	29.99	124.16	3.31	
Viscount Extra Mild King Size	53.90	34.94	35.87	145.21	3.18	
Sportsman Plain Regular Size	31.32	26.85	22.03	75.37	2.07	
Vatnage Medium 7 King Size	42.16	26.10	27.52	121.33	2.73	10.61
Benson & Hedges Deluxe Menthol Ultra Lights 100's	44.00	27.93	28.52	114.01	3.11	
Player's Light Regular Size	48.40	30.33	29.70	100.46	2.73	
Vantage Max 15 King Size	35.81	24.71	24.52	104.84	2.56	11.84
Craven Menthol King Size	49.98	35.84	34.45	133.70	3.42	
Matinee Silver Regular Size	49.64	31.32	32.44	116.24	3.56	
Belmont Milds Regular Size	38.33	19.59	23.85	88.15	2.34	
Belmont Milds King Size	42.76	20.10	25.66	97.06	2.57	

Player's Light King Size	49.04	30.73	31.51	133.89	3.14	
Gauloises Blondes Lights King Size	56.40	29.47	35.57	172.76	3.10	17.28
Vantage Rich 12 King Size	40.00	26.54	26.92	103.46	2.77	12.65
Gauloises Blondes Ultra Light King Size	65.31	33.25	40.37	203.05	3.68	18.76
Mark ten Plain King Size	34.91	29.61	24.62	85.08	2.09	
Du Maurier Light Regular Size	53.57	33.04	34.97	138.46	3.62	
Du Maurier King Size	47.45	30.73	30.50	116.93	2.76	
Player's Regular Size	39.72	24.58	25.27	106.29	2.59	
Du Maurier Extra Light King Size	51.64	30.99	32.66	124.39	3.31	
Player's Special Blend King Size	41.44	25.36	27.64	112.17	2.71	
Player's Special Blend Regular Size	42.62	25.78	27.83	114.75	2.83	
Player's Plain Regular Size	34.14	29.51	22.80	94.78	2.75	13.73
Player's Extra Light King Size	49.54	29.10	32.08	131.05	3.04	
Du Maurier Regular Size	47.76	29.85	31.22	128.35	3.30	
Canyon Regular Size	54.01	35.99	37.06	170.05	2.94	21.82
Dakar Regular Size	54.01	35.99	37.06	170.05	2.94	21.82
Discretion Regular Size	54.01	35.99	37.06	170.05	2.94	21.82
Fine Regular Size	54.01	35.99	37.06	170.05	2.94	21.82
Gipsy Regular Size	54.01	35.99	37.06	170.05	2.94	21.82
Selesta Regular Size	54.01	35.99	37.06	170.05	2.94	21.82
Smoking Regular Size	54.01	35.99	37.06	170.05	2.94	21.82
Tremblay Regular Size	54.01	35.99	37.06	170.05	2.94	21.82
Canyon King Size	53.99	34.69	37.04	160.09	2.78	20.61
Dakar King Size	53.99	34.69	37.04	160.09	2.78	20.61
Discretion King Size	53.99	34.69	37.04	160.09	2.78	20.61
Fine King Size	53.99	34.69	37.04	160.09	2.78	20.61

Gipsy King Size	53.99	34.69	37.04	160.09	2.78	20.61
Selesta King Size	53.99	34.69	37.04	160.09	2.78	20.61
Smoking King Size	53.99	34.69	37.04	160.09	2.78	20.61
Tremblay King Size	53.99	34.69	37.04	160.09	2.78	20.61
Dakar Light King Size	54.85	35.68	37.38	170.39	3.25	23.25
Fine Light King Size	54.85	35.68	37.38	170.39	3.25	23.25
Gipsy Light King Size	54.85	35.68	37.38	170.39	3.25	23.25
Rodeo King Size	54.85	35.68	37.38	170.39	3.25	23.25
Selesta Light King Size	54.85	35.68	37.38	170.39	3.25	23.25
Smoking Light King Size	54.85	35.68	37.38	170.39	3.25	23.25
Tremblay Light King Size	54.85	35.68	37.38	170.39	3.25	23.25
Dakar Light Regular Size	53.31	35.19	36.63	163.54	3.04	21.82
Fine Light Regular Size	53.31	35.19	36.63	163.54	3.04	21.82
Gipsy Light Regular Size	53.31	35.19	36.63	163.54	3.04	21.82
Rodeo Regular Size	53.31	35.19	36.63	163.54	3.04	21.82
Selesta Light Regular Size	53.31	35.19	36.63	163.54	3.04	21.82
Smoking Light Regular Size	53.31	35.19	36.63	163.54	3.04	21.82
*** Means ***	48.21	30.35	32.28	142.91	2.94	18.75
*** Standard deviation ***	7.35	4.80	5.37	35.92	0.43	4.44
*** Coefficient of variation ***	0.15	0.16	0.17	0.25	0.15	0.24
Maximum	65.31	39.62	41.30	230.38	4.05	23.25
75th percentile	53.99	35.19	37.04	170.05	3.25	21.82
9th percentile	54.85	35.87	37.38	196.48	3.35	23.25
Median	49.54	29.89	34.45	145.21	2.94	20.61
Minimum	31.32	19.59	22.03	75.37	1.97	9.76

Brand	Cadmium	Nitric oxide	Nitrogen oxides	NNN	NNK	NAT
Export 'A' Ultra Light Regular Size	72.54	47.64	51.45	26.40	50.87	39.01
Vantage Slims Extra Light 4 100's	65.39	41.62	43.94	20.69	49.03	38.38
Export 'A' Medium King Size	61.13	60.75	63.02	28.68	42.26	41.13
Export 'A' Full Flavour King Size	64.16	60.93	63.44	28.67	44.80	38.71
Craven A Extra Light King Size	79.97	57.41	61.44	16.64	33.68	27.32
Export 'A' Medium Regular Size	75.75	58.58	62.97	27.00	50.03	42.66
Export 'A' Extra Light Regular Size	70.84	43.74	47.12	23.71	50.34	38.65
More Regular 120's	62.22	130.37	141.48	132.59	81.85	10.74
Export 'A' Light / Special Light King Size	61.54	57.69	59.62	33.46	46.58	40.77
Export 'A' Light / Special Light Regular Size	75.96	57.56	61.37	26.77	54.40	44.78
More Menthol 120's	59.62	145.77	160.38	131.92	87.69	11.15
Vantage Ultra Light 1 King Size	80.68	59.06	64.19	26.06	51.04	42.40
Export 'A' Extra Light King Size	63.88	65.20	67.40	28.19	39.65	37.00
Export 'A' Mild King Size	58.46	47.31	49.62	24.62	41.54	34.23
Export 'A' Mild Regular Size	58.46	47.31	49.62	24.62	41.54	34.23
Export 'A' Ultra Light King Size	59.14	47.86	50.19	24.90	42.02	34.63
Number 7 King Size	86.67	59.11	62.38	20.79	35.49	27.52
Craven Milds Ultra Mild King Size	72.88	63.30	67.20	31.37	45.66	35.09
Camel Light King Size	82.76	188.51	205.17	155.17	97.70	12.64
Winston Light King Size	82.76	188.51	205.17	155.17	97.70	12.64
Export Plain Regular Size	60.77	46.54	49.23	29.69	43.85	40.00
Rothmans Special Mild King Size	83.30	56.92	60.70	21.63	37.46	29.12

Winston Light 100's	79.91	177.17	193.61	151.14	90.87	11.87
Winston 100's	77.31	157.31	171.15	153.46	96.54	13.08
Gauloises Blondes King Size	52.14	214.43	233.63	128.19	45.86	138.38
Player's Extra Light Regular Size	76.43	53.95	57.79	19.59	37.62	31.87
Camel King Size	76.65	175.33	192.51	160.35	100.44	12.78
Salem King Size	76.65	175.33	192.51	160.35	100.44	12.78
Winston King Size	76.65	175.33	192.51	160.35	100.44	12.78
Export 'A' Full Flavour Regular Size	79.93	53.16	57.42	27.47	58.37	43.28
Du Maurier Extra Light Regular Size	84.65	61.83	66.84	17.16	32.59	30.90
Craven A King Size	79.39	52.69	56.53	18.14	36.59	28.36
Salem Light King Size	77.59	164.22	179.31	142.24	92.24	11.64
Matinee Extra Light King Size	80.06	68.79	74.52	19.85	36.14	35.59
Camel Plain Regular Size	74.69	116.33	126.12	163.27	103.67	13.47
Du Maurier Light King Size	81.90	67.78	74.02	17.07	34.91	31.57
Viscount Extra Mild King Size	77.05	65.21	70.77	29.06	42.93	32.59
Sportsman Plain Regular Size	64.36	30.98	31.32	19.62	25.81	23.75
Vatnage Medium 7 King Size	90.32	58.09	62.85	26.81	55.32	48.27
Benson & Hedges Deluxe Menthol Ultra Lights 100's	70.15	54.26	59.24	16.34	36.75	26.95
Player's Light Regular Size	76.82	47.80	50.91	17.07	39.54	33.16
Vantage Max 15 King Size	69.52	56.13	60.65	20.00	27.10	30.65
Craven Menthol King Size	79.02	64.11	69.64	15.56	34.77	26.94
Matinee Silver Regular Size	66.50	44.72	46.04	8.07	17.11	18.32
Belmont Milds Regular Size	37.90	40.46	41.31	14.48	20.02	19.16
Belmont Milds King Size	40.19	45.75	47.04	26.94	30.79	27.79

Player's Light King Size	85.41	61.82	65.97	18.83	40.07	34.66
Gauloises Blondes Lights King Size	53.35	254.56	277.93	139.73	49.79	152.94
Vantage Rich 12 King Size	71.15	53.46	56.54	21.92	37.85	38.85
Gauloises Blondes Ultra Light King Size	58.78	284.39	310.52	156.74	57.00	169.21
Mark ten Plain King Size	57.03	28.36	28.67	8.73	13.40	14.65
Du Maurier Light Regular Size	88.75	73.60	77.35	17.54	36.06	32.41
Du Maurier King Size	88.57	58.26	61.12	18.12	35.68	30.77
Player's Regular Size	79.46	51.71	56.37	15.89	38.42	29.53
Du Maurier Extra Light King Size	87.08	61.80	66.36	17.24	36.20	30.95
Player's Special Blend King Size	51.33	55.89	58.56	19.85	20.99	24.45
Player's Special Blend Regular Size	52.05	51.64	54.92	20.00	19.34	24.47
Player's Plain Regular Size	79.85	34.66	35.34	9.89	22.43	21.27
Player's Extra Light King Size	93.22	68.47	73.61	17.47	38.46	31.56
Du Maurier Regular Size	90.06	59.68	63.93	15.88	36.67	30.30
Canyon Regular Size	70.59	70.05	78.61	27.17	70.05	42.83
Dakar Regular Size	70.59	70.05	78.61	27.17	70.05	42.83
Discretion Regular Size	70.59	70.05	78.61	27.17	70.05	42.83
Fine Regular Size	70.59	70.05	78.61	27.17	70.05	42.83
Gipsy Regular Size	70.59	70.05	78.61	27.17	70.05	42.83
Selesta Regular Size	70.59	70.05	78.61	27.17	70.05	42.83
Smoking Regular Size	70.59	70.05	78.61	27.17	70.05	42.83
Tremblay Regular Size	70.59	70.05	78.61	27.17	70.05	42.83
Canyon King Size	68.08	82.63	92.02	28.12	73.24	44.98
Dakar King Size	68.08	82.63	92.02	28.12	73.24	44.98
Discretion King Size	68.08	82.63	92.02	28.12	73.24	44.98
Fine King Size	68.08	82.63	92.02	28.12	73.24	44.98

Gipsy King Size	68.08	82.63	92.02	28.12	73.24	44.98
Selesta King Size	68.08	82.63	92.02	28.12	73.24	44.98
Smoking King Size	68.08	82.63	92.02	28.12	73.24	44.98
Tremblay King Size	68.08	82.63	92.02	28.12	73.24	44.98
Dakar Light King Size	70.87	80.10	89.32	28.88	73.79	45.29
Fine Light King Size	70.87	80.10	89.32	28.88	73.79	45.29
Gipsy Light King Size	70.87	80.10	89.32	28.88	73.79	45.29
Rodeo King Size	70.87	80.10	89.32	28.88	73.79	45.29
Selesta Light King Size	70.87	80.10	89.32	28.88	73.79	45.29
Smoking Light King Size	70.87	80.10	89.32	28.88	73.79	45.29
Tremblay Light King Size	70.87	80.10	89.32	28.88	73.79	45.29
Dakar Light Regular Size	70.72	70.72	79.01	26.91	63.54	41.05
Fine Light Regular Size	70.72	70.72	79.01	26.91	63.54	41.05
Gipsy Light Regular Size	70.72	70.72	79.01	26.91	63.54	41.05
Rodeo Regular Size	70.72	70.72	79.01	26.91	63.54	41.05
Selesta Light Regular Size	70.72	70.72	79.01	26.91	63.54	41.05
Smoking Light Regular Size	70.72	70.72	79.01	26.91	63.54	41.05
*** Means ***	71.35	81.55	88.84	43.54	56.05	37.76
*** Standard deviation ***	10.31	48.55	53.46	46.49	22.36	24.42
*** Coefficient of variation ***	0.14	0.60	0.60	1.07	0.40	0.65
Maximum	93.22	284.39	310.52	163.27	103.67	169.21
75th percentile	77.59	80.10	89.32	28.88	73.24	42.83
9th percentile	83.57	166.45	181.95	144.02	88.33	45.29
Median	70.72	68.79	74.52	27.17	51.04	38.38
Minimum	37.90	28.36	28.67	8.07	13.40	10.74

Brand	NAB	Pyridine	Quinoline	Hydroquinone	Resorcinol	Catechol	Phenol	*m*- and *p*-Cresols
Export 'A' Ultra Light Regular Size	2.93	14.64	0.28	62.53	1.05	68.38	17.03	8.23
Vantage Slims Extra Light 4 100's	2.84	12.40	0.27	58.80	0.88	65.67	18.64	8.76
Export 'A' Medium King Size	2.94	14.42	0.26	44.91	0.98	55.47	11.32	7.40
Export 'A' Full Flavour King Size	3.01	14.01	0.28	47.31	0.99	59.86	12.54	7.56
Craven A Extra Light King Size	2.05	14.42	0.26	65.72	1.06	70.53	14.05	7.38
Export 'A' Medium Regular Size	3.21	15.51	0.29	62.18	0.91	66.12	16.01	8.29
Export 'A' Extra Light Regular Size	2.76	14.60	0.27	63.48	0.91	68.42	19.05	8.62
More Regular 120's	36.93	17.00	0.39	58.89	1.12	69.26	19.33	12.26
Export 'A' Light / Special Light King Size	3.35	15.08	0.28	47.31	1.00	59.62	12.69	8.00
Export 'A' Light / Special Light Regular Size	3.30	15.20	0.27	64.47	1.07	68.20	18.14	9.63
More Menthol 120's	37.23	17.27	0.40	59.23	1.19	71.54	18.54	12.12
Vantage Ultra Light 1 King Size	2.99	14.85	0.26	60.36	0.80	67.89	13.93	7.33
Export 'A' Extra Light King Size	3.00	15.51	0.27	47.58	1.07	59.47	11.76	7.53
Export 'A' Mild King Size	2.38	13.15	0.30	48.46	0.86	59.23	13.50	7.77
Export 'A' Mild Regular Size	2.38	13.15	0.30	48.46	0.86	59.23	13.50	7.77
Export 'A' Ultra Light King Size	2.41	13.31	0.30	49.03	0.87	59.92	13.66	7.86
Number 7 King Size	2.29	14.72	0.32	71.27	1.12	79.13	18.55	9.86
Craven Milds Ultra Mild King Size		17.99	0.30	71.87	1.31	77.47	14.75	8.51
Camel Light King Size	41.55	21.61	0.32	59.77	1.11	64.37	12.13	8.39
Winston Light King Size	41.55	21.61	0.32	59.77	1.11	64.37	12.13	8.39
Export Plain Regular Size	3.14	13.65	0.55	53.46	0.76	72.69	45.00	21.58
Rothmans Special Mild King Size	2.33	13.72	0.30	68.19	1.08	74.10	18.68	9.97

Winston Light 100's	37.67	20.55	0.35	61.19	1.17	70.78	17.12	11.23
Winston 100's	41.15	18.08	0.39	60.00	1.05	71.54	18.92	12.15
Gauloises Blondes King Size	16.07	18.82	0.29	44.30	0.78	47.43	10.98	6.98
Player's Extra Light Regular Size	1.98	15.67	0.30	68.60	1.07	70.79	16.86	8.58
Camel King Size	43.35	22.11	0.40	63.00	1.15	70.93	17.67	11.54
Salem King Size	43.35	22.11	0.40	63.00	1.15	70.93	17.67	11.54
Winston King Size	43.35	22.11	0.40	63.00	1.15	70.93	17.67	11.54
Export 'A' Full Flavour Regular Size	2.72	16.52	0.33	69.46	1.02	72.36	18.01	9.00
Du Maurier Extra Light Regular Size	2.13	15.10	0.26	58.01	1.09	65.50	12.78	7.05
Craven A King Size	1.74	13.78	0.27	72.51	1.04	76.43	15.50	7.84
Salem Light King Size	40.99	21.38	0.39	64.66	1.18	73.71	18.88	12.16
Matinee Extra Light King Size	2.94	16.42	0.28	60.10	0.89	68.17	14.01	7.83
Camel Plain Regular Size	42.78	20.69	0.80	64.90	1.13	83.27	53.88	27.14
Du Maurier Light King Size	2.66	14.68	0.27	61.55	1.04	70.22	14.47	7.83
Viscount Extra Mild King Size		17.48	0.29	74.63	1.14	76.50	15.23	7.92
Sportsman Plain Regular Size	1.72	11.36	0.55	66.08	1.20	93.96	53.69	23.20
Vatnage Medium 7 King Size	3.47	15.26	0.26	68.63	1.14	71.46	15.14	7.83
Benson & Hedges Deluxe Menthol Ultra Lights 100's	1.73	14.19	0.28	67.70	1.17	71.78	16.38	8.43
Player's Light Regular Size	1.92	14.73	0.27	65.31	1.11	70.40	16.46	9.13
Vantage Max 15 King Size	2.35	12.42	0.31	50.97	0.90	65.48	16.06	9.29
Craven Menthol King Size	2.13	15.40	0.29	71.39	1.08	74.01	12.40	7.49
Matinee Silver Regular Size		15.23	0.29	63.45	1.15	69.04	16.95	9.19
Belmont Milds Regular Size		10.65	0.32	62.60	1.32	82.19	15.76	8.77
Belmont Milds King Size	1.71	9.83	0.30	64.57	1.33	79.53	15.39	9.32

Player's Light King Size	2.54	14.93	0.30	64.59	0.93	71.77	18.12	9.40
Gauloises Blondes Lights King Size	18.29	19.82	0.30	47.25	0.86	50.30	10.67	7.06
Vantage Rich 12 King Size	2.96	13.81	0.33	55.77	1.12	71.92	19.15	10.92
Gauloises Blondes Ultra Light King Size	19.00	21.37	0.31	54.03	1.13	55.81	11.87	7.96
Mark ten Plain King Size		12.78	0.57	68.57	1.43	95.68	54.54	23.75
Du Maurier Light Regular Size		15.59	0.24	62.87	1.21	66.59	12.81	7.52
Du Maurier King Size	2.05	14.20	0.25	66.23	1.23	74.44	15.48	8.11
Player's Regular Size	1.86	15.21	0.28	66.08	1.02	68.46	15.47	7.83
Du Maurier Extra Light King Size		17.57	0.30	63.14	1.20	73.68	15.47	8.38
Player's Special Blend King Size	2.34	15.21	0.37	65.78	0.96	65.40	19.73	10.27
Player's Special Blend Regular Size	2.41	14.84	0.32	66.39	1.19	63.52	15.74	8.81
Player's Plain Regular Size	1.90	12.16	0.53	65.67	1.16	81.72	54.10	22.46
Player's Extra Light King Size	2.03	16.03	0.29	69.10	1.15	73.39	14.98	7.96
Du Maurier Regular Size	2.34	16.35	0.30	65.88	1.10	71.31	13.82	7.39
Canyon Regular Size	3.90	18.18	0.39	78.07	1.47	85.56	16.04	11.18
Dakar Regular Size	3.90	18.18	0.39	78.07	1.47	85.56	16.04	11.18
Discretion Regular Size	3.90	18.18	0.39	78.07	1.47	85.56	16.04	11.18
Fine Regular Size	3.90	18.18	0.39	78.07	1.47	85.56	16.04	11.18
Gipsy Regular Size	3.90	18.18	0.39	78.07	1.47	85.56	16.04	11.18
Selesta Regular Size	3.90	18.18	0.39	78.07	1.47	85.56	16.04	11.18
Smoking Regular Size	3.90	18.18	0.39	78.07	1.47	85.56	16.04	11.18
Tremblay Regular Size	3.90	18.18	0.39	78.07	1.47	85.56	16.04	11.18
Canyon King Size	4.34	17.09	0.40	75.59	1.61	88.73	19.39	13.05
Dakar King Size	4.34	17.09	0.40	75.59	1.61	88.73	19.39	13.05
Discretion King Size	4.34	17.09	0.40	75.59	1.61	88.73	19.39	13.05
Fine King Size	4.34	17.09	0.40	75.59	1.61	88.73	19.39	13.05

Gipsy King Size	4.34	17.09	0.40	75.59	1.61	88.73	19.39	13.05
Selesta King Size	4.34	17.09	0.40	75.59	1.61	88.73	19.39	13.05
Smoking King Size	4.34	17.09	0.40	75.59	1.61	88.73	19.39	13.05
Tremblay King Size	4.34	17.09	0.40	75.59	1.61	88.73	19.39	13.05
Dakar Light King Size	4.10	16.99	0.43	72.82	1.78	87.38	19.08	12.91
Fine Light King Size	4.10	16.99	0.43	72.82	1.78	87.38	19.08	12.91
Gipsy Light King Size	4.10	16.99	0.43	72.82	1.78	87.38	19.08	12.91
Rodeo King Size	4.10	16.99	0.43	72.82	1.78	87.38	19.08	12.91
Selesta Light King Size	4.10	16.99	0.43	72.82	1.78	87.38	19.08	12.91
Smoking Light King Size	4.10	16.99	0.43	72.82	1.78	87.38	19.08	12.91
Tremblay Light King Size	4.10	16.99	0.43	72.82	1.78	87.38	19.08	12.91
Dakar Light Regular Size	4.01	18.56	0.40	74.59	1.73	85.64	15.52	10.72
Fine Light Regular Size	4.01	18.56	0.40	74.59	1.73	85.64	15.52	10.72
Gipsy Light Regular Size	4.01	18.56	0.40	74.59	1.73	85.64	15.52	10.72
Rodeo Regular Size	4.01	18.56	0.40	74.59	1.73	85.64	15.52	10.72
Selesta Light Regular Size	4.01	18.56	0.40	74.59	1.73	85.64	15.52	10.72
Smoking Light Regular Size	4.01	18.56	0.40	74.59	1.73	85.64	15.52	10.72
*** Means ***	8.77	16.46	0.35	65.96	1.25	75.30	18.26	10.70
*** Standard deviation ***	13.08	2.62	0.09	9.11	0.30	10.74	8.72	3.76
*** Coefficient of variation ***	1.49	0.16	0.24	0.14	0.24	0.14	0.48	0.35
Maximum	43.35	22.11	0.80	78.07	1.78	95.68	54.54	27.14
75th percentile	4.34	18.18	0.40	74.59	1.47	85.64	19.08	12.15
9th percentile	37.63	19.96	0.43	75.59	1.73	88.73	19.39	13.05
Median	3.90	16.99	0.33	66.08	1.15	73.39	16.04	9.97
Minimum	1.71	9.83	0.24	44.30	0.76	47.43	10.67	6.98

Brand	*o*-Cresol	1,3-Butadiene	Isoprene	Acrylonitrile	Benzene	Toluene	Styrene
Export 'A' Ultra Light Regular Size	3.73	30.24	163.91	7.08	30.35	54.92	9.00
Vantage Slims Extra Light 4 100's	3.93	29.91	156.33	6.86	28.80	52.17	7.58
Export 'A' Medium King Size	2.75	32.57	215.47	8.75	33.36	54.72	10.34
Export 'A' Full Flavour King Size	3.00	32.62	215.41	9.03	34.55	56.27	9.75
Craven A Extra Light King Size	3.15	43.22	268.65	9.28	39.13	67.93	11.39
Export 'A' Medium Regular Size	3.74	33.78	194.92	8.39	33.14	59.68	10.65
Export 'A' Extra Light Regular Size	4.10	30.52	159.13	7.45	30.38	55.02	9.12
More Regular 120's	4.26	43.70	320.00	9.26	36.41	65.93	10.04
Export 'A' Light / Special Light King Size	3.10	31.46	208.85	8.31	32.42	54.23	10.54
Export 'A' Light / Special Light Regular Size	4.08	36.80	201.66	8.85	34.68	63.16	9.83
More Menthol 120's	4.35	44.62	330.38	9.27	36.19	65.38	10.54
Vantage Ultra Light 1 King Size	3.37	37.73	222.31	9.04	39.13	66.87	10.72
Export 'A' Extra Light King Size	2.96	35.24	233.48	9.47	35.90	58.59	11.19
Export 'A' Mild King Size	3.37	35.58	219.62	9.23	31.81	55.77	9.42
Export 'A' Mild Regular Size	3.37	35.58	219.62	9.23	31.81	55.77	9.42
Export 'A' Ultra Light King Size	3.40	35.99	222.18	9.34	32.18	56.42	9.53
Number 7 King Size	4.06	38.13	249.66	8.75	35.67	64.43	10.62
Craven Milds Ultra Mild King Size	3.38	56.54	345.77	13.15	46.00	82.44	13.87
Camel Light King Size	3.15	53.68	398.85	13.39	51.84	93.68	13.91
Winston Light King Size	3.15	53.68	398.85	13.39	51.84	93.68	13.91
Export Plain Regular Size	9.27	29.19	186.92	6.38	26.96	46.54	8.19
Rothmans Special Mild King Size	4.10	38.89	245.84	9.04	35.62	63.03	10.12

Winston Light 100's	5.04	52.05	380.37	12.56	46.62	82.65	13.33
Winston 100's	4.46	40.77	305.00	9.27	37.19	66.54	10.81
Gauloises Blondes King Size	3.14	35.67	299.10	9.13	34.10	61.54	10.98
Player's Extra Light Regular Size	3.88	36.87	228.75	7.76	36.16	64.98	10.94
Camel King Size	4.43	43.61	319.38	11.10	40.62	72.25	12.91
Salem King Size	4.43	43.61	319.38	11.10	40.62	72.25	12.91
Winston King Size	4.43	43.61	319.38	11.10	40.62	72.25	12.91
Export 'A' Full Flavour Regular Size	4.22	33.23	175.63	7.83	31.60	57.06	10.24
Du Maurier Extra Light Regular Size	3.13	40.07	248.37	8.29	37.66	63.77	10.66
Craven A King Size	3.38	38.86	236.09	9.12	35.33	63.58	10.10
Salem Light King Size	5.08	45.69	326.29	10.86	42.46	75.43	12.76
Matinee Extra Light King Size	3.47	49.68	304.26	10.04	44.90	72.35	12.84
Camel Plain Regular Size	10.57	34.53	261.63	8.73	31.84	56.73	9.55
Du Maurier Light King Size	3.43	41.67	255.71	8.12	38.74	63.37	11.13
Viscount Extra Mild King Size	3.41	50.54	295.00	11.29	45.67	79.38	12.89
Sportsman Plain Regular Size	9.98	32.01	178.97	6.95	27.19	45.09	6.88
Vatnage Medium 7 King Size	3.51	37.64	201.64	9.60	38.40	66.85	10.61
Benson & Hedges Deluxe Menthol Ultra Lights 100's	3.87	37.99	232.38	8.80	34.32	59.78	10.89
Player's Light Regular Size	3.92	38.27	217.41	8.01	34.72	60.06	10.08
Vantage Max 15 King Size	3.87	31.61	190.32	7.45	33.19	9.03	56.23
Craven Menthol King Size	3.36	46.84	281.33	9.51	43.62	73.23	12.86
Matinee Silver Regular Size	4.31	42.69	263.96	7.72	39.70	65.99	11.22
Belmont Milds Regular Size	3.41	37.90	215.06	8.09	29.81	46.84	7.24
Belmont Milds King Size	3.42	46.18	245.01	8.55	33.78	51.31	6.84

Player's Light King Size	4.05	41.00	247.00	9.53	39.79	70.32	10.73
Gauloises Blondes Lights King Size	3.05	44.71	375.49	12.04	42.17	76.72	12.19
Vantage Rich 12 King Size	4.50	34.62	200.38	8.42	37.15	9.62	61.81
Gauloises Blondes Ultra Light King Size	3.56	51.06	438.17	14.01	48.09	85.50	14.25
Mark ten Plain King Size	10.28	28.98	173.91	6.70	26.49	46.13	8.10
Du Maurier Light Regular Size	3.15	45.75	273.34	10.20	41.33	71.25	11.91
Du Maurier King Size	3.51	37.71	211.08	8.70	38.12	65.80	10.36
Player's Regular Size	3.69	36.42	210.05	8.29	35.45	61.37	10.18
Du Maurier Extra Light King Size	3.73	42.39	255.24	9.46	41.20	72.69	12.55
Player's Special Blend King Size	4.75	33.42	258.17	7.03	32.70	58.17	9.13
Player's Special Blend Regular Size	3.93	36.52	277.05	8.11	35.08	58.61	9.51
Player's Plain Regular Size	11.08	29.85	192.16	5.56	28.13	48.13	7.35
Player's Extra Light King Size	3.57	45.74	267.49	10.50	42.67	75.76	11.84
Du Maurier Regular Size	3.61	42.32	238.40	9.14	40.22	70.33	11.69
Canyon Regular Size	4.22	49.84	355.08	11.93	48.56	91.44	12.67
Dakar Regular Size	4.22	49.84	355.08	11.93	48.56	91.44	12.67
Discretion Regular Size	4.22	49.84	355.08	11.93	48.56	91.44	12.67
Fine Regular Size	4.22	49.84	355.08	11.93	48.56	91.44	12.67
Gipsy Regular Size	4.22	49.84	355.08	11.93	48.56	91.44	12.67
Selesta Regular Size	4.22	49.84	355.08	11.93	48.56	91.44	12.67
Smoking Regular Size	4.22	49.84	355.08	11.93	48.56	91.44	12.67
Tremblay Regular Size	4.22	49.84	355.08	11.93	48.56	91.44	12.67
Canyon King Size	4.84	46.95	342.25	11.55	47.42	88.26	11.88
Dakar King Size	4.84	46.95	342.25	11.55	47.42	88.26	11.88
Discretion King Size	4.84	46.95	342.25	11.55	47.42	88.26	11.88
Fine King Size	4.84	46.95	342.25	11.55	47.42	88.26	11.88

Gipsy King Size	4.84	46.95	342.25	11.55	47.42	88.26	11.88
Selesta King Size	4.84	46.95	342.25	11.55	47.42	88.26	11.88
Smoking King Size	4.84	46.95	342.25	11.55	47.42	88.26	11.88
Tremblay King Size	4.84	46.95	342.25	11.55	47.42	88.26	11.88
Dakar Light King Size	4.76	48.01	364.56	11.50	47.48	88.35	11.84
Fine Light King Size	4.76	48.01	364.56	11.50	47.48	88.35	11.84
Gipsy Light King Size	4.76	48.01	364.56	11.50	47.48	88.35	11.84
Rodeo King Size	4.76	48.01	364.56	11.50	47.48	88.35	11.84
Selesta Light King Size	4.76	48.01	364.56	11.50	47.48	88.35	11.84
Smoking Light King Size	4.76	48.01	364.56	11.50	47.48	88.35	11.84
Tremblay Light King Size	4.76	48.01	364.56	11.50	47.48	88.35	11.84
Dakar Light Regular Size	3.87	51.60	377.35	11.99	50.11	92.27	12.49
Fine Light Regular Size	3.87	51.60	377.35	11.99	50.11	92.27	12.49
Gipsy Light Regular Size	3.87	51.60	377.35	11.99	50.11	92.27	12.49
Rodeo Regular Size	3.87	51.60	377.35	11.99	50.11	92.27	12.49
Selesta Light Regular Size	3.87	51.60	377.35	11.99	50.11	92.27	12.49
Smoking Light Regular Size	3.87	51.60	377.35	11.99	50.11	92.27	12.49
*** Means ***	4.33	42.60	288.66	10.02	40.63	71.56	12.28
*** Standard deviation ***	1.57	7.19	71.97	1.88	7.19	17.66	7.32
*** Coefficient of variation ***	0.36	0.17	0.25	0.19	0.18	0.25	0.60
Maximum	11.08	56.54	438.17	14.01	51.84	93.68	61.81
75th percentile	4.75	48.01	355.08	11.55	47.48	88.35	12.55
9th percentile	4.84	51.60	377.35	11.99	48.56	91.44	12.91
Median	4.05	43.61	295.00	9.53	40.62	71.25	11.84
Minimum	2.75	28.98	156.33	5.56	26.49	9.03	6.84

Table A1.2.

Yields per milligram of nicotine of toxicants in Philip Morris international brands reported by Counts et al. (2004)

Brand	Nicotine	Tar	Carbon monoxide	Acetaldehyde	Acetone	Acrolein
Marlboro Long Size F hard pack/Argentina	2.12	15.19	12.74	586.79	316.51	58.54
Marlboro Long Size Filter hard pack/Venezuela	1.99	15.78	12.91	661.81	346.23	61.11
SG Ventil Regular Filter soft pack/European Union	1.48	18.92	13.92	777.70	397.30	75.81
Petra Regular Filter hard pack/CEMA	1.85	17.51	13.08	634.05	334.05	59.46
Marlboro King Size Filter soft pack/USA	2.25	16.71	13.82	574.67	302.67	58.13
Marlboro King Size Filter hard pack/Norway	2.08	15.24	13.08	660.10	350.48	64.42
L & M King Size Filter hard pack/European Union	1.88	17.66	15.27	783.51	408.51	74.73
Marlboro King Size Filter hard pack/Malaysia	2.21	16.74	12.81	655.66	317.65	62.31
Chesterfield Originals King Size Filter hard pack	1.94	16.39	14.59	672.68	345.88	64.64
L & M King Size Filter hard pack/Malaysia	2.40	14.58	10.79	547.50	262.08	53.50
Marlboro King Size Filter hard pack 25 s/Australia	2.38	14.71	13.07	584.03	310.08	59.24
Marlboro King Size Filter hard pack/Taiwan	2.27	15.07	12.56	555.51	281.06	55.02
Marlboro 100 Filter hard pack/European Union	2.27	15.55	14.93	662.56	330.84	64.54
Marlboro King Size Filter hard pack Medium/European Union	1.94	15.31	14.74	635.05	340.21	60.31
Parliament 100 Filter soft pack Light/USA	2.41	14.40	13.73	596.68	292.95	54.65
Marlboro King Size Filter hard pack/Japan	2.56	12.93	11.13	451.17	261.72	40.66
L & M King Size Filter hard pack Light/European Union	1.50	16.93	17.27	870.00	448.00	84.93
Filter 6 King Size Filter hard pack Light/European Union	1.79	14.64	14.36	697.21	360.89	73.85
Chesterfield Originals King Size Filter hard pack	1.67	16.11	15.63	718.56	381.44	71.14
Diana King Size Filter soft pack Specially Mild/E	1.94	15.52	13.35	688.14	350.52	72.94
Muratti Ambassador King Size Filter hard pack/European Union	1.80	16.11	14.67	766.11	378.89	69.17
Merit King Size Filter hard pack/European Union	1.47	15.51	16.87	804.76	427.21	77.76

Parliament 100 Filter soft pack/CEMA	2.17	14.15	13.59	658.53	344.70	62.49
Marlboro King Size Filter hard pack Light/Germany/United Kingdom	1.58	15.32	15.57	741.14	373.42	78.86
Marlboro King Size Filter hard pack Light/Japan	1.43	16.22	18.60	723.08	381.12	66.78
Marlboro 100 Filter hard pack Light/Germany	2.06	13.74	14.47	747.57	366.02	74.81
Merit King Size Filter soft pack Ultra-light/USA	1.58	14.37	16.71	750.00	403.80	70.44
Marlboro King Size Filter hard pack Ultra-light Menthol/USA	1.58	16.52	17.03	827.22	422.15	88.23
Parliament King Size Filter hard pack Light/Japan	1.79	15.03	15.20	656.42	347.49	62.51
Virginia Slims 100 Filter hard pack Ultra-light Menthol	1.88	14.73	14.26	661.17	339.36	67.34
Chesterfield INTL King Size Filter hard pack Ultra-light/	1.40	14.00	15.86	782.86	413.57	78.43
Philip Morris 100 Filter hard pack Super L	1.85	14.16	16.00	722.16	375.14	69.84
Marlboro King Size Filter hard pack Ultra-light/European Union	1.47	14.76	16.94	750.34	378.23	69.32
Diana King Size Filter hard pack Ultra-light/European Union	1.41	15.82	17.02	777.30	392.20	84.40
Virginia Slims 100 Filter hard pack Ultra-light Menthol	1.39	20.07	27.27	986.33	491.37	99.50
Philip Morris One King Size Filter hard pack/European Union	1.16	14.48	17.84	886.21	445.69	88.36
Muratti King Size Filter hard pack Ultra-light 1 mg/CEMA	1.07	17.38	20.65	997.20	500.93	92.71
Longbeach One King Size Filter hard pack/Australia	1.19	13.70	16.30	857.98	470.59	89.50
Virginia Slims 100 Filter hard pack Menthol 1	1.30	17.85	25.54	902.31	452.31	81.54
Marlboro King Size Filter hard pack/Mexico	2.47	13.44	10.69	466.80	256.28	47.00
Raffles 100 Filter hard pack/European Union	2.70	11.22	10.93	517.04	266.30	49.70
Marlboro King Size Filter hard pack/Brazil	2.24	15.67	12.68	546.43	290.18	52.10
Peter Jackson King Size Filter hard pack Menthol/Australia	1.78	13.03	12.08	535.96	286.52	56.24
Marlboro 100 Filter hard pack Light/USA	2.15	14.51	14.65	565.58	306.98	54.74
Marlboro King Size Filter hard pack Light/Norway	1.82	15.05	14.45	612.64	319.78	57.20
Chesterfield King Size Filter hard pack Light/European Union	1.54	14.74	15.13	687.01	352.60	66.49
Philip Morris King Size Filter hard pack Super Light	1.73	14.68	14.86	615.61	315.61	61.10
Merit King Size Filter soft pack Ultra-light/USA	1.34	15.60	17.99	694.03	364.93	66.57

1R4Filter Kentucky Reference	1.83	14.37	16.45	791.26	412.57	66.89
1R4Filter Kentucky Reference	1.93	14.20	15.23	704.15	355.96	57.62
** Mean **		15.33	15.19	694.97	359.42	67.55
** Standard deviation **		1.55	3.12	121.70	59.72	12.51
** Coefficient of variation **		0.10	0.21	0.18	0.17	0.19
Maximum	2.70	20.07	27.27	997.20	500.93	99.50
75th percentile	2.14	16.11	16.41	774.51	396.02	74.79
90th percentile	2.38	17.40	17.86	859.18	445.92	85.26
Median	1.84	15.13	14.70	687.58	351.56	66.53
Minimum	1.07	11.22	10.69	451.17	256.28	40.66

Brand	Butyraldehyde	Crotonaldehyde	Methyl ethyl ketone	Propionaldehyde
Marlboro Long Size F hard pack/Argentina	34.72	28.58	88.54	50.00
Marlboro Long Size Filter hard pack/Venezuela	39.95	31.01	95.23	57.54
SG Ventil Regular Filter soft pack/European Union	48.45	36.35	112.97	68.78
Petra Regular Filter hard pack/CEMA	42.11	30.27	97.30	58.27
Marlboro King Size Filter soft pack/USA	36.18	22.49	76.36	50.13
Marlboro King Size Filter hard pack/Norway	41.15	34.04	103.27	56.68
L & M King Size Filter hard pack/European Union	48.94	34.41	110.96	67.50
Marlboro King Size Filter hard pack/Malaysia	41.22	30.00	82.26	57.10
Chesterfield Originals King Size Filter hard pack	42.63	29.74	90.21	58.66
L & M King Size Filter hard pack/Malaysia	35.92	23.67	64.00	48.29
Marlboro King Size Filter hard pack 25 s/Australia	37.56	26.60	79.96	52.69
Marlboro King Size Filter hard pack/Taiwan	33.00	17.67	65.86	47.62
Marlboro 100 Filter hard pack/European Union	40.84	26.74	88.11	58.81
Marlboro King Size Filter hard pack Medium/European Union	38.09	25.93	84.33	55.52
Parliament 100 Filter soft pack Light/USA	34.36	17.51	68.76	50.66
Marlboro King Size Filter hard pack/Japan	26.25	15.55	61.02	39.57
L & M King Size Filter hard pack Light/European Union	52.27	37.27	123.07	74.33
Filter6 King Size Filter hard pack Light/European Union	44.92	29.05	95.70	62.07
Chesterfield Originals King Size Filter hard pack	45.27	31.50	97.96	64.61
Diana King Size Filter soft pack Specially Mild/E	43.76	33.66	96.49	60.82
Muratti Ambassador King Size Filter hard pack/European Union	43.06	27.94	98.11	66.61
Merit King Size Filter hard pack/European Union	48.91	36.94	119.93	67.01

Parliament 100 Filter soft pack/CEMA	37.97	25.99	92.26	57.97
Marlboro King Size Filter hard pack Light/Germany/United Kingdom	44.94	27.59	95.44	64.30
Marlboro King Size Filter hard pack Light/Japan	38.74	22.87	85.10	62.52
Marlboro 100 Filter hard pack Light/Germany	45.63	28.25	95.10	65.00
Merit King Size Filter soft pack Ultra-light/USA	47.66	31.96	99.56	69.05
Marlboro King Size Filter hard pack Ultra-light Menthol/USA	51.46	36.58	105.57	75.38
Parliament King Size Filter hard pack Light/Japan	36.82	23.63	85.47	53.07
Virginia Slims 100 Filter hard pack Ultra-light Menthol	41.49	29.10	82.34	56.65
Chesterfield INTL King Size Filter hard pack Ultra-light/	46.14	36.43	117.71	63.93
Philip Morris 100 Filter hard pack Super L	45.78	31.57	94.86	63.57
Marlboro King Size Filter hard pack Ultra-light/European Union	45.65	30.00	91.77	64.56
Diana King Size Filter hard pack Ultra-light/European Union	47.73	33.83	100.28	70.35
Virginia Slims 100 Filter hard pack Ultra-light Menthol	60.00	38.27	115.97	88.42
Philip Morris One King Size Filter hard pack/European Union	56.38	33.88	106.55	72.76
Muratti King Size Filter hard pack Ultra-light 1 mg/CEMA	63.55	41.31	124.39	85.98
Longbeach One King Size Filter hard pack/Australia	53.87	39.58	119.16	76.30
Virginia Slims 100 Filter hard pack Menthol 1	54.62	33.31	104.92	74.00
Marlboro King Size Filter hard pack/Mexico	29.88	19.96	67.09	39.92
Raffles 100 Filter hard pack/European Union	36.85	23.07	78.11	43.56
Marlboro King Size Filter hard pack/Brazil	35.04	23.62	79.06	47.77
Peter Jackson King Size Filter hard pack Menthol/Australia	33.37	23.93	79.10	45.73
Marlboro 100 Filter hard pack Light/USA	37.26	22.79	80.19	49.02
Marlboro King Size Filter hard pack Light/Norway	37.86	24.78	86.65	51.59
Chesterfield King Size Filter hard pack Light/European Union	41.43	27.21	91.88	57.60
Philip Morris King Size Filter hard pack Super Light	38.21	24.39	80.58	52.02
Merit King Size Filter soft pack Ultra-light/USA	45.52	27.39	87.84	59.03

1R4Filter Kentucky Reference	51.04	28.52	114.21	70.44
1R4Filter Kentucky Reference	43.06	25.44	98.29	59.90
** Mean **	42.95	28.84	93.20	60.27
** Standard deviation **	7.55	5.89	15.78	10.73
** Coefficient of variation **	0.18	0.20	0.17	0.18
Maximum	63.55	41.31	124.39	88.42
75th percentile	47.28	33.57	102.52	66.91
90th percentile	52.43	36.62	116.15	74.03
Median	42.37	28.55	93.56	58.92
Minimum	26.25	15.55	61.02	39.57

Brand	Formaldehyde	Acrylonitrile	Benzene	1,3-Butadiene	Isoprene
Marlboro Long Size F hard pack/Argentina	45.57	9.34	34.34	46.79	443.87
Marlboro Long Size Filter hard pack/Venezuela	44.87	10.00	34.57	49.30	440.20
SG Ventil Regular Filter soft pack/European Union	73.72	10.88	37.91	52.03	343.92
Petra Regular Filter hard pack/CEMA	57.73	10.27	39.19	45.73	323.78
Marlboro King Size Filter soft pack/USA	29.16	13.38	37.24	50.13	468.89
Marlboro King Size Filter hard pack/Norway	49.04	10.19	39.57	53.08	433.17
L & M King Size Filter hard pack/European Union	52.98	11.49	43.88	56.86	423.94
Marlboro King Size Filter hard pack/Malaysia	28.01	11.72	34.30	43.39	352.49
Chesterfield Originals King Size Filter hard pack	46.44	9.23	34.69	47.27	369.59
L & M King Size Filter hard pack/Malaysia	33.75	10.25	33.58	44.83	406.67
Marlboro King Size Filter hard pack 25 s/Australia	28.19	9.92	33.15	41.43	357.14
Marlboro King Size Filter hard pack/Taiwan	28.77	10.97	30.70	44.05	389.87
Marlboro 100 Filter hard pack/European Union	36.61	12.03	36.87	49.69	424.67
Marlboro King Size Filter hard pack Medium/European Union	44.38	10.88	37.22	48.35	400.00
Parliament 100 Filter soft pack Light/USA	25.39	11.12	31.66	46.60	421.99
Marlboro King Size Filter hard pack/Japan	29.41	6.72	25.70	35.78	283.20
L & M King Size Filter hard pack Light/European Union	53.00	12.00	47.00	62.40	464.67
Filter6 King Size Filter hard pack Light/European Union	71.79	11.62	41.01	54.80	400.00
Chesterfield Originals King Size Filter hard pack	44.07	12.51	42.81	55.69	444.31
Diana King Size Filter soft pack Specially Mild/E	49.23	10.52	38.09	49.23	352.58
Muratti Ambassador King Size Filter hard pack/European Union	59.39	10.00	34.44	53.28	364.44
Merit King Size Filter hard pack/European Union	43.81	12.65	43.88	60.48	482.99

Parliament 100 Filter soft pack/CEMA	30.78	9.08	31.24	48.11	383.41
Marlboro King Size Filter hard pack Light/Germany/United Kingdom	46.58	13.61	39.81	61.65	517.09
Marlboro King Size Filter hard pack Light/Japan	52.31	9.93	34.76	56.08	377.62
Marlboro 100 Filter hard pack Light/Germany	40.05	12.33	36.26	54.03	473.30
Merit King Size Filter soft pack Ultra-light/USA	24.18	14.94	47.66	59.24	510.13
Marlboro King Size Filter hard pack Ultra-light Menthol/USA	36.77	13.67	44.37	59.11	487.97
Parliament King Size Filter hard pack Light/Japan	24.80	9.66	32.01	50.67	443.58
Virginia Slims 100 Filter hard pack Ultra-light Menthol	32.23	12.02	36.54	50.48	445.21
Chesterfield INTL King Size Filter hard pack Ultra-light/	46.86	12.57	45.57	65.79	503.57
Philip Morris 100 Filter hard pack Super L	35.41	11.89	41.41	54.11	478.38
Marlboro King Size Filter hard pack Ultra-light/European Union	45.85	11.09	37.62	53.40	463.27
Diana King Size Filter hard pack Ultra-light/European Union	40.28	13.05	43.55	61.35	468.79
Virginia Slims 100 Filter hard pack Ultra-light Menthol	36.62	18.85	51.08	74.89	693.53
Philip Morris One King Size Filter hard pack/European Union	26.21	17.33	50.00	75.52	745.69
Muratti King Size Filter hard pack Ultra-light 1 mg/CEMA	28.79	17.01	47.85	75.14	644.86
Longbeach One King Size Filter hard pack/Australia	90.50	10.17	44.29	65.46	499.16
Virginia Slims 100 Filter hard pack Menthol 1	26.15	17.31	41.62	67.62	700.77
Marlboro King Size Filter hard pack/Mexico	35.51	9.92	30.12	39.39	363.16
Raffles 100 Filter hard pack/European Union	35.89	10.19	32.26	43.22	397.78
Marlboro King Size Filter hard pack/Brazil	38.97	12.63	37.86	52.05	421.43
Peter Jackson King Size Filter hard pack Menthol/Australia	73.20	10.67	37.19	55.73	424.72
Marlboro 100 Filter hard pack Light/USA	24.56	15.95	45.72	55.02	539.53
Marlboro King Size Filter hard pack Light/Norway	38.57	12.31	35.44	47.75	410.44
Chesterfield King Size Filter hard pack Light/European Union	47.01	15.26	43.12	59.61	522.08
Philip Morris King Size Filter hard pack Super Light	33.53	14.97	39.77	56.71	540.46
Merit King Size Filter soft pack Ultra-light/USA	21.87	19.48	44.70	64.18	701.49

1R4Filter Kentucky Reference	33.06	16.01	45.52	57.38	520.22
1R4Filter Kentucky Reference	31.09	15.44	39.43	48.65	481.35
** Mean **	41.06	12.30	38.97	54.07	459.03
** Standard deviation **	14.48	2.73	5.69	8.85	99.48
** Coefficient of variation **	0.35	0.22	0.15	0.16	0.22
Maximum	90.50	19.48	51.08	75.52	745.69
75th percentile	46.79	13.55	43.79	59.21	496.36
90th percentile	57.90	16.11	45.85	65.49	550.90
Median	37.67	11.81	38.00	53.34	443.72
Minimum	21.87	6.72	25.70	35.78	283.20

Brand	Styrene	Toluene	Ammonia	Total hydrogen cyanide
Marlboro Long Size F hard pack/Argentina	12.31	59.95	16.51	150.61
Marlboro Long Size Filter hard pack/Venezuela	12.76	64.92	22.96	169.70
SG Ventil Regular Filter soft pack/European Union	15.07	68.24	22.43	180.07
Petra Regular Filter hard pack/CEMA	15.08	73.62	21.51	155.24
Marlboro King Size Filter soft pack/USA	13.51	71.87	27.73	214.89
Marlboro King Size Filter hard pack/Norway	13.85	71.83	20.67	145.24
L & M King Size Filter hard pack/European Union	16.91	81.54	21.22	202.55
Marlboro King Size Filter hard pack/Malaysia	14.89	69.00	40.72	201.27
Chesterfield Originals King Size Filter hard pack	14.02	66.55	21.29	182.37
L & M King Size Filter hard pack/Malaysia	13.17	64.13	23.04	198.42
Marlboro King Size Filter hard pack 25 s/Australia	13.07	62.48	25.13	203.28
Marlboro King Size Filter hard pack/Taiwan	8.90	56.78	26.12	192.38
Marlboro 100 Filter hard pack/European Union	14.67	72.69	26.48	200.48
Marlboro King Size Filter hard pack Medium/European Union	13.81	69.95	17.89	170.36
Parliament 100 Filter soft pack Light/USA	8.88	54.90	26.72	201.54
Marlboro King Size Filter hard pack/Japan	8.36	45.59	16.95	115.70
L & M King Size Filter hard pack Light/European Union	18.53	84.13	20.20	199.53
Filter6 King Size Filter hard pack Light/European Union	14.13	73.74	14.97	177.54
Chesterfield Originals King Size Filter hard pack	14.13	77.13	20.36	192.57
Diana King Size Filter soft pack Specially Mild/E	14.85	70.57	18.30	180.26
Muratti Ambassador King Size Filter hard pack/European Union	10.61	58.83	19.17	143.17
Merit King Size Filter hard pack/European Union	15.71	81.02	22.45	203.06

Parliament 100 Filter soft pack/CEMA	8.76	53.41	23.32	173.69
Marlboro King Size Filter hard pack Light/Germany/United Kingdom	14.94	77.22	20.06	206.71
Marlboro King Size Filter hard pack Light/Japan	10.77	61.12	19.79	187.83
Marlboro 100 Filter hard pack Light/Germany	14.22	72.04	17.82	169.22
Merit King Size Filter soft pack Ultra-light/USA	16.01	87.97	26.27	267.53
Marlboro King Size Filter hard pack Ultra-light Menthol/USA	15.13	79.43	27.53	276.39
Parliament King Size Filter hard pack Light/Japan	8.77	53.63	27.32	196.15
Virginia Slims 100 Filter hard pack Ultra-light Menthol	12.61	69.20	28.78	229.89
Chesterfield INTL King Size Filter hard pack Ultra-light/	15.43	80.50	21.14	202.21
Philip Morris 100 Filter hard pack Super L	14.49	75.62	19.51	218.59
Marlboro King Size Filter hard pack Ultra-light/European Union	14.35	71.84	16.73	211.70
Diana King Size Filter hard pack Ultra-light/European Union	16.17	77.87	18.30	237.73
Virginia Slims 100 Filter hard pack Ultra-light Menthol	16.62	90.86	24.96	390.22
Philip Morris One King Size Filter hard pack/European Union	16.72	93.02	21.81	287.33
Muratti King Size Filter hard pack Ultra-light 1 mg/CEMA	16.36	83.18	24.86	322.80
Longbeach One King Size Filter hard pack/Australia	16.64	72.44	9.24	157.90
Virginia Slims 100 Filter hard pack Menthol 1	15.15	75.31	22.69	374.31
Marlboro King Size Filter hard pack/Mexico	10.45	52.06	19.27	148.70
Raffles 100 Filter hard pack/European Union	11.00	56.93	11.19	135.07
Marlboro King Size Filter hard pack/Brazil	12.81	65.00	17.46	148.17
Peter Jackson King Size Filter hard pack Menthol/Australia	11.40	57.53	10.06	114.66
Marlboro 100 Filter hard pack Light/USA	11.63	81.07	24.51	220.51
Marlboro King Size Filter hard pack Light/Norway	13.24	65.82	20.05	178.08
Chesterfield King Size Filter hard pack Light/European Union	13.25	75.84	18.12	172.99
Philip Morris King Size Filter hard pack Super Light	12.83	71.97	19.42	201.04
Merit King Size Filter soft pack Ultra-light/USA	13.43	78.36	20.82	319.33

1R4Filter Kentucky Reference	16.45	96.28	16.99	233.28
1R4Filter Kentucky Reference	13.06	80.98	17.20	218.76
** Mean **	13.60	71.12	21.16	203.62
** Standard deviation **	2.41	11.11	5.19	57.34
** Coefficient of variation **	0.18	0.16	0.25	0.28
Maximum	18.53	96.28	40.72	390.22
75th percentile	15.12	78.24	24.21	217.67
90th percentile	16.47	83.27	26.78	277.49
Median	13.93	71.92	20.75	198.98
Minimum	8.36	45.59	9.24	114.66

Brand	Impinger hydrogen cyanide	Pad hydrogen cyanide	Nitric oxide	Nitrogen oxides	1 Aminonaphthalene
Marlboro Long Size F hard pack/Argentina	91.98	58.63	144.81	159.91	16.75
Marlboro Long Size Filter hard pack/Venezuela	106.18	63.52	144.72	158.79	18.94
SG Ventil Regular Filter soft pack/European Union	113.18	66.89	131.76	156.76	17.50
Petra Regular Filter hard pack/CEMA	100.97	54.27	99.46	111.89	19.89
Marlboro King Size Filter soft pack/USA	139.69	75.20	212.44	234.67	16.80
Marlboro King Size Filter hard pack/Norway	88.89	56.35	153.37	167.31	17.21
L & M King Size Filter hard pack/European Union	131.70	70.85	153.19	168.09	18.83
Marlboro King Size Filter hard pack/Malaysia	123.39	77.83	214.93	247.06	24.80
Chesterfield Originals King Size Filter hard pack	112.32	70.05	134.54	153.09	17.84
L & M King Size Filter hard pack/Malaysia	126.17	72.25	166.25	187.08	20.63
Marlboro King Size Filter hard pack 25 s/Australia	135.76	67.52	183.61	207.98	17.52
Marlboro King Size Filter hard pack/Taiwan	127.67	64.71	208.37	223.35	16.70
Marlboro 100 Filter hard pack/European Union	126.56	73.92	168.72	184.58	17.27
Marlboro King Size Filter hard pack Medium/European Union	107.89	62.47	134.02	150.52	17.53
Parliament 100 Filter soft pack Light/USA	132.66	68.88	222.41	238.59	16.39
Marlboro King Size Filter hard pack/Japan	68.71	46.95	144.53	158.59	18.79
L & M King Size Filter hard pack Light/European Union	126.27	73.27	161.33	177.33	20.07
Filter6 King Size Filter hard pack Light/European Union	117.93	59.61	83.80	91.06	10.11
Chesterfield Originals King Size Filter hard pack	124.19	68.32	128.74	148.50	16.53
Diana King Size Filter soft pack Specially Mild/E	116.44	63.81	134.02	152.06	16.29
Muratti Ambassador King Size Filter hard pack/European Union	87.67	55.50	110.00	127.78	16.17
Merit King Size Filter hard pack/European Union	132.38	70.68	191.16	208.16	15.78

Parliament 100 Filter soft pack/CEMA	113.36	60.28	173.27	186.64	18.76
Marlboro King Size Filter hard pack Light/Germany/United Kingdom	138.67	68.04	132.91	148.10	12.85
Marlboro King Size Filter hard pack Light/Japan	118.18	69.65	179.72	196.50	16.85
Marlboro 100 Filter hard pack Light/Germany	105.15	64.13	123.30	135.44	12.72
Merit King Size Filter soft pack Ultra-light/USA	182.09	85.44	278.48	312.03	17.53
Marlboro King Size Filter hard pack Ultra-light Menthol/USA	185.38	91.01	297.47	331.65	16.52
Parliament King Size Filter hard pack Light/Japan	131.28	64.86	243.58	262.57	17.37
Virginia Slims 100 Filter hard pack Ultra-light Menthol	157.23	72.61	243.09	276.60	18.51
Chesterfield INTL King Size Filter hard pack Ultra-light/	133.21	69.00	140.71	152.86	14.21
Philip Morris 100 Filter hard pack Super L	145.51	73.14	158.92	176.22	18.49
Marlboro King Size Filter hard pack Ultra-light/European Union	134.83	76.87	142.86	160.54	15.51
Diana King Size Filter hard pack Ultra-light/European Union	156.10	81.63	177.30	204.96	16.81
Virginia Slims 100 Filter hard pack Ultra-light Menthol	253.67	136.55	348.92	389.93	13.88
Philip Morris One King Size Filter hard pack/European Union	192.07	95.26	241.38	262.93	16.12
Muratti King Size Filter hard pack Ultra-light 1 mg/CEMA	213.93	108.88	273.83	302.80	16.73
Longbeach One King Size Filter hard pack/Australia	97.48	60.34	85.71	98.32	9.83
Virginia Slims 100 Filter hard pack Menthol 1	233.77	140.46	320.77	352.31	14.00
Marlboro King Size Filter hard pack/Mexico	94.45	54.25	121.46	131.58	13.16
Raffles 100 Filter hard pack/European Union	86.00	49.07	118.52	129.26	11.59
Marlboro King Size Filter hard pack/Brazil	93.08	55.04	118.30	129.46	13.79
Peter Jackson King Size Filter hard pack Menthol/Australia	69.04	45.62	64.61	71.91	9.10
Marlboro 100 Filter hard pack Light/USA	152.56	67.95	246.51	267.44	15.86
Marlboro King Size Filter hard pack Light/Norway	117.97	60.11	165.93	180.22	14.45
Chesterfield King Size Filter hard pack Light/European Union	112.40	60.58	123.38	137.66	14.94
Philip Morris King Size Filter hard pack Super Light	133.99	67.11	152.02	168.21	12.49
Merit King Size Filter soft pack Ultra-light/USA	219.48	99.85	251.49	272.39	19.33

1R4Filter Kentucky Reference	163.44	69.84	334.43	354.64	15.79
1R4Filter Kentucky Reference	153.63	65.13	301.55	325.91	14.35
** Mean **	132.53	71.08	179.73	198.64	16.20
** Standard deviation **	39.64	18.60	68.45	74.36	2.89
** Coefficient of variation **	0.30	0.26	0.38	0.37	0.18
Maximum	253.67	140.46	348.92	389.93	24.80
75th percentile	144.06	73.23	220.54	244.94	17.53
90th percentile	186.05	91.44	280.38	313.41	18.98
Median	126.42	68.00	160.13	176.77	16.61
Min mum	68.71	45.62	64.61	71.91	9.10

Brand	2-Aminonaphthalene	3-Aminobiphenyl	4-Aminobiphenyl
Marlboro Long Size F hard pack/Argentina	10.19	3.11	2.23
Marlboro Long Size Filter hard pack/Venezuela	11.46	3.41	2.49
SG Ventil Regular Filter soft pack/European Union	10.74	3.29	2.57
Petra Regular Filter hard pack/CEMA	10.92	3.21	2.31
Marlboro King Size Filter soft pack/USA	10.31	2.94	2.21
Marlboro King Size Filter hard pack/Norway	10.53	3.08	2.26
L & M King Size Filter hard pack/European Union	11.97	3.52	2.66
Marlboro King Size Filter hard pack/Malaysia	14.34	4.14	3.18
Chesterfield Originals King Size Filter hard pack	10.67	2.69	2.08
L & M King Size Filter hard pack/Malaysia	11.79	2.92	2.17
Marlboro King Size Filter hard pack 25 s/Australia	11.01	3.00	2.30
Marlboro King Size Filter hard pack/Taiwan	10.22	2.75	2.09
Marlboro 100 Filter hard pack/European Union	9.91	2.82	2.16
Marlboro King Size Filter hard pack Medium/European Union	10.82	2.68	2.10
Parliament 100 Filter soft pack Light/USA	9.54	2.71	2.00
Marlboro King Size Filter hard pack/Japan	10.55	2.86	2.10
L & M King Size Filter hard pack Light/European Union	12.80	3.94	3.09
Filter6 King Size Filter hard pack Light/European Union	6.03	1.68	1.31
Chesterfield Originals King Size Filter hard pack	10.96	2.77	2.16
Diana King Size Filter soft pack Specially Mild/E	10.15	2.66	2.15
Muratti Ambassador King Size Filter hard pack/European Union	9.56	2.74	2.06
Merit King Size Filter hard pack/European Union	11.16	3.40	2.78

Parliament 100 Filter soft pack/CEMA	11.61	3.36	2.59
Marlboro King Size Filter hard pack Light/Germany/United Kingdom	8.10	2.44	1.87
Marlboro King Size Filter hard pack Light/Japan	10.98	2.92	2.17
Marlboro 100 Filter hard pack Light/Germany	8.01	2.17	1.70
Merit King Size Filter soft pack Ultra-light/USA	11.14	3.19	2.56
Marlboro King Size Filter hard pack Ultra-light Menthol/USA	11.20	3.37	2.65
Parliament King Size Filter hard pack Light/Japan	11.34	3.29	2.59
Virginia Slims 100 Filter hard pack Ultra-light Menthol	12.39	2.88	2.24
Chesterfield INTL King Size Filter hard pack Ultra-light/	10.00	3.04	2.49
Philip Morris 100 Filter hard pack Super L	11.19	2.62	2.08
Marlboro King Size Filter hard pack Ultra-light/European Union	10.27	2.52	2.09
Diana King Size Filter hard pack Ultra-light/European Union	10.92	3.22	2.50
Virginia Slims 100 Filter hard pack Ultra-light Menthol	8.78	2.55	2.10
Philip Morris One King Size Filter hard pack/European Union	11.47	3.71	3.09
Muratti King Size Filter hard pack Ultra-light 1 mg/CEMA	10.56	3.37	2.86
Longbeach One King Size Filter hard pack/Australia	6.55	1.78	1.37
Virginia Slims 100 Filter hard pack Menthol 1	8.38	2.55	2.11
Marlboro King Size Filter hard pack/Mexico	7.81	2.30	1.79
Raffles 100 Filter hard pack/European Union	6.56	1.79	1.30
Marlboro King Size Filter hard pack/Brazil	8.08	2.46	1.84
Peter Jackson King Size Filter hard pack Menthol/Australia	5.00	1.53	1.16
Marlboro 100 Filter hard pack Light/USA	10.65	2.78	2.17
Marlboro King Size Filter hard pack Light/Norway	9.18	2.70	2.14
Chesterfield King Size Filter hard pack Light/European Union	9.09	2.49	2.01
Philip Morris King Size Filter hard pack Super Light	7.98	2.36	1.86
Merit King Size Filter soft pack Ultra-light/USA	10.45	2.67	2.33

1R4Filter Kentucky Reference	10.22	2.95	2.49
1R4Filter Kentucky Reference	9.43	2.96	2.28
** Mean **	10.06	2.85	2.22
** Standard deviation **	1.76	0.53	0.43
** Coefficient of variation **	0.18	0.19	0.19
Maximum	14.34	4.14	3.18
75th percentile	11.11	3.21	2.49
90th percentile	11.63	3.40	2.67
Median	10.49	2.84	2.17
Minimum	5.00	1.53	1.16

Brand	Benzo[a]pyrene	Catechol	m- and p-Cresol	o-Cresol
Marlboro Long Size F hard pack/Argentina	7.70	48.73	9.15	3.65
Marlboro Long Size Filter hard pack/Venezuela	8.60	53.07	10.55	4.51
SG Ventil Regular Filter soft pack/European Union	8.85	58.18	11.42	4.08
Petra Regular Filter hard pack/CEMA	13.82	62.16	13.68	5.00
Marlboro King Size Filter soft pack/USA	9.86	44.84	7.91	3.19
Marlboro King Size Filter hard pack/Norway	7.10	53.41	9.38	4.11
L & M King Size Filter hard pack/European Union	9.99	63.78	11.33	4.84
Marlboro King Size Filter hard pack/Malaysia	11.77	54.30	12.53	4.45
Chesterfield Originals King Size Filter hard pack	10.35	53.45	9.79	3.81
L & M King Size Filter hard pack/Malaysia	12.04	54.83	9.79	3.65
Marlboro King Size Filter hard pack 25 s/Australia	9.08	41.89	8.61	2.74
Marlboro King Size Filter hard pack/Taiwan	9.15	47.18	9.74	3.76
Marlboro 100 Filter hard pack/European Union	10.44	51.89	8.55	3.35
Marlboro King Size Filter hard pack Medium/European Union	9.79	47.68	7.63	2.98
Parliament 100 Filter soft pack Light/USA	9.76	46.64	8.17	3.07
Marlboro King Size Filter hard pack/Japan	8.21	47.30	9.41	3.65
L & M King Size Filter hard pack Light/European Union	9.61	61.60	8.60	3.47
Filter6 King Size Filter hard pack Light/European Union	13.84	65.36	6.03	2.39
Chesterfield Originals King Size Filter hard pack	9.98	49.64	6.65	2.48
Diana King Size Filter soft pack Specially Mild/E	9.77	56.65	10.82	3.94
Muratti Ambassador King Size Filter hard pack/European Union	12.55	65.11	12.94	4.59
Mer t King Size Filter hard pack/European Union	9.18	49.25	6.46	2.62

Parliament 100 Filter soft pack/CEMA	7.71	57.93	10.83	3.79
Marlboro King Size Filter hard pack Light/Germany/United Kingdom	9.97	49.49	5.51	2.29
Marlboro King Size Filter hard pack Light/Japan	9.57	57.20	7.69	2.80
Marlboro 100 Filter hard pack Light/Germany	9.44	48.20	7.09	2.78
Merit King Size Filter soft pack Ultra-light/USA	7.69	38.86	7.59	2.66
Marlboro King Size Filter hard pack Ultra-light Menthol/USA	8.85	38.23	5.76	2.10
Parliament King Size Filter hard pack Light/Japan	7.00	43.52	7.04	2.59
Virginia Slims 100 Filter hard pack Ultra-light Menthol	7.03	39.10	6.06	2.00
Chesterfield INTL King Size Filter hard pack Ultra-light/	7.96	49.57	6.29	2.61
Philip Morris 100 Filter hard pack Super L	8.16	47.35	8.05	2.89
Marlboro King Size Filter hard pack Ultra-light/European Union	7.72	42.18	5.51	2.08
Diana King Size Filter hard pack Ultra-light/European Union	9.35	47.87	6.67	2.42
Virginia Slims 100 Filter hard pack Ultra-light Menthol	8.37	36.91	4.46	1.76
Philip Morris One King Size Filter hard pack/European Union	5.67	38.36	6.03	2.03
Muratti King Size Filter hard pack Ultra-light 1 mg/CEMA	7.16	42.43	7.20	2.74
Longbeach One King Size Filter hard pack/Australia	8.08	46.81	6.55	2.69
Virginia Slims 100 Filter hard pack Menthol 1	6.67	34.00	4.69	1.65
Marlboro King Size Filter hard pack/Mexico	9.26	41.46	6.92	2.98
Raffles 100 Filter hard pack/European Union	11.09	61.96	9.81	4.32
Marlboro King Size Filter hard pack/Brazil	9.94	49.33	7.99	3.54
Peter Jackson King Size Filter hard pack Menthol/Australia	8.23	48.76	5.28	2.39
Marlboro 100 Filter hard pack Light/USA	9.47	43.02	5.53	2.24
Marlboro King Size Filter hard pack Light/Norway	9.08	46.10	6.04	2.58
Chesterfield King Size Filter hard pack Light/European Union	8.32	45.45	4.68	1.90
Philip Morris King Size Filter hard pack Super Light	7.68	40.98	5.09	2.08
Merit King Size Filter soft pack Ultra-light/USA	6.21	34.10	7.01	2.83

1R4Filter Kentucky Reference	7.44	47.60	5.52	2.31
1R4Filter Kentucky Reference	6.99	46.32	5.39	2.36
** Mean **	9.03	48.80	7.83	3.03
** Standard deviation **	1.76	7.93	2.30	0.86
** Coefficient of variation **	0.19	0.16	0.29	0.28
Maximum	13.84	65.36	13.68	5.00
75th percentile	9.84	53.44	9.40	3.65
90th percentile	11.15	61.64	10.88	4.33
Median	9.08	47.78	7.40	2.79
Minimum	5.67	34.00	4.46	1.65

Brand	Hydroquinone	Phenol	Resorcinol	Pyridine	Quinoline
Marlboro Long Size F hard pack/Argentina	49.72	12.55	0.88	24.81	0.36
Marlboro Long Size Filter hard pack/Venezuela	67.79	16.98	0.66	25.83	0.44
SG Ventil Regular Filter soft pack/European Union	85.00	15.61	1.05	23.78	0.41
Petra Regular Filter hard pack/CEMA	75.73	19.35	1.47	23.30	0.46
Marlboro King Size Filter soft pack/USA	48.36	11.64	1.04	24.80	0.34
Marlboro King Size Filter hard pack/Norway	56.63	14.04	0.76	24.38	0.37
L & M King Size Filter hard pack/European Union	80.48	17.98	1.35	28.14	0.44
Marlboro King Size Filter hard pack/Malaysia	71.04	18.46	1.24	27.24	0.44
Chesterfield Originals King Size Filter hard pack	61.44	13.04	1.13	22.94	0.39
L & M King Size Filter hard pack/Malaysia	59.21	14.33	0.90	21.38	0.42
Marlboro King Size Filter hard pack 25 s/Australia	46.09	11.01	0.78	24.20	0.33
Marlboro King Size Filter hard pack/Taiwan	50.62	15.02	1.40	17.36	0.39
Marlboro 100 Filter hard pack/European Union	61.98	12.11	1.28	22.56	0.36
Marlboro King Size Filter hard pack Medium/European Union	50.57	10.21	0.68	19.95	0.29
Parliament 100 Filter soft pack Light/USA	49.63	11.54	0.98	15.64	0.35
Marlboro King Size Filter hard pack/Japan	45.94	13.98	0.75	13.32	0.35
L & M King Size Filter hard pack Light/European Union	79.87	12.40	1.39	27.33	0.33
Filter6 King Size Filter hard pack Light/European Union	79.33	8.66	1.49	17.37	0.27
Chesterfield Originals King Size Filter hard pack	59.76	8.20	0.79	20.72	0.29
Diana King Size Filter soft pack Specially Mild/E	63.35	15.77	0.71	22.78	0.38
Muratti Ambassador King Size Filter hard pack/European Union	83.33	18.28	1.06	16.61	0.42
Merit King Size Filter hard pack/European Union	53.33	9.12	0.90	23.20	0.28

Parliament 100 Filter soft pack/CEMA	58.34	15.16	1.03	14.47	0.35
Marlboro King Size Filter hard pack Light/Germany/United Kingdom	65.70	7.85	1.60	21.14	0.25
Marlboro King Size Filter hard pack Light/Japan	58.11	9.09	1.23	14.97	0.32
Marlboro 100 Filter hard pack Light/Germany	60.19	10.39	1.18	20.34	0.32
Merit King Size Filter soft pack Ultra-light/USA	45.06	9.30	1.12	25.82	0.28
Marlboro King Size Filter hard pack Ultra-light Menthol/USA	48.29	7.66	0.84	24.18	0.23
Parliament King Size Filter hard pack Light/Japan	45.98	10.00	0.74	17.09	0.28
Virginia Slims 100 Filter hard pack Ultra-light Menthol	38.51	7.82	0.70	19.47	0.28
Chesterfield INTL King Size Filter hard pack Ultra-light/	62.29	9.43	1.25	22.93	0.28
Philip Morris 100 Filter hard pack Super L	49.08	10.76	1.23	20.16	0.30
Marlboro King Size Filter hard pack Ultra-light/European Union	49.59	6.94	0.90	21.56	0.25
Diana King Size Filter hard pack Ultra-light/European Union	59.57	7.59	0.94	22.20	0.26
Virginia Slims 100 Filter hard pack Ultra-light Menthol	44.96	5.90	1.15	24.24	0.24
Philip Morris One King Size Filter hard pack/European Union	45.78	8.02	1.14	23.71	0.22
Muratti King Size Filter hard pack Ultra-light 1 mg/CEMA	54.21	10.65	1.23	24.77	0.27
Longbeach One King Size Filter hard pack/Australia	51.60	7.73	1.11	20.00	0.24
Virginia Slims 100 Filter hard pack Menthol 1	39.46	6.23	1.02	21.92	0.25
Marlboro King Size Filter hard pack/Mexico	43.60	12.19	0.71	18.87	0.36
Raffles 100 Filter hard pack/European Union	63.07	19.78	0.94	17.22	0.39
Marlboro King Size Filter hard pack/Brazil	62.68	14.24	0.99	22.32	0.39
Peter Jackson King Size Filter hard pack Menthol/Australia	57.13	9.55	0.92	15.62	0.25
Marlboro 100 Filter hard pack Light/USA	44.05	8.56	0.78	18.79	0.28
Marlboro King Size Filter hard pack Light/Norway	49.12	9.34	0.87	21.37	0.32
Chesterfield King Size Filter hard pack Light/European Union	59.87	6.95	0.86	20.06	0.28
Philip Morris King Size Filter hard pack Super Light	46.71	8.03	0.87	20.81	0.28
Merit King Size Filter soft pack Ultra-light/USA	35.37	12.61	0.99	25.37	0.40

1R4Filter Kentucky Reference	57.81	7.54	0.72	22.95	0.29
1R4Filter Kentucky Reference	52.28	8.24	0.88	20.00	0.30
** Mean **	56.55	11.36	1.01	21.40	0.33
** Standard deviation **	11.90	3.72	0.24	3.52	0.06
** Coefficient of variation **	0.21	0.33	0.23	0.16	0.20
Maximum	85.00	19.78	1.60	28.14	0.46
75th percentile	62.21	14.02	1.18	24.08	0.37
90th percentile	76.09	17.08	1.35	25.42	0.42
Median	55.42	10.52	0.98	21.74	0.32
Minimum	35.37	5.90	0.66	13.32	0.22

Brand	NNN	NNK	NAT	NAB	Mercury	Cadmium	Lead
Marlboro Long Size F hard pack/Argentina	103.30	79.10	104.81	15.19	2.69	27.17	19.67
Marlboro Long Size Filter hard pack/Venezuela	118.34	73.27	85.73	16.08	2.86	47.49	25.18
SG Ventil Regular Filter soft pack/European Union	80.74	49.32	71.15	9.86	3.65	41.82	22.30
Petra Regular Filter hard pack/CEMA	61.89	43.51	57.73	7.46	2.92	48.05	21.19
Marlboro King Size Filter soft pack/USA	151.33	111.11	130.62	17.11	2.93	63.60	26.31
Marlboro King Size Filter hard pack/Norway	189.04	101.97	151.11	15.87	2.50	50.48	18.61
L & M King Size Filter hard pack/European Union	92.71	57.02	78.78	10.80	3.51	53.56	24.52
Marlboro King Size Filter hard pack/Malaysia	185.79	80.54	140.59	20.90	2.90	70.72	32.08
Chesterfield Originals King Size Filter hard pack	75.00	54.85	69.18	8.87	2.89	44.64	23.71
L & M King Size Filter hard pack/Malaysia	100.08	52.33	76.42	11.63	2.50	41.04	26.04
Marlboro King Size Filter hard pack 25 s/Australia	133.78	97.52	122.31	15.50	2.86	57.18	21.30
Marlboro King Size Filter hard pack/Taiwan	169.74	97.53	143.39	17.53	2.51	37.53	24.32
Marlboro 100 Filter hard pack/European Union	110.26	83.08	95.02	11.32	2.91	50.88	25.33
Marlboro King Size Filter hard pack Medium/European Union	83.87	70.88	76.60	10.41	3.09	47.89	19.38
Parliament 100 Filter soft pack Light/USA	162.49	109.13	143.20	20.79	2.57	31.83	23.98
Marlboro King Size Filter hard pack/Japan	125.27	71.02	121.45	14.06	2.85	45.00	22.66
L & M King Size Filter hard pack Light/European Union	94.60	59.13	83.00	13.87	4.13	55.87	25.13
Filter5 King Size Filter hard pack Light/European Union	17.09	24.97	24.30	2.96	3.07	35.81	18.66
Chesterfield Originals King Size Filter hard pack	86.29	60.54	77.54	10.24	2.51	41.20	24.85
Diana King Size Filter soft pack Specially Mild/E	51.19	41.13	49.69	7.63	3.35	42.89	27.16
Muratti Ambassador King Size Filter hard pack/European Union	54.72	52.56	57.39	6.61	3.06	24.44	20.67
Merit King Size Filter hard pack/European Union	128.44	63.40	108.91	14.42	3.88	61.09	23.81

Parliament 100 Filter soft pack/CEMA	165.48	76.96	130.83	19.72	2.76	28.66	22.03
Marlboro King Size Filter hard pack Light/Germany/United Kingdom	63.54	50.32	57.85	6.84	3.48	43.67	16.27
Marlboro King Size Filter hard pack Light/Japan	116.92	82.66	101.47	11.26	3.43	38.46	32.87
Marlboro 100 Filter hard pack Light/Germany	65.68	51.80	60.39	7.33	3.11	36.70	15.49
Merit King Size Filter soft pack Ultra-light/USA	175.82	99.68	152.09	20.95	3.92	64.62	23.73
Marlboro King Size Filter hard pack Ultra-light Menthol/USA	157.85	94.75	143.99	20.13	4.18	66.96	25.13
Parliament King Size Filter hard pack Light/Japan	149.55	94.30	135.47	23.46	3.13	29.89	22.40
Virginia Slims 100 Filter hard pack Ultra-light Menthol	145.96	91.01	129.41	16.81	3.09	60.11	24.89
Chesterfield INTL King Size Filter hard pack Ultra-light/	75.71	38.71	65.86	10.57	3.86	50.14	22.93
Philip Morris 100 Filter hard pack Super L	117.84	79.30	107.24	12.65	3.57	47.89	16.11
Marlboro King Size Filter hard pack Ultra-light/European Union	74.35	51.90	82.11	8.98	3.67	38.23	17.48
Diana King Size Filter hard pack Ultra-light/European Union	56.17	42.27	57.52	8.37	4.11	42.98	26.31
Virginia Slims 100 Filter hard pack Ultra-light Menthol	120.72	94.24	106.19	12.88	4.68	60.94	33.17
Philip Morris One King Size Filter hard pack/European Union	161.29	62.24	147.84	21.38	5.09	47.07	22.16
Muratti King Size Filter hard pack Ultra-light 1 mg/CEMA	182.99	85.98	161.50	18.79	5.51	40.65	24.02
Longbeach One King Size Filter hard pack/Australia	17.31	32.86	41.43	3.61	3.70	38.32	21.60
Virginia Slims 100 Filter hard pack Menthol 1	174.38	77.54	164.62	19.31	4.92	46.46	19.77
Marlboro King Size Filter hard pack/Mexico	89.51	42.83	75.71	10.24	3.24	79.80	18.66
Raffles 100 Filter hard pack/European Union	17.22	23.33	29.07	4.37	2.59	24.93	14.11
Marlboro King Size Filter hard pack/Brazil	60.45	48.71	48.62	6.96	2.50	46.12	19.78
Peter Jackson King Size Filter hard pack Menthol/Australia	16.29	28.20	33.54	3.15	2.75	36.18	14.44
Marlboro 100 Filter hard pack Light/USA	132.79	98.00	121.67	18.51	3.53	60.37	24.14
Marlboro King Size Filter hard pack Light/Norway	174.01	108.19	140.60	17.36	3.08	55.38	21.87
Chesterfield King Size Filter hard pack Light/European Union	61.10	35.58	57.86	7.92	3.44	48.64	23.51
Philip Morris King Size Filter hard pack Super Light	105.09	79.02	102.20	11.10	3.18	43.35	20.23
Merit King Size Filter soft pack Ultra-light/USA	185.82	86.34	182.91	23.21	3.96	47.31	19.18

1R4Filter Kentucky Reference	126.28	109.23	136.12	20.98	5.52	87.49	48.63
1R4Filter Kentucky Reference	133.11	103.01	142.85	23.94	5.54	78.13	48.29
** Mean **	109.98	70.06	99.72	13.40	3.43	48.19	23.52
** Standard deviation **	49.38	25.10	40.64	5.80	0.82	13.82	6.58
** Coefficient of variation **	0.45	0.36	0.41	0.43	0.24	0.29	0.28
Maximum	189.04	111.11	182.91	23.94	5.54	87.49	48.63
75th percentile	150.89	93.44	135.96	18.27	3.82	55.75	25.07
90th percentile	174.53	102.07	148.17	20.95	4.70	64.85	27.66
Median	113.59	72.14	101.83	12.76	3.15	46.77	22.79
Min mum	16.29	23.33	24.30	2.96	2.50	24.44	14.11

Brand	Chromium	Nickel	Arsenic	Selenium
Marlboro Long Size F hard pack/Argentina			4.06	
Marlboro Long Size Filter hard pack/Venezuela				
SG Ventil Regular Filter soft pack/European Union				
Petra Regular Filter hard pack/CEMA			4.92	
Marlboro King Size Filter soft pack/USA			3.78	
Marlboro King Size Filter hard pack/Norway			3.70	
L & M King Size Filter hard pack/European Union				
Marlboro King Size Filter hard pack/Malaysia			5.38	
Chesterfield Originals King Size Filter hard pack				
L & M King Size Filter hard pack/Malaysia			4.71	
Marlboro King Size Filter hard pack 25 s/Australia			4.41	
Marlboro King Size Filter hard pack/Taiwan			4.45	
Marlboro 100 Filter hard pack/European Union				
Marlboro King Size Filter hard pack Medium/European Union				
Parliament 100 Filter soft pack Light/USA			3.86	
Marlboro King Size Filter hard pack/Japan				
L & M King Size Filter hard pack Light/European Union				
Filter6 King Size Filter hard pack Light/European Union				
Chesterfield Originals King Size Filter hard pack				
Diana King Size Filter soft pack Specially Mild/E			4.38	
Muratti Ambassador King Size Filter hard pack/European Union			4.89	
Merit King Size Filter hard pack/European Union				

Parliament 100 Filter soft pack/CEMA	4.70
Marlboro King Size Filter hard pack Light/Germany/United Kingdom	
Marlboro King Size Filter hard pack Light/Japan	
Marlboro 100 Filter hard pack Light/Germany	
Merit King Size Filter soft pack Ultra-light/USA	
Marlboro King Size Filter hard pack Ultra-light Menthol/USA	4.75
Parliament King Size Filter hard pack Light/Japan	4.25
Virginia Slims 100 Filter hard pack Ultra-light Menthol	5.16
Chesterfield INTL King Size Filter hard pack Ultra-light/	
Philip Morris 100 Filter hard pack Super L	
Marlboro King Size Filter hard pack Ultra-light/European Union	
Diana King Size Filter hard pack Ultra-light/European Union	
Virginia Slims 100 Filter hard pack Ultra-light Menthol	
Philip Morris One King Size Filter hard pack/European Union	
Muratti King Size Filter hard pack Ultra-light 1 mg/CEMA	
Longbeach One King Size Filter hard pack/Australia	
Virginia Slims 100 Filter hard pack Menthol 1	
Marlboro King Size Filter hard pack/Mexico	5.87
Raffles 100 Filter hard pack/European Union	
Marlboro King Size Filter hard pack/Brazil	
Peter Jackson King Size Filter hard pack Menthol/Australia	
Marlboro 100 Filter hard pack Light/USA	
Marlboro King Size Filter hard pack Light/Norway	
Chesterfield King Size Filter hard pack Light/European Union	
Philip Morris King Size Filter hard pack Super Light	
Merit King Size Filter soft pack Ultra-light/USA	

1R4Filter Kentucky Reference			6.50	
1R4Filter Kentucky Reference			6.37	
** Mean **			4.79	
** Standard deviation **			0.82	
** Coefficient of variation **			0.17	
Maximum	0.00	0.00	6.50	0.00
75th percentile	#NUM!	#NUM!	5.10	#NUM!
90th percentile	#NUM!	#NUM!	6.02	#NUM!
Median	#NUM!	#NUM!	4.70	#NUM!
Minimum	0.00	0.00	3.70	0.00

NNK, 4-(*N*-nitrosomethylamino)-1-(3-pyridyl)-1-butanone; NNN, *N*′-nitrosonornicotine; NAT, *N*′-nitrosoanatabine; NAB, *N*′-nitrosoanabasine; CEMA, central Europe, Middle East and Africa

Table A1.3.

Constituents per milligram of nicotine for Australian brands, modified intense machine regimen

Brand	Nicotine	Acetaldehyde	Acetone	Acrolein	Acrylonitrile	Ammonia
Longbeach Mild	2.50	429.32	189.32	45.88	6.80	10.24
Longbeach Super Mild	2.00	494.15	223.90	52.70	7.90	10.20
Longbeach Ultra Mild	1.60	574.50	258.63	61.94	8.56	9.63
Peter Jackson Extra Mild	2.40	546.96	242.25	58.83	6.92	9.21
Peter Jackson Super Mild	2.00	586.30	268.85	63.55	8.50	8.90
Peter Jackson Ultra Mild	1.60	677.56	295.50	71.44	10.63	10.31
Horizon Mild	2.10	612.38	265.24	67.62	9.91	10.95
Horizon Super Mild	2.20	562.27	245.00	62.73	9.46	11.64
Horizon Ultra Mild	1.54	683.12	292.21	72.73	11.04	12.40
Benson & Hedges Extra Mild 8	1.97	564.47	277.67	61.42	10.10	11.32
Benson & Hedges Special Filter King Size hard pack	2.49	466.67	232.93	50.20	8.80	11.45
Holiday 8 Super Mild hard pack	1.48	508.11	260.14	53.18	8.18	13.11
Winfield Extra Mild 25 hard pack	2.06	512.62	260.19	54.85	8.45	11.60
Winfield Filter King Size hard pack	2.27	486.78	244.93	51.10	8.15	10.93
Winfield Super Mild King Size hard pack	2.09	538.28	276.08	56.94	7.99	10.86
Mean	2.02	549.57	255.52	59.01	8.76	10.85
Standard deviation	0.34	71.75	27.35	7.90	1.25	1.15
Coefficient of variation	0.17	0.13	0.11	0.13	0.14	0.11
Maximum	2.50	683.12	295.50	72.73	11.04	13.11
75th percentile	2.24	580.40	272.46	63.14	9.68	11.52
90th percentile	2.45	651.49	286.39	69.91	10.42	12.10
Median	2.06	546.96	260.14	58.83	8.50	10.93

Brand	Benzene	Benzo[a]pyrene	Butyraldehyde	Cadmium	Carbon monoxide	Catechol	Crotonaldehyde
Longbeach Mild	24.20	8.40	23.24	25.16	8.72	51.08	16.12
Longbeach Super Mild	30.30	9.10	24.75	27.95	10.10	51.90	17.80
Longbeach Ultra Mild	34.19	10.00	31.19	34.38	11.94	45.56	20.00
Peter Jackson Extra Mild	30.75	10.54	28.79	30.17	10.13	51.25	21.08
Peter Jackson Super Mild	35.80	10.05	32.20	33.65	10.95	44.60	21.85
Peter Jackson Ultra Mild	45.31	9.00	35.81	29.56	13.56	44.56	23.06
Horizon Mild	34.86	9.24	33.33	39.52	11.05	50.48	23.05
Horizon Super Mild	33.36	9.46	31.64	44.86	10.86	47.73	20.55
Horizon Ultra Mild	39.55	12.27	38.77	39.55	12.40	48.70	23.51
Benson & Hedges Extra Mild 8	37.41	6.90	38.27	43.86	10.96	52.79	20.71
Benson & Hedges Special Filter King Size hard pack	32.81	7.39	32.65	44.58	9.36	54.62	17.23
Holiday 8 Super Mild hard pack	35.95	8.24	32.91	42.91	11.08	51.69	19.39
Winfield Extra Mild 25 hard pack	35.49	7.38	35.49	39.13	10.44	51.46	19.66
Winfield Filter King Size hard pack	31.45	7.49	33.61	36.61	9.69	54.63	16.96
Winfield Super Mild King Size hard pack	33.88	7.37	37.70	35.26	10.57	50.24	21.15
Mean	34.35	8.86	32.69	36.48	10.79	50.09	20.14
Standard deviation	4.68	1.48	4.50	6.32	1.21	3.24	2.31
Coefficient of variation	0.14	0.17	0.14	0.17	0.11	0.06	0.11
Maximum	45.31	12.27	38.77	44.86	13.56	54.63	23.51
75th percentile	35.87	9.73	35.65	41.23	11.06	51.79	21.50
90th percentile	38.69	10.35	38.05	44.29	12.22	53.89	23.06
Median	34.19	9.00	32.91	36.61	10.86	51.08	20.55

Brand	Formaldehyde	Hydrogen cyanide	Hydroquinone	Isoprene	Lead	Mercury	Methyl ethyl ketone
Longbeach Mild	54.60	88.44	62.56	293.08	.	1.84	45.96
Longbeach Super Mild	63.95	101.50	68.90	328.45	.	2.10	51.85
Longbeach Ultra Mild	62.31	112.56	61.94	378.00	.	2.63	58.81
Peter Jackson Extra Mild	71.17	94.42	67.83	290.38	11.04	1.92	57.29
Peter Jackson Super Mild	70.80	103.95	56.35	363.50	.	2.35	65.65
Peter Jackson Ultra Mild	64.81	142.06	60.81	438.44	.	2.75	69.75
Horizon Mild	75.24	123.81	60.48	357.14	.	2.61	62.86
Horizon Super Mild	58.64	121.82	55.91	333.18	13.55	2.46	73.64
Horizon Ultra Mild	55.97	142.86	60.07	411.04	.	3.25	67.53
Benson & Hedges Extra Mild 8	55.33	127.92	57.87	411.68	.	3.12	77.16
Benson & Hedges Special Filter King Size hard pack	49.80	111.65	60.24	359.84	11.93	2.54	67.47
Holiday 8 Super Mild hard pack	58.65	138.51	62.70	343.92	.	2.96	71.62
Winfield Extra Mild 25 hard pack	55.83	116.51	59.71	396.12	.	2.71	74.76
Winfield Filter King Size hard pack	49.78	112.78	64.32	355.51	12.12	2.41	70.49
Winfield Super Mild King Size hard pack	53.59	118.18	60.77	382.78	.	2.57	80.38
Mean	60.03	117.13	61.36	362.87	12.16	2.55	66.35
Standard deviation	7.82	16.37	3.64	42.08	1.04	0.40	9.54
Coefficient of variation	0.13	0.14	0.06	0.12	0.09	0.16	0.14
Maximum	75.24	142.86	68.90	438.44	13.55	3.25	80.38
75th percentile	64.38	125.86	62.63	389.45	12.47	2.73	72.63
90th percentile	71.02	140.64	66.43	411.42	13.12	3.06	76.20
Median	58.64	116.51	60.77	359.84	12.02	2.57	67.53

Brand	NNN	NNK	NAT	NAB	Nitrogen oxides	Nitric oxide	Phenol
Longbeach Mild	19.12	22.84	4.04	33.08	68.80	61.68	13.56
Longbeach Super Mild	16.00	27.15	5.25	27.95	74.50	68.00	10.20
Longbeach Ultra Mild	15.31	24.44	4.06	36.94	77.13	69.63	7.31
Peter Jackson Extra Mild	14.08	18.83	4.96	27.63	76.00	68.92	12.58
Peter Jackson Super Mild	10.95	20.30	5.10	26.30	86.30	77.75	8.70
Peter Jackson Ultra Mild	20.06	26.25	7.69	35.88	105.13	95.06	6.25
Horizon Mild	15.00	19.86	4.66	31.57	101.43	91.43	11.38
Horizon Super Mild	18.59	24.86	7.64	35.86	88.64	79.09	11.14
Horizon Ultra Mild	19.55	23.31	4.64	31.62	103.25	92.86	8.70
Benson & Hedges Extra Mild 8	23.91	32.64	6.50	41.73	85.28	77.67	11.83
Benson & Hedges Special Filter King Size hard pack	25.02	37.63	6.10	45.78	87.55	80.32	14.18
Holiday 8 Super Mild hard pack	33.24	25.61	7.77	49.73	93.24	85.81	13.31
Winfield Extra Mild 25 hard pack	28.59	38.20	8.69	48.54	89.32	82.04	13.50
Winfield Filter King Size hard pack	25.33	33.70	6.83	44.93	73.57	67.40	14.67
Winfield Super Mild King Size hard pack	27.13	34.59	8.13	48.33	72.25	66.03	13.16
Mean	20.79	27.35	6.14	37.72	85.49	77.58	11.36
Standard deviation	6.22	6.43	1.58	8.19	11.71	10.52	2.61
Coefficient of variation	0.30	0.24	0.26	0.22	0.14	0.14	0.23
Maximum	33.24	38.20	8.69	49.73	105.13	95.06	14.67
75th percentile	25.18	33.17	7.66	45.36	91.28	83.93	13.40
90th percentile	28.01	36.42	7.99	48.46	102.52	92.29	13.93
Median	19.55	25.61	6.10	35.88	86.30	77.75	11.83

Brand	Propionaldehyde	Pyridine	Quinoline	Resorcinol	Styrene	Toluene	1,3-Butadiene
Longbeach Mild	34.88	12.56	0.28	1.00	7.12	39.16	33.72
Longbeach Super Mild	40.90	11.45	0.20	1.20	7.75	45.65	39.40
Longbeach Ultra Mild	46.06	13.56	0.19	1.44	9.44	51.69	45.56
Peter Jackson Extra Mild	46.17	13.58	0.25	0.92	8.54	45.42	38.04
Peter Jackson Super Mild	47.20	12.90	0.20	0.90	9.90	54.85	44.55
Peter Jackson Ultra Mild	57.63	13.56	0.19	1.31	10.50	65.25	53.63
Horizon Mild	50.00	15.33	0.29	1.13	10.38	53.81	44.19
Horizon Super Mild	47.73	14.46	0.28	0.86	9.68	52.73	43.50
Horizon Ultra Mild	58.12	16.17	0.24	.	12.21	60.00	51.43
Benson & Hedges Extra Mild 8	47.82	15.43	0.29	1.22	11.47	59.90	52.28
Benson & Hedges Special Filter King Size hard pack	40.16	15.34	0.32	1.57	10.12	52.21	43.78
Holiday 8 Super Mild hard pack	42.30	15.54	0.29	1.78	10.74	57.23	49.53
Winfield Extra Mild 25 hard pack	43.93	17.67	0.31	1.56	11.31	56.31	47.33
Winfield Filter King Size hard pack	41.45	16.74	0.33	1.68	10.66	48.90	42.51
Winfield Super Mild King Size hard pack	46.51	16.84	0.30	1.34	10.81	55.02	47.85
Mean	46.06	14.74	0.26	1.28	10.04	53.21	45.15
Standard deviation	6.14	1.77	0.05	0.30	1.38	6.58	5.48
Coefficient of variation	0.13	0.12	0.19	0.23	0.14	0.12	0.12
Maximum	58.12	17.67	0.33	1.78	12.21	65.25	53.63
75th percentile	47.77	15.86	0.30	1.53	10.78	56.77	48.69
90th percentile	54.58	16.80	0.32	1.65	11.41	59.96	51.94
Median	46.17	15.33	0.28	1.27	10.38	53.81	44.55

Brand	1-Aminonaphthalene	2-Aminonaphthalene	3-Aminobiphenyl
Longbeach Mild	8.80	5.36	1.16
Longbeach Super Mild	7.55	4.60	1.15
Longbeach Ultra Mild	8.13	5.19	1.31
Peter Jackson Extra Mild	7.50	4.63	1.08
Peter Jackson Super Mild	7.05	4.35	1.15
Peter Jackson Ultra M ld	7.75	5.13	1.31
Horizon Mild	9.62	5.81	1.50
Horizon Super Mild	9.23	5.55	1.46
Horizon Ultra Mild	10.00	7.14	1.65
Benson & Hedges Extra Mild 8	10.86	6.90	1.71
Benson & Hedges Special Filter King Size hard pack	10.36	6.43	1.65
Holiday 8 Super Mild hard pack	11.42	7.30	2.03
Winfield Extra Mild 25 hard pack	10.73	6.94	1.73
Winfield Filter King Size hard pack	11.67	7.23	1.82
Winfield Super Mild King Size hard pack	10.14	6.56	1.72
Mean	9.39	5.94	1.50
Standard deviation	1.52	1.04	0.29
Coefficient of variatior	0.16	0.18	0.19
Maximum	11.67	7.30	2.03
75th percentile	10.54	6.92	1.71
90th percentile	11.20	7.19	1.78
Median	9.62	5.81	1.50

Brand	4-Aminobiphenyl	*m*- and *p*-Cresol	*o*-Cresol
Longbeach Mild	0.88	8.00	3.12
Longbeach Super Mild	0.90	6.30	2.40
Longbeach Ultra Mild	1.06	5.19	1.88
Peter Jackson Extra Mild	0.83	7.92	3.08
Peter Jackson Super Mild	0.90	6.25	2.45
Peter Jackson Ultra Mild	1.00	4.56	1.69
Horizon Mild	1.14	7.10	2.67
Horizon Super Mild	1.06	6.64	2.54
Horizon Ultra Mild	1.30	6.24	2.31
Benson & Hedges Extra Mild 8	1.39	7.11	2.75
Benson & Hedges Special Filter King Size hard pack	1.26	9.24	3.28
Holiday 8 Super Mild hard pack	1.63	8.99	3.54
Winfield Extra Mild 25 hard pack	1.33	8.35	3.03
Winfield Filter King Size hard pack	1.39	9.34	3.54
Winfield Super Mild King Size hard pack	1.33	7.94	3.23
Mean	1.16	7.28	2.77
Standard deviation	0.24	1.43	0.56
Coefficient of variation	0.20	0.20	0.20
Maximum	1.63	9.34	3.54
75th percentile	1.33	8.18	3.18
90th percentile	1.39	9.14	3.43
Median	1.14	7.11	2.75

NNK 4-(N-nitrosomethylamino)-1-(3-pyridyl)-1-butanone; NNN, N´-nitrosonornicotine; NAT, N´-nitrosoanatabine; NAB, N´-nitrosoanabasine

Annex 3.2 **Basis for calculation of toxicant animal carcinogenicity index and toxicant non-cancer response index**

The T25 value is the long-term daily dose that will cause tumours in 25% of the animals above the background level at a specific tissue site. The T25 is determined by linear extrapolation from the lowest dose that gives a statistically significant increase in tumours (referred to herein as the critical dose) (Dybing et al., 1997). T25 values are derived from the following equations:

$$C = [(B/100 - A/100)/(1 - A/100)] \times 100$$

$$T25 = (25/C) \times \text{critical dose}$$

where A is the proportion (%) of animals with the tumour in the control group, B is the proportion (%) of animals with the tumour in an exposed group and C is the net increase in tumour frequency (%).

The default values used to convert feed and drinking-water concentrations into doses per kilogram bodyweight are given below. Most of the T25 values were derived from oral feeding studies. Concentrations used in inhalation bioassays were converted to oral doses by using the default values for inhalation volumes reported in Table A2.1.

Table A2.1

Default values for dose calculation, weight and intake by diet, water and inhalation, for a standard experimental period of 2 years

Experimental animal	Sex	Weight(g)	Food/day(g)	Water/day(ml)	Inhalation volume(l/h)
Mouse	Male	30	3.60	5	1.8
	Female	25	3.25	5	1.8
Rat	Male	500	20.00	25	6.0
	Female	350	17.50	20	6.0
Hamster	Male	125	11.50	15	3.6
	Female	110	11.50	15	3.6

From Gold et al. (1984)

Acetaldehyde

Groups of 105 male and 105 female 6-week-old Wistar rats were exposed by inhalation to acetaldehyde at a concentration of 0 ppm (control), 750 ppm, 1500 ppm or 3000 ppm, 6 h/day, 5 days/week for 28 months. Control measurements showed that the mean concentrations of acetaldehyde in the low and intermediate doses were 735 and 1412 ppm, respectively, while that in the high dose was 3033 ppm from day 0 to day 141, 2167 ppm from day 142 to day 210, 2039 ppm from day 211 to day 238, 1433 ppm from day 239 to day 300, 1695 ppm from day 301 to day 312, 1472 ppm from day 313 to day 359, and 977 ppm for the rest of the study. The reason for the gradual lowering of the high dose was its considerable toxicity, causing growth retardation, respiratory problems and death. All the animals at the high dose died after 100 weeks. The incidences of squamous epithelial carcinomas in the nasal cavity were: control males 1/49 (2%), low-dose males 1/52 (2%), intermediate-dose males 5/53 (9%) and high-dose males 15/49 (31%); control females 0/50 (0%), low-dose females 0/48 (0%), intermediate-dose females 5/5 (9%) and high-dose females 17/53 (32%). The incidences of adenocarcinomas in the nasal cavity were: control males 0/59 (0%), low-dose males 16/52 (31%), intermediate-dose males 31/53 (59%) and high-dose males 21/49 (43%); control females 0/50 (0%), low-dose females 6/48 (13%), intermediate-dose females 26/53 (49%) and high-dose females 21/53 (40%) (Woutersen et al., 1986).

Remarks on the study

Species, strain, sex:	Rat, Wistar, male
Route:	Inhalation
Critical end-point:	Nasal adenocarcinomas
Duration:	104 weeks (default)
Critical dose:	735 ppm = 735 × 44.1/24.45 (conversion factor) mg/m^3 = 1326 mg/m^3; inhalation volume per day 6 l/h × 6 h for 5 days/week = 25.7 l/day; inhalation dose per day for specified body weight 450 g = 1350 mg/m^3 × 25.7 l/day × 1000/450 kg = 75.8 mg/kg bw per day; daily dose for 24 months with treatment and observation time of 28 months: 75.8 mg/kg bw per day × 28/24 × 28/24 = 102.1 mg/kg bw per day

Lowest dose causing significantly increased tumour incidence

Control:	0%
Dose 102.1 mg/kg bw per day:	31%
Net increase:	31%

T25 calculation

T25 = 25/31 × 82.1 mg/kg bw per day = 82.4 mg/kg bw per day

Acrylonitrile

A study was conducted by Biodynamics Inc. (1980) in which acrylonitrile was administered in drinking-water to groups of 100 Fischer 344 rats of each sex at doses of 1, 3, 10, 30 (stated to correspond to 2.5 mg/kg bw per day) and 100 ppm, with a control group of 200 rats of each sex for 2 years. Interim necropsies were performed at 6, 12 and 18 months (10 per sex per exposed group and 20 per sex in the control group). The study was terminated early because of the low survival rate. An increased incidence of tumours (astrocytomas of the brain and spinal cord and carcinomas of the Zymbal gland) was seen in the groups at 3 ppm (3/200 in controls, 10/99 in 30 ppm group) or higher, and the incidence was dose-dependent. An increased incidence of mammary gland tumours was seen in females at 100 ppm.

Remarks on the study

Species, strain, sex:	Rat, Fischer 344, male
Route:	Drinking-water
Critical end-point:	Brain and spinal cord astrocytoma
Duration:	104 weeks
Critical dose:	2.5 mg/kg bw per day

Lowest dose causing significantly increased tumour incidence

Control:	3/200 (0.2%)
Dose 0.04 mg/kg bw per day:	10/99 (10%)
Net increase:	$[(10/99-3/200) \times 100]/(1-3/200) = 9\%$

T25 calculation

$T25 = 25/9 \times 2.5$ mg/kg bw per day = 6.9 mg/kg bw per day

1-Aminonaphthalene

Solutions of 0.01% 1-naphthylamine hydrochloride (freed from 2-naphthylamine by multiple fractional recrystallization) were added to the drinking-water of 61 male and female stock mice for 84 weeks. In males, the incidence of hepatomas was 4/18 (22%) in treated animals and 4/24 (17%) in the controls. In females, the corresponding incidences were 5/43 (11%) and 0/36 (0%) (Clayson, Ashton, 1963).

Remarks on the study

Species, strain, sex:	Mouse, stock (strain not specified), female
Route:	Drinking-water
Critical end-point:	Hepatoma
Duration:	84 weeks
Critical dose:	0.01% = 0.1 mg/ml, female mice weighing 25 g, drinking 5 ml per day: $0.1 \times 5 \times 1000/25$ mg/kg bw per day = 20 mg/kg bw per day

Lowest dose causing significantly increased tumour incidence

Control:	0%
Dose 20 mg/kg bw per day:	11%
Net increase:	11%

T25 calculation
T25 = 25/11 × 20 mg/kg bw per day × 84/104 × 84/104 = 29.7 mg/kg bw per day

2-Aminonaphthalene

In groups of 23 DBA and 25 IF mice given 2-naphthylamine by stomach tube at a dose of 240 or 400 mg/kg bw per week in arachis oil, respectively, for 90 weeks, liver tumours developed in 50% of the animals. In two similar groups of control mice given arachis oil alone, no hepatomas were found (Bonser et al., 1952).

Remarks on the study

Species, strain, sex:	Mice, DBA, sex not specified
Route:	Gavage
Critical end-point:	Liver tumours
Duration:	90 weeks
Critical dose:	240 mg/kg bw once a week, 240/7 mg/kg bw per day = 34.3 mg/kg bw per day dose with administration and observation for 104 weeks = 34.3 × 90/104 × 90/104 mg/kg bw per day = 25.7 mg/kg bw per day

Lowest dose causing significantly increased tumour incidence

Control:	0%
Dose 25.7 mg/kg bw per day:	50%
Net increase:	50%

T25 calculation
T25 = 25/50 × 25.7 mg/kg bw per day = 12.8 mg/kg bw per day

Benzene

Benzene in corn oil was administered to groups of 50 B6C3F1 mice of each sex by gavage on 5 days per week for 103 weeks. Both sexes were exposed to a dose of 0, 25, 50 or 100 mg/kg bw per day. Benzene mainly caused significantly increased incidences of malignant lymphomas in both sexes at doses ≥ 25 mg/kg bw per day, Zymbal gland carcinomas in males at doses ≥ 50 mg/kg bw per day and females at doses ≥ 100 mg/kg bw per day, lung alveolar and bronchiolar adenomas and carcinomas in males at ≥ 100 mg/kg bw per day and females at ≥ 50 mg/kg bw per day, Harderian gland adenomas in males at ≥ 25 mg/kg bw per day, preputial gland squamous cell carcinomas in males at incidences of 0/21, 5/28, 19/29 (66%) and 31/35 at 0, 25, 50 and 100 mg/kg bw per day, respectively, and mammary gland carcinomas in females at ≥ 50 mg/kg bw per day (National Toxicology Program, 1986).

Remarks on the study

Species, strain, sex:	Mouse, B6C3F1, male
Route:	Gavage
Critical end-point:	Preputial gland, carcinoma (all types)
Duration:	104 weeks, dosing for 103 weeks
Critical dose:	50 mg/kg bw per day, 5 days/week; daily dose 50 mg/kg bw × 5/7 = 35.7 mg/kg bw per day; daily dose for 104 weeks = 35.7 mg/kg bw × 103/104 = 35.4 mg/kg bw per day

Lowest dose causing significantly increased tumour incidence

Control:	0/21 (0%)
Dose 35.4 mg/kg bw per day:	19/29 (66%)
Net increase:	66%

T25 calculation

T25 = 25/66 × 35.4 mg/kg bw per day = 13.4 mg/kg bw per day

Benzo[a]pyrene

Groups of 24 male Syrian golden hamsters were exposed by inhalation to air containing benzo[*a*]pyrene at 0, 2.2, 9.5 and 46.5 mg/m^3, corresponding to total average doses of 0, 29, 127 and 383 mg benzo[*a*]pyrene per animal. The average survival time was 96.4 weeks, with the exception of animals at the high dose (59 weeks). Of the animals at the intermediate dose, 34.6% developed respiratory tract tumours and 26.9% developed tumours of the upper digestive tract. None of the controls or low-dose animals developed such tumours (Thyssen et al., 1981).

Remarks on the study

Species, strain, sex: Hamster, Syrian golden, male
Route: Inhalation
Critical end-point: Respiratory tract tumours
Duration: 96.4 weeks average survival time for control, low and intermediate dose
Critical dose: 127 mg total dose in 657 days (96.4 weeks) = 0.19 mg per animal per day; default body weight of male hamsters 125 g; daily dose = 0.19 mg × 1000/125 = 1.5 mg/kg bw per day

Lowest dose causing significantly increased tumour incidence

Control: 0/24 (0%)
Dose 1.5 mg/kg bw per day: 9/26 (34.6%)
Net increase: 34.6%

T25 calculation
T25 = 25/34.6 × 1.5 mg/kg bw per day = 1.1 mg/kg bw per day

1,3-Butadiene

Groups of 70 male and 70 female B6C3F1 mice aged 8–9 weeks were exposed to air containing 0, 625 or 1250 ppm 1,3-butadiene, 6 h/day, 5 times per week for 2 years (Melnick et al., 1990). The results with the two lowest concentrations used are shown in Table A2.2.

Table A2.2
Tumours induced by aerosol exposure to 1,3-butadiene in B6C3F1 mice

Tumour type	0 ppm		6.25 ppm		20 ppm	
	Males	Females	Males	Females	Males	Females
Alveolar or bronchiolar adenoma or carcinoma	22/70 (31%)	4/70 (6%)	23/60 (38%)	15/60* (25%)	20/60 (33%)	19/60* (32%)
Lymphoma, all malignant	4/70 (6%)	10/70 (14%)	3/70 (4%)	14/70 (20%)	8/70 (11%)	18/49* (26%)
Haemangiosarcoma, heart	0/70 (0%)	0/70 (0%)	0/70 (0%)	0/70 (0%)	1/70 (1%)	0/70 (0%)
Papilloma or carcinoma of the fore-stomach	1/70 (1%)	2/70 (3%)	0/70 0%)	2/70 (3%)	1/70 (1%)	3/70 (4%)

* $p < 0.01$, Fisher exact test

Remarks on the study

Species, strain, sex:	Mouse, B6C3F1, female
Route:	Inhalation
Critical end-point:	Alveolar or bronchiolar adenoma or carcinoma
Duration:	104 weeks
Critical dose:	6.25 ppm = (6.25 × 2.21)/1000 mg/m³ = 13.8 µg/m³; inhalation volume per day 2.5 l/h × 6 h for 5 days per week = 15 l × 5/7 = 10.7 l/day; inhalation dose per day for specified body weight 39 g = 13.8 µg/m³ × 10.7 l/day × 1000/39kg = 3.8 mg/kg bw per day

Lowest dose causing significantly increased tumour incidence

Control:	4/7 (6%)
Dose 3.8 mg/kg bw per day:	15/60 (25%)
Net increase:	[(25/100−6/100)/(1−6/100)] × 100 = 20%

T25 calculation

T25 = 25/20 × 3.8 mg/kg bw per day = 4.8 mg/kg bw per day

Cadmium

Four groups of 40 male SPF Wistar (TNO/W75) rats, 6 weeks old, were exposed to 12.5, 25 or 50 µg/m³ cadmium as cadmium chloride aerosol (mass median aerodynamic diameter, 0.55 µm; geometric standard deviation, 1.8) for 23 h/day on 7 days/week for 18 months. Animals were observed for an additional 13 months, at which time the experiment was ended. A group of 41 rats exposed to filtered air served as controls. Histological examination was performed on all animals. Body weights and survival were not affected by cadmium treatment. A dose-related increase in the incidence of malignant pulmonary tumours (mostly adenocarcinomas) was observed in cadmium chloride-treated rats (12.5 µg/m³, 6/39 [15%]; 25 µg/m³, 20/38 [53%]; 50 µg/m³, 25/35 [71%]) compared with controls (0/38). Multiple pulmonary tumours were observed frequently; several tumours showed metastases or were regionally invasive. The incidence of adenomatous hyperplasia was also increased by cadmium treatment (Takenaka et al., 1983).

Remarks on the study

Species, strain, sex:	Rats, SPF Wistar, male
Route:	Inhalation
Duration:	23 h/day, 7 days/week for 18 months, observation for additional 13 months before termination of experiment
Critical dose:	25 μg/m³; inhalation volume per 23 h = 0.06 m³ × 23 = 0.138 m³; male rats weigh 500 g; daily dose: 0.138 × 25 μg/0.5 kg = 6.9 μg/kg

Lowest dose causing significantly increased tumour incidence

Control:	0%
Dose 6.9 μg/kg bw per day:	53%
Net increase:	53%

T25 calculation
T25 = 25/53 × 6.9 × 18/24 × 31/24 = 3 μg/kg bw per day

Catechol

Groups of 20 or 30 male Wistar, WKY, Lewis and Sprague-Dawley rats (6 weeks of age) were given catechol in the diet at 0 or 0.8% for 104 weeks. The incidence of hyperplasia in the forestomach was significantly increased in exposed WKY and Sprague-Dawley rats compared with controls. Papillomas occurred in 6/30 Sprague-Dawley rats, 2/30 Wistar rats and 1/30 WKY rats and carcinomas in 1/30 Sprague-Dawley and 1/30 Wistar rats, with none in controls. All strains developed 97–100% incidence of adenomas in the glandular stomach, with none in controls, and adenocarcinomas in the glandular stomach occurred in 23/30 Sprague-Dawley, 22/30 Lewis, 20/30 Wistar and 3/30 Wistar rats, with none in controls (Tanaka et al., 1995).

Remarks on the study

Species, strain, sex:	Rats, Sprague-Dawley, male
Route:	Diet
Critical end-point:	Glandular stomach adenocarcinomas
Duration:	104 weeks
Critical dose:	0.8% in diet = 8000 mg/kg diet, male rats eat 20 g per day and weigh 500 g, daily dose: (8000 mg/kg × 0.02 kg)/0.5 kg = 320 mg/kg bw per day

Lowest dose causing significantly increased tumour incidence

Control:	0/20 (0%)
Dose 320 mg/kg bw per day:	23/30 (77%)
Net increase:	77%

T25 calculation

T25 = 25/77 × 320 mg/kg bw per day = 104 mg/kg bw per day

Formaldehyde

Groups of 119–120 male and 120 female Fischer 344 rats, 7 weeks of age, were exposed to 0, 2.0, 5.6 or 14.3 ppm (0, 2.5, 6.9 or 17.6 mg/m^3) formaldehyde (> 97.5% pure) vapour by whole-body exposure for 6 h/day on 5 days/week for up to 24 months and were then observed for 6 months with no further exposure. While no nasal cavity malignancies were found in rats exposed to 0 or 2.0 ppm formaldehyde, two squamous-cell carcinomas (one among 119 males and one among 116 females examined) occurred in the group exposed to 5.6 ppm and 107 (51 among 117 males and 52 among 115 females examined) in those exposed to 14.3 ppm ($p < 0.001$). Five additional nasal cavity tumours (classified as carcinoma, undifferentiated carcinoma or sarcoma and carcinosarcoma) were identified in rats exposed to 14.3 ppm; two of these tumours were found in rats that also had squamous-cell carcinomas of the nasal cavity. There was a significant overall increase in the incidence of polypoid adenomas in treated animals (males and females combined) when compared with controls ($p = 0.02$, Fisher exact test). The incidences of polypoid adenomas were marginally significantly elevated in females at the low dose and in males at the intermediate dose (Swenberg et al., 1980; Kerns et al., 1983).

Because of the highly nonlinear dose–response relation for formaldehyde-induced nasal tumours, no T25 value was calculated for this compound.

Hydroquinone

Groups of 65 male and 65 female Fischer 344 rats (7–9 weeks of age) were given hydroquinone by gavage at 0, 25 or 50 mg/kg bw, 5 days/week for 103 weeks. The animals were sacrificed when they were 111–113 weeks old. In the males, renal adenomas were found in 0/55 (0%) controls, 4/55 ($p = 0.069$) (7%) at the low dose and 8/55 ($p = 0.003$) (14.5%) at the high dose. In the females mononuclear leukaemia was found in 9/55 (16%) controls, 15/55 ($p = 0.048$) (27%) at the low dose and 22/55 ($p = 0.003$) (40%) at the high dose (National Toxicology Program, 1989).

Remarks on the study

Species, strain, sex:	Rats, Fischer 344, male
Route:	Gavage
Critical end-point:	Renal tubular adenoma
Duration:	103 weeks
Critical dose:	50 mg/kg bw per day and 5 days per week, daily dose for 104 weeks with observation for 112 weeks: 50 mg/kg bw per day × 5/7 × 103/104 = 35.4 mg/kg bw per day

Lowest dose causing significantly increased tumour incidence

Control:	0/55 (0%)
Dose 35.4 mg/kg bw per day:	8/55 (14.5%)
Net increase:	14.5%

T25 calculation
T25 = 25/14.5 × 35.4 mg/kg bw per day = 61.0 mg/kg bw per day

Isoprene

Groups of 50 male and 50 female B6C3F1 mice (age unspecified) were exposed to isoprene by whole- body inhalation at a concentration of 0, 10, 70, 140, 280, 700 or 2200 ppm (0, 28, 200, 400, 800, 2000 or 6160 mg/m^3) for 4 or 8 h/day on 5 days/week for 20, 40 or 80 weeks, followed by holding periods until termination of the experiment at 96 or 104 weeks. Increases in tumour incidence were found in the lung, liver, heart, spleen and Harderian gland in males at an exposure of ≥ 140 ppm for ≥ 40 weeks. In female mice, increased incidences of Harderian gland adenomas (2/49 controls, 3/49 at 10 ppm and 8/49 ($p < 0.005$) at 70 ppm) and pituitary adenomas (1/49 controls, 6/46 at 10 ppm and 9/49 ($p < 0.05$) at 70 ppm) were seen after exposure for 80 weeks (Cox, Bird, Griffis, 1996; Placke et al., 1996).

Remarks on the study

Species, strain, sex:	Mice, B6C3F1, female
Route:	Inhalation
Critical end-point:	Pituitary adenomas
Duration:	80 weeks
Critical dose:	200 mg/m^3; inhalation volume per 8 h/day = 0.0018 m^3/h 8 h 5/7 = 0.0103 m^3; female mice weigh 25 g; daily dose: (0.103 × 200 mg/0.025 kg = 82.3 mg/kg bw per day; daily dose for 104 weeks = 82.3 mg/kg bw per day 80/104 = 63.3 mg/kg bw per day

Lowest dose causing significantly increased tumour incidence

Control:	1/49 (2%)
Dose 63.3 mg/kg bw per day:	9/49 (18%)
Net increase:	[(18/100−2/100)/(1−2/100)] 100 = 16.7%

T25 calculation
T25 = 25/16.7 × 63.3 mg/kg bw per day = 94.8 mg/kg bw per day

Lead

Basic lead acetate has been shown to induce kidney tumours in several experiments with rats. In one experiment, Wistar rats received feed containing 0.1% and 1% basic lead acetate for 29 and 24 months, respectively. Two control groups consisted of 24–30 rats. In the low-dose group, 11/32 (34%) developed kidney tumours (three carcinomas), and in the high dose 13/24 (54%) developed kidney tumours (six carcinomas). No kidney tumours were found among the control animals (van Esch, van Genderen, Vink, 1962).

Remarks on the study

Species, strain, sex:	Rat, Wistar, sex not specified
Route:	Feed
Critical end-point:	Renal tumours
Duration:	29 months
Critical dose:	1000 mg/kg diet, default feed intake 18.8 g/day (mean of male and female), default body weight 425 g (mean of male and female), daily dose = 1000 mg/kg 0.0188 kg × 1000/425 = 44.2 mg/kg bw per day; daily dose for 2 years = 44.2 mg/kg bw per day × 29/24 = 53.4 mg/kg bw per day

Lowest dose causing significantly increased tumour incidence

Control:	No renal tumours found (number of control animals not reported)
Dose 53.4 mg/kg bw per day:	11/32 (34%)
Net increase:	34%

T25 calculation
T25 = 25/34 × 53.4 mg/kg bw per day = 39.3 mg/kg bw per day

NNK

Male Fischer rats were treated with NNK dissolved in trioctanoin at 0.03, 0.1, 0.3, 1.0, 10 or 50 mg/kg bw or trioactanoin alone subcutaneously three times per week for 20 weeks. Animals were killed over the course of 104 weeks after cessation of treatment. The following lung tumour incidences were found: 2.5% (control), 6.7% (0.03 mg/kg bw), 10.0% (0.1 mg/kg bw), 13.3% (0.3 mg/kg bw), 53.3% (1.0 mg/kg bw), 73.3% (10 mg/kg bw), 73.3% (10 mg/kg bw) and 87.1% (50 mg/kg bw). Tumour incidence increased with dose, and the trend was strongly significant. The respective incidences of alveolar hyperplasia were 2.5%, 16.4%, 16.0%, 40.0%, 73.3%, 93.3% and 93.5% (Belinsky et al., 1990).

Remarks on the study

Species, strain, sex:	Rats, Fischer, male
Route:	Subcutaneous
Critical end-point:	Lung adenomas and carcinomas
Duration:	20 weeks
Critical dose:	0.03 mg/kg bw 3 times per week, daily dose: 0.03 mg/kg bw × 3/7 = 00.013 mg/kg bw per day, daily dose for 2 years: 12.9 µg/kg bw per day × 20/104 = 2.5 µg/kg bw per day

Lowest dose causing significantly increased tumour incidence

Control:	1/40 (2.5%)
Dose 2.5 µg/kg bw per day:	4/60 (6.7%)%
Net increase:	[(6.7/100−2.5/100)/(1−2.5/100)] × 100 = 4.3

T25 calculation

T25 = 25/4.3 × 2.5 µg/kg bw per day = 0.015 mg/kg bw per day

NNN

A group of 20 male Fischer rats, 7 weeks old, was given 200 mg/l NNN in the drinking-water on 5 days/week for 30 weeks (estimated total, 630 mg). Animals were killed when moribund or after 11 months, and all animals, except those lost to cannibalism or autolysis, were necropsied. All 12 rats in the treated groups that were necropsied had developed oesophageal tumours (11 papillomas and three carcinomas); in addition, one pharyngeal papilloma and three carcinomas of the nasal cavity with invasion of the brain were observed. No tumours were observed in 19 untreated controls (Hoffmann et al., 1975).

Remarks on the study

Species, strain, sex:	Rat, Fischer, male
Route:	Drinking-water
Critical end-point:	Oesophageal papillomas and carcinomas
Duration:	30-week treatment period, necropsied after 11 months
Critical dose:	630 mg total for 210 days, male rats weigh 500 g = daily dose 630/210 × 1000/500 kg = 6.0 mg/kg bw per day; daily dose for 24 months = 6.0 mg/kg bw per day × 210/728 × 11/24 = 0.8 mg/kg bw per day

Lowest dose causing significantly increased tumour incidence

Control:	0%
Dose 0.4 mg/kg bw per day:	12/12 (100%)
Net increase:	100%

T25 calculation
T25 = 25/100 × 0.4 mg/kg bw per day = 0.2 mg/kg bw per day

References

Belinsky SA et al. (1990) Dose–response relationships beteen O^6-methylguanine formation in Clara cells and induction of pulmonary neoplasia in the rat by 4-(methylnitrosamino)-1-(3-pyridyl)-1-butanone. *Cancer Research*, 50:3772–3780.

Biodynamics, Inc. (1990) *A twenty-four month oral toxicity/carcinogenicity study of arcrylonitrile administered in the drinking water to Fischer 344 rats.* Division of Biology and Safety Evaluation, East Millstone, New Jersey, under project No 77-1746 for Monsanto Company, St Louis, Missouri.

Bonser GM et al. (1952) The carcinogenic properties of 2-amino-1-naphthol hydrochloride and its parent amine 2- naphthylamine. *British Journal of Cancer*, 6:412–424.

Clayson DB, Ashton MJ (1963) The metabolism of 1-naphthylamine and its bearing on the mode of carcinogenesis of the aromatic amines. *Acta Unio International Contra Cancrum*, 19:539–542.

Cox LA, Bird MG, Griffis L (1996) Isoprene cancer risk and the time pattern of dose administration. *Toxicology*, 113:263–272.

Dybing E et al. (1997) T25: a simplified carcinogenic potency index. Description of the system and study of correlations between carcinogenic potency and species/site specificity and mutagenicity. *Pharmacology and Toxicology*, 80:272–279.

van Esch GJ, van Genderen H, Vink HH (1962) The induction of renal tumours by feeding of basic lead acetate to rats. *British Journal of Cancer*, 16:289–297.

Gold LS et al. (1984) A carcinogenic potency database of the standardized results of animal bioassays. *Environmental Health Perspectives*, 58:9–319.

Hoffmann D et al. (1975) A study of tobacco carcinogenesis. XIV. Effects of *N′*-nitrosonornicotine and *N′*- nitrosoanabasine in rats. *Journal of the National Cancer Institute*, 55:977–981.

Kerns WD et al. (1983) Carcinogenicity of formaldehyde in rats and mice after long-term inhalation exposure. *Cancer Research*, 43:4382–4392.

Melnick Rl, Huff J, Chou BJ, Miller RA. Carcinogenicity of 1,3-butadiene in C57Bl/6 x C3HF1 mice at low exposure concentrations. Cancer Res 1990; 50: 6592-6599.

National Toxicology Program (1986) *Toxicology and carcinogenesis studies of benzene (CAS No. 71-43-2) in F344/N rats and B6C3F1 mice (gavage studies)*. Research Triangle Park, North Carolina. (NTP TR 289; National Institutes of Health Publication No. 86-2545).

National Toxicology Program (1989) *NTP toxicology and carcinogenesis studies of hydroquinone (CAS No. 123- 31-9) in F344/N rats and B6C3F1 mice (gavage studies)*. Research Triangle Park, North Carolina. (NTP TR 366).

Placke ME et al. (1996) Chronic inhalation oncogenicity study of isoprene in B6C3F1 mice. *Toxicology*, 110:253262.

Swenberg JA et al. (1980) Induction of squamous cell carcinomas of the rat nasal cavity by inhalation exposure to formaldehyde vapor. *Cancer Research*, 40:3398–3402.

Takenaka S et al. (1983) Carcinogenicity of cadmium chloride aerosols in W rats. *Journal of the National Cancer Institute*, 70:367–373.

Tanaka H et al. (1995) Rat strain differences in catechol carcinogenicity to the stomach. *Food and Chemical Toxicology*, 33:93–98.

Thyssen J et al. (1981) Inhalation studies with benzo(a)pyrene in Syrian golden hamsters. *Journal of the National Cancer Institute*, 66:575–577.

Woutersen RA et al. (1986) Inhalation toxicity of acetaldehyde in rats. III. Carcinogenicity study. *Toxicology*, 41:213–231.

Annex 3.3 Calculation of toxicant animal carcinogenicity index and toxicant non-cancer response index for international Philip Morris brands, Canadian brands and Australian brands

In this report, the T25 carcinogenic potency method (Dybing et al., 1997) was used, rather than cancer potency factors published by the US Environmental Protection Agency (www.epa.gov/iris) or the California Environmental Protection Agency (www.oehha.ca.gov) and used in the study of Fowles and Dybing (2003). The latter potency factors are derived from the lower 95% confidence limit of a modelled benchmark dose for 10% tumour incidence. The authors examined the usefulness of the T25 carcinogenic potency method extensively (Dybing et al., 1997; Sanner et al., 2001; Sanner, Dybing, 2005a,b). Furthermore, the T25 method has been used in European chemical product regulation (European Commission, 1999; Scientific Committee on Cosmetic and Non-food Products, 2003). The choice of method for estimating carcinogenic potency does not have much effect on calculations of the toxicant animal carcinogenicity index, as the various methods for estimating potency factors show good correlation. For instance, Dybing et al. (1997) found a correlation coefficient of 0.96 between the T25 values for 110 US National Cancer Institute/National Toxicology Program carcinogens and the TD50 carcinogenic potency indices derived with the method of Gold et al. (1984). Interestingly, using the T25 method, Sanner and Dybing (2005b) found good agreement between the hazard characterization based on epidemiological data and that based on animal experiments, although the data available for such comparisons were limited.

Tables A3.1–A3.3 show the cancer and toxicant non-cancer response indices per milligram of nicotine of toxicants in smoke generated by the modified intense smoking regimen based on data from Counts et al. (2005), the Canadian brands and the Australian brands. Tables A3.4–A3.9 show the ranking of toxicants in smoke with respect to toxicant animal carcinogenicity and toxicant non-cancer response indices for the three data sets. Table A3.10 and A3.11 show comparisons of the three data sets for the two indices.

Table A3.1

Cancer and toxicant non-cancer response indices per milligram of nicotine of toxicants in smoke generated by the modified intense smoking regimen based on data from Counts et al. (2005) on smoke toxicant levels

Toxicant	Level in smoke (µg/mg nicotine)			T25[a] (mg/kg bw per day)	Potency per mg/kg bw per day	Toxicant animal carcinogenicity index			Tolerable level (µg/m)[3]	Toxicant non-cancer response index		
	Mean	90%ile	Maximum			Mean	90%ile	Maximum		Mean	90%ile	Maximum
Acetaldehyde	695	859	997	82.4	0.01	7.0	8.6	10.0	9	77.2	95.4	111
Acetone	359	446	501	ND	–	–	–	–	None	–	–	–
Acrolein	67.6	85.3	99.5	I	–	–	–	–	0.06	1127	1422	1658
Acrylonitrile	12.3	16.1	19.5	6.9	0.14	1.7	2.3	2.7	5	2.5	3.2	3.9
1-Aminonaphthalene	16.2[b]	19.0[b]	24.8[b]	29.7	0.03	0.00049	0.00057	0.00074	None	–	–	–
2-Aminonaphthalene	10.1[b]	11.6[b]	14.3[b]	12.8	0.08	0.00081	0.00093	0.0011	None	–	–	–
3-Aminobiphenyl	2.9[b]	3.4[b]	4.1[b]	ND	–	–	–	–	None	–	–	–
4-Aminobiphenyl	2.2[b]	2.7b	3.2[b]	ND[c]	–	–	–	–	None	–	–	–
Ammonia	21.2	26.8	40.7	ND	–	–	–	–	200	0.11	0.13	0.20
Arsenic	4.8[b]	6.0[b]	6.5[b]	NQ	–	–	–	–	0.03	0.16	0.20	0.22
Benzene	39.0	45.8	51.1	13.4	0.07	2.7	3.2	3.6	60	0.66	0.76	0.85
Benzo[*a*]pyrene	9.0[b]	11.2[b]	13.8[b]	1.1[d]	0.91	0.0082	0.0102	0.0126	None	–	–	–
1,3-Butadiene	54.1	65.5	75.5	4.8	0.21	11.4	13.8	15.9	20	2.7	3.3	3.8
Butyraldehyde	43.0	52.4	63.6	ND	–	–	–	–	None	–	–	–
Cadmium	48.2[b]	64.9[b]	87.5[b]	0.03	33	1.6	2.1	2.2	0.02	2.4	3.2	4.4
Carbon monoxide	15.2[e]	17.9[e]	27.3[e]	ND	–	–	–	–	10 000	1.5	1.8	2.7

Catechol	48.8	61.6	65.4	104	0.01	0.49	0.62	0.65	None	–	–	–
Chromium	NQ	NQ	NQ	NQ	–	–	–	–	0.2f	–	–	–
m– and *p*-Cresol	7.8	10.9	13.7	ND	–	–	–	–	600g	0.01	0.02	0.02
o-Cresol	3.0	4.3	5.0	ND	–	–	–	–	600g	0.01	0.01	0.01
Crotonaldehyde	28.8	36.6	41.3	I	–	–	–	–	None	–	–	–
Formaldehyde	41.1	57.9	90.5	NQh	–	–	–	–	3	13.7	19.3	30.2
Hydrogen cyanide	204	277	390	ND	–	–	–	–	9	22.7	30.8	43.3
Hydroquinone	56.6	76.1	85.0	61.0	0.02	1.1	1.5	1.7	None	–	–	–
Isoprene	459	551	746	94.8[d]	0.01	4.6	5.5	7.5	None	–	–	–
Lead	23.5[b]	27.7[b]	48.6[b]	39.3[i]	0.03	0.00	0.00	0.00	None	–	–	–
Mercury	3.4[b]	4.7[b]	5.5[b]	L	–	–	–	–	0.09	0.04	0.05	0.06
Methyl ethyl ketone	93.2	116	124	ND	–	–	–	–	1000	0.09	0.12	0.12
N´-Nitrosoanabasine	13.4[b]	21.0[b]	23.9[b]	L	–	–	–	–	None	–	–	–
N´-Nitrosoanatabine	99.7[b]	148[b]	183[b]	I	–	–	–	–	None	–	–	–
Nickel	NQ	NQ	NQ	NQ	–	–	–	–	0.05	–	–	–
Nitric oxide	180	280	349	ND	–	–	–	–	None	–	–	–
Nitrogen oxides	199	313	390	ND	–	–	–	–	40[j]	5.0	7.8	9.8
NNK	70.1[b]	102[b]	111[b]	0.015[k]	67	4.7	6.8	7.4	None	–	–	–
NNN	110[b]	175[b]	189[b]	0.2	5.0	0.55	0.88	0.95	None	–	–	–
Phenol	11.4	17.1	19.8	I	–	–	–	–	200	0.06	0.09	0.10
Propionaldehyde	60.3	74.0	88.4	ND	–	–	–	–	None	–	–	–
Pyridine	21.4	25.4	28.1	L	–	–	–	–	None	–	–	–
Quinoline	0.33	0.42	0.46	ND	–	–	–	–	None	–	–	–
Resorcinol	1.0	1.4	1.6	I	–	–	–	–	None	–	–	–

Selenium	NQ	NQ	NQ	ND	–	–	–	–	20	–	–	–
Styrene	13.6	16.5	18.5	L	–	–	–	–	900	0.02	0.02	0.02
Toluene	71.1	83.3	96.3	E	–	–	–	–	300	0.24	0.28	0.32

ND, no data; I, insufficient evidence of carcinogenicity; NQ, not quantifiable; L, limited evidence of carcinogenicity; NNN, *N*′-nitrosonornicotine; NNK, 4-(*N*-nitrosomethylamino)-1-(3-pyridyl)-1-butanone; E, evidence of noncarcinogenicity

[a] Values are from studies by oral administration, unless otherwise stated.

[b] ng/mg nicotine

[c] No proper data for T25 calculation

[d] Inhalation administration

[e] mg/mg nicotine

[f] Hexavalent chromium

[g] Cresol mixture

[h] Highly non-linear dose-response relation

[i] Lead subacetate

[j] WHO guideline for nitrogen dioxide, not listed by the Califronia Environmental Protection Agency in 2005

[k] Subcutaneous administration

Table A3.2

Cancer and toxicant non-cancer response indices per milligram of nicotine of toxicants in smoke generated by the modified intense smoking regimen based on Canadian data on smoke toxicant levels

Toxicant	Level in smoke (µg/mg nicotine)			T25[a] (mg/kg bw per day)	Potency per mg/kg bw per day	Toxicant animal carcinogenicity index			Tolerable level (µg/m³)	Toxicant non-cancer response index		
	Mean	90%ile	Maximum			Mean	90%ile	Maximum		Mean	90%ile	Maximum
Acetaldehyde	567	658	766	82	0.01	5.7	6.6	7.7	9	62.9	73.1	85.2
Acetone	289	323	386	ND[b]	–	–	–	–	None	–	–	–
Acrolein	71.3	81.7	99.5	I	–	–	–	–	0.06	1188	1362	1659
Acrylonitrile	10.0	12.0	14.0	6.9	0.14	1.4	1.7	2.0	5	2.0	2.4	2.8
1-Aminonaphthalene	10.8[b]	15.1[b]	19.6[b]	29.7	0.03	0.00032	0.00045	0.00059	None	–	–	–
2-Aminonaphthalene	9.7[b]	14.2[b]	14.5[b]	12.8	0.08	0.00077	0.0011	0.0012	None	–	–	–
3-Aminobiphenyl	1.8[b]	2.5[b]	2.8[b]	ND	–	–	–	–	None	–	–	–
4-Aminobiphenyl	1.8[b]	2.4[b]	2.6[b]	ND[c]	–	–	–	–	None	–	–	–
Ammonia	12.7	18.1	19.0	ND	–	–	–	–	200	0.06	0.08	0.09
Arsenic	ND[b]	ND[b]	ND[b]	NQ	–	–	–	–	0.03			
Benzene	40.6	48.6	51.8	13.4	0.07	2.8	3.4	3.6	60	0.68	0.81	0.86
Benzo[*a*]pyrene	10.5[b]	17.4[b]	17.9[b]	1.1[d]	0.91	0.0096	0.0158	0.0163	None	–	–	–
1,3-Butadiene	42.6	51.6	56.5	4.8	0.21	8.9	0.0108	11.9	20	2.1	2.6	2.8
Butyraldehyde	32.3	37.4	41.3	ND	–	–	–	–	None	–	–	
Cadmium	71.4[b]	83.6[b]	93.2[b]	0.03	33	2.4	2.8	3.1	0.02	3.6	4.2	4.7
Carbon monoxide	11.8[e]	14.6[e]	15.7[e]	ND	–	–	–	–	10000	1.2	1.5	1.6

Catechol	75.3	88.7	95.7	104	0.01	0.75	0.89	0.96	None	–	–	–
Chromium	ND	ND	ND	NQ	–	–	–	–	0.2[f]	–	–	–
m- and *p*-Cresol	10.7	13.1	27.1	ND	–	–	–	–	600[g]	0.02	0.02	0.05
o-Cresol	4.3	4.8	11.1	ND	–	–	–	–	600[g]	0.01	0.01	0.02
Crotonaldehyde	30.3	35.9	39.6	I	–	–	–	–	None	–	–	–
Formaldehyde	77.3	116	118	NQ[h]	–	–	–	–	3	25.8	38.7	39.4
Hydrogen cyanide	143	196	230	ND	–	–	–	–	9	15.9	21.8	25.6
Hydroquinone	66.0	75.6	78.1	61.0	0.02	1.3	1.5	1.6	None	–	–	–
Isoprene	289	377	438	94.8[d]	0.01	2.9	3.8	4.4	None	–	–	
Lead	18.7[b]	23.3[b]	23.3[b]	39.3[i]	0.03	0.00	0.00	0.00	None	–	–	–
Mercury	2.9[b]	3.3[b]	4.0[b]	L	–	–	–	–	0.09	0.03	0.04	0.04
Methyl ethyl ketone	ND	ND	ND	ND	–	–	–	–	1000	0.09	0.12	0.12
N′-Nitrosoanabasine	8.8[b]	37.6[b]	43.3[b]	L	–	–	–	–	None	–	–	–
N′-Nitrosoanatabine	37.8[b]	45.3[b]	169[b]	I	–	–	–	–	None	–	–	–
Nickel	ND	ND	ND	ND	–	–	–	–	0.05	–	–	–
Nitric oxide	81.5	166	284	ND	–	–	–	–	None	–	–	–
Nitrogen oxides	88.8	182	311	ND	–	–	–	–	20[j]	2.2	4.6	7.8
NNK	56.1[b]	88.3[b]	104[b]	0.015[k]	67	3.8	5.9	7.0	None	–	–	–
NNN	43.5[b]	144[b]	163[b]	0.2	5.0	0.22	0.72	0.82	None	–	–	–
Phenol	18.3	19.4	54.5	I	–	–	–	–	200	0.09	0.10	0.27
Propionaldehyde	48.2	54.9	65.3	ND	–	–	–	–	None	–	–	–
Pyridine	16.5	20.0	22.1	L	–	–	–	–	None	–	–	–
Quinoline	0.35	0.43	0.80	ND	–	–	–	–	None	–	–	–
Resorcinol	1.3	1.7	1.8	I	–	–	–	–	None	–	–	–

Selenium	ND	ND	ND	ND	–	–	–	–	20	–	–	–
Styrene	12.3	12.9	61.8	L	–	–	–	–	900	0.01	0.01	0.07
Toluene	71.6	91.4	93.7	E	–	–	–	–	300	0.24	0.30	0.31

ND, no data; I, insufficient evidence of carcinogenicity; NQ, not quantifiable; L, limited evidence of carcinogenicity; NNN, *N*′-nitrosonornicotine; NNK, 4-(*N*-nitrosomethylamino)-1-(3-pyridyl)-1-butanone; E, evidence of noncarcinogenicity

[a]Values are from studies by oral administration, unless otherwise stated.

[b]ng/mg nicotine

[c]No proper data for T25 calculation

[d]Inhalation administration

[e]mg/mg nicotine

[f]Hexavalent chromium

[g]Cresol mixture

[h]Highly non-linear dose-response relation

[i]Lead subacetate

[j]WHO guideline for nitrogen dioxide, not listed by the Califronia Environmental Protection Agency in 2005

[k]Subcutaneous administration

Table A3.3

Cancer and toxicant non-cancer response indices per milligram nicotine of toxicants in smoke generated by the modified intense smoking regimen based on Australian data on smoke toxicant levels

Toxicant	Level in smoke (µg/mg nicotine)			T25[a] (mg/kg bw per day)	Potency per mg/kg bw per day	Toxicant animal carcinogenicity index			Tolerable level (µg/m³)	Toxicant non-cancer response index		
	Mean	90%ile	Maximum			Mean	90%ile	Maximum		Mean	90%ile	Maximum
Acetaldehyde	550	651	683	82	0.01	5.5	6.5	6.8	9	61.1	72.3	75.9
Acetone	253	286	296	ND	–	–	–	–	None	–	–	–
Acrolein	59.0	69.9	72.7	I	–	–	–	–	0.06	983	1165	1212
Acrylonitrile	8.8	10.4	11.0	6.9	0.14	1.2	1.5	1.5	5	1.8	2.1	2.2
1-Aminonaphthalene	9.4[b]	11.2[b]	11.7[b]	29.7	0.03	0.000028	0.00034	0.00035	None	–	–	–
2-Aminonaphthalene	5.9[b]	7.2[b]	7.3[b]	12.8	0.08	0.00047	0.00058	0.00058	None	–	–	–
3-Aminobiphenyl	1.5[b]	1.9[b]	2.0[b]	ND	–	–	–	–	None	–	–	–
4-Aminobiphenyl	1.2[b]	1.4[b]	1.6[b]	ND[c]	–	–	–	–	None	–	–	–
Ammonia	10.8	12.1	13.1	ND	–	–	–	–	200	0.05	0.06	0.07
Arsenic	ND[b]	ND[b]	ND[b]	NQ	–	–	–	–	0.03	–	–	–
Benzene	34.4	38.7	45.3	13.4	0.07	2.4	2.7	3.2	60	0.57	0.65	0.76
Benzo[*a*]pyrene	8.9[b]	10.3[b]	12.3[b]	1.1[d]	0.91	0.0081	0.0094	0.0112	None	–	–	–
1,3-Butadiene	45.2	51.9	53.6	4.8	0.21	9.5	10.9	11.3	20	2.3	2.6	2.7
Butyraldehyde	32.7	38.0	38.8	ND	–	–	–	–	None	–	–	–
Cadmium	36.5[b]	44.3[b]	44.9[b]	0.03	33	1.2	1.5	1.5	0.02	1.8	2.2	2.2
Carbon monoxide	10.8[e]	12.2[e]	13.6[e]	ND	–	–	–	–	10000	1.1	1.2	1.4

Catechol	50.1	53.9	54.6	104	0.01	0.50	0.54	0.55	None	–	–	–
Chromium	ND	ND	ND	NQ	–	–	–	–	0.2[f]	–	–	–
m- and *p*-Cresol	7.3	9.1	9.3	ND	–	–	–	–	600[g]	0.01	0.02	0.02
o-Cresol	2.8	3.4	3.5	ND	–	–	–	–	600[g]	0.00	0.01	0.01
Crotonaldehyde	20.1	23.1	23.5	I	–	–	–	–	None	–	–	–
Formaldehyde	60.0	71.0	75.2	NQ[h]	–	–	–	–	3	20.0	23.7	25.1
Hydrogen cyanide	117	141	143	ND	–	–	–	–	9	13.0	15.7	15.9
Hydroquinone	61.4	66.4	68.9	61.0	0.02	1.2	1.3	1.4	None	–	–	–
Isoprene	363	411	438	94.8[d]	0.01	3.6	4.1	4.4	None	–	–	–
Lead	12.2[b]	13.1[b]	13.5[b]	39.3[i]	0.03	0.00	0.00	0.00	None	–	–	–
Mercury	2.5[b]	3.1[b]	3.3[b]	L	–	–	–	–	0.09	0.00	0.00	0.00
Methyl ethyl ketone	66.3	76.2	80.4	ND	–	–	–	–	1000	0.07	0.08	0.08
N´-Nitrosoanabasine	6.1[b]	8.0[b]	8.7[b]	L	–	–	–	–	None	–	–	–
N´-Nitrosoanatabine	37.7[b]	48.5[b]	49.7[b]	I	–	–	–	–	None	–	–	–
Nickel	ND	ND	ND	NQ	–	–	–	–	0.05	–	–	–
Nitric oxide	77.6	92.3	95.1	ND	–	–	–	–	None	–	–	–
Nitrogen oxides	85.5	103	105	ND	–	–	–	–	20[j]	2.1	2.6	2.6
NNK	27.3[b]	36.4[b]	38.2[b]	0.015[k]	67	1.8	2.4	2.6	None	–	–	–
NNN	20.8[b]	28.0[b]	33.2[b]	0.2	5.0	0.10	0.14	0.17	None	–	–	–
Phenol	11.4	13.9	14.7	I	–	–	–	–	200	0.06	0.07	0.07
Propionaldehyde	46.1	54.6	58.1	ND	–	–	–	–	None	–	–	–
Pyridine	14.7	16.8	17.7	L	–	–	–	–	None	–	–	–
Quinoline	0.26	0.32	0.33	ND	–	–	–	–	None	–	–	–
Resorcinol	1.33	1.6	1.8	I	–	–	–	–	None	–	–	–

Selenium	ND	ND	ND	ND	–	–	–	–	20[g]	–	–	–
Styrene	10.0	11.4	12.2	L	–	–	–	–	900	0.01	0.01	0.01
Toluene	53.2	60.0	65.3	E	–	–	–	–	300	0.18	0.20	0.22

ND, no data; I, insufficient evidence of carcinogenicity; NQ, not quantifiable; L, limited evidence of carcinogenicity; NNN, *N′*-nitrosonornicotine; NNK, 4-(*N*-nitrosomethylamino)-1-(3-pyridyl)-1-butanone; E, evidence of noncarcinogenicity

[a] Values are from studies by oral administration, unless otherwise stated.

[b] ng/mg nicotine

[c] No proper data for T25 calculation

[d] Inhalation administration

[e] mg/mg nicotine

[f] Hexavalent chromium

[g] Cresol mixture

[h] Highly non-linear dose-response relation

[i] Lead subacetate

[j] WHO guideline for nitrogen dioxide, not listed by the Califronia Environmental Protection Agency in 2005

[k] Subcutaneous administration

Table A3.4

Ranking of toxicants in smoke with respect to toxicant animal carcinogenicity indices: data from Counts et al. (2005)

Toxicant	Mean	90th percentile	Maximum
1,3-Butadiene	11.4	13.8	15.9
Acetaldehyde	7.0	8.6	10.0
NNK	4.7	6.8	7.4
Isoprene	4.6	5.5	7.5
Benzene	2.7	3.2	3.6
Acrylonitrile	1.7	2.3	2.7
Cadmium	1.6	2.1	2.2
Hydroquinone	1.1	1.5	1.7
NNN	0.55	0.88	0.95
Catechol	0.49	0.62	0.65
Benzo[*a*]pyrene	0.0082	0.0102	0.0126
2-Aminonaphthalene	0.00081	0.00093	0.0011
Lead	0.00	0.00	0.00
1-Aminonaphthalene	0.00049	0.00057	0.00074

NNK, 4-(*N*-nitrosomethylamino)-1-(3-pyridyl)-1-butanone; NNN, *N*′-nitrosonornicotine

Table A3.5

Ranking of toxicants in smoke with respect to toxicant non-cancer response indices: data from Counts et al. (2005)

Toxicant	Mean	90th percentile	Maximum
Acrolein	1127	1422	1658
Acetaldehyde	77.2	95.4	111
Hydrogen cyanide	22.7	30.8	43.3
Formaldehyde	13.7	19.3	30.2
Nitrogen oxides	5.0	7.8	9.8
Cadmium	2.4	3.2	4.4
1,3-Butadiene	2.7	3.3	3.8
Acrylonitrile	2.5	3.3	3.9
Carbon monoxide	1.5	1.8	2.7
Benzene	0.66	0.76	0.85
Toluene	0.24	0.28	0.32
Arsenic	0.16	0.20	0.22
Ammonia	0.11	0.13	0.20
Methyl ethyl ketone	0.09	0.12	0.12
Phenol	0.06	0.09	0.10
Mercury	0.04	0.05	0.06
Styrene	0.02	0.02	0.02
m- and *p*-Cresol	0.01	0.02	0.02
o-Cresol	0.01	0.01	0.01

Table A3.6
Ranking of toxicants in smoke with respect to toxicant animal carcinogenicity indices: Canadian data

Toxicant	Mean	90th percentile	Maximum
1,3-Butadiene	8.9	10.8	11.9
Acetaldehyde	5.7	6.6	7.7
NNK	3.8	5.9	7.0
Isoprene	2.9	3.8	4.4
Benzene	2.8	3.4	3.6
Cadmium	2.4	2.8	3.1
Acrylonitrile	1.4	1.7	2.0
Hydroquinone	1.3	1.5	1.6
Catechol	0.75	0.89	0.96
NNN	0.22	0.72	0.82
Benzo[*a*]pyrene	0.0096	0.0158	0.0163
2-Aminonapthalene	0.00077	0.0011	0.0012
Lead	0.00	0.00	0.00
1-Aminonaphthalene	0.00032	0.00045	0.00059

NNK, 4-(*N*-nitrosomethylamino)-1-(3-pyridyl)-1-butanone; NNN, *N*′-nitrosonornicotine

Table A3.7
Ranking of toxicants in smoke with respect to toxicant non-cancer response indices: Canadian data

Toxicant	Mean	90th percentile	Maximum
Acrolein	1188	1362	1659
Acetaldehyde	62.9	73.1	85.2
Formaldehyde	25.8	38.7	39.4
Hydrogen cyanide	15.9	21.8	25.6
Cadmium	3.6	4.2	4.7
Nitrogen oxides	2.2	4.6	4.6
1,3-Butadiene	2.1	2.6	2.8
Acrylonitrile	2.0	2.4	2.8
Carbon monoxide	1.2	1.5	1.6
Benzene	0.68	0.81	0.86
Toluene	0.24	0.30	0.31
Phenol	0.09	0.10	0.27
Ammonia	0.06	0.08	0.09
Styrene	0.01	0.01	0.07
m- and *p*-Cresol	0.02	0.02	0.05
Mercury	0.03	0.04	0.04
o-Cresol	0.01	0.01	0.02

Table A3.8
Ranking of toxicants in smoke with respect to toxicant animal carcinogenicity indices: Australian data

Toxicant	Mean	90 percentile	Max
1,3-Butadiene	9.5	10.9	11.3
Acetaldehyde	5.5	6.5	6.8
Isoprene	3.6	4.1	4.4
Benzene	2.4	2.7	3.2
NNK	1.8	2.4	2.6
Acrylonitrile	1.2	1.5	1.5
Cadmium	1.2	1.5	1.5
Hydroquinone	1.2	1.3	1.4
Catechol	0.50	0.54	0.55
NNN	0.10	0.14	0.17
Benzo[a]pyrene	0.0081	0.0094	0.0112
2-Aminonaphthalene	0.00047	0.00058	0.00058
Lead	0.00	0.00	0.00
1-Aminonaphthalene	0.00028	0.00034	0.00035

NNK, 4-(N-nitrosomethylamino)-1-(3-pyridyl)-1-butanone; NNN, N′-nitrosonornicotine

Table A3.9
Ranking of toxicants in smoke with respect to toxicant non-cancer response indices: Australian data

Toxicant	Mean	90th percentile	Max
Acrolein	983	1165	1212
Acetaldehyde	61.1	72.3	75.9
Formaldehyde	20.0	23.7	25.1
Hydrogen cyanide	13.0	15.7	15.9
1,3-Butadiene	2.3	2.6	2.7
Nitrogen oxides	2.1	2.6	2.6
Cadmium	1.8	2.2	2.2
Acrylonitrile	1.8	2.1	2.2
Carbon monoxide	1.1	1.2	1.4
Benzene	0.57	0.65	0.76
Toluene	0.18	0.20	0.22
Methyl ethyl ketone	0.07	0.08	0.08
Phenol	0.06	0.07	0.07
Ammonia	0.05	0.06	0.07
m- and p-Cresol	0.01	0.02	0.02
Styrene	0.01	0.01	0.01
o-Cresol	0.00	0.01	0.01
Mercury	0.00	0.00	0.00

Table A3.10
Ranking of toxicants in smoke with respect to toxicant animal carcinogenicity indices

Toxicant	Mean			
	Counts et al. (2005)	Canadian data	Australian data	Mean
1,3-Butadiene	11.4	8.9	9.5	9.9
Acetaldehyde	7.0	5.7	5.5	6.1
Isoprene	4.6	2.9	3.6	3.7
NNK	4.7	3.8	1.8	3.4
Benzene	2.7	2.8	2.4	2.6
Cadmium	1.6	2.4	1.2	1.7
Acrylonitrile	1.7	1.4	1.2	1.4
Hydroquinone	1.1	1.3	1.2	1.2
Catechol	0.49	0.75	0.50	0.58
NNN	0.55	0.22	0.10	0.29
Benzo[a]pyrene	0.0082	0.0096	0.0081	0.0086
2-Aminonaphthalene	0.00081	0.00077	0.00047	0.00068
Lead	0.00	0.00	0.00	0.00
1-Aminonaphthalene	0.00049	0.00032	0.00028	0.00036

NNK, 4-(N-nitrosomethylamino)-1-(3-pyridyl)-1-butanone; NNN, N´-nitrosonornicotine

Table A3.11
Ranking of toxicants in smoke with respect to toxicant non-cancer response indices

Toxicant	Mean			
	Counts et al. (2005)	Canadian data	Australian data	Mean
Acrolein	1127	1188	983	1099
Acetaldehyde	77.2	62.9	61.1	67.1
Formaldehyde	13.7	25.8	20.0	19.8
Hydrogen cyanide	22.7	15.9	13.0	17.2
Nitrogen oxides	5.0	2.2	2.1	3.1
Cadmium	2.4	3.6	1.8	2.6
1,3-Butadiene	2.7	2.1	2.3	2.4
Acrylonitrile	2.5	2.0	1.8	2.1
Carbon monoxide	1.5	1.2	1.1	1.3
Benzene	0.66	0.68	0.57	0.64
Toluene	0.24	0.24	0.18	0.22
Arsenic	0.16	–	–	0.16
Methyl ethyl ketone	0.09	–	0.07	0.08
Ammonia	0.11	0.06	0.05	0.07
Phenol	0.06	0.09	0.06	0.07
Mercury	0.04	0.03	0.00	0.02
Styrene	0.02	0.01	–	0.02
m- and p-Cresol	0.01	0.02	0.01	0.01
o-Cresol	0.01	0.01	0.0	00.01

Some of the calculated T25 values are less certain than others, for instance, when data from older experiments that did not adhere to modern bioassay testing conditions were used (e.g. for 1- and 2-aminonaphthalene). The value for NNN is highly uncertain, as only one dose resulted in a 100% tumour incidence. The reported T25 value for NNK is also rather uncertain because the value was derived from an experiment by subcutaneous injection three times a week for 20 weeks and normalization of this regime to daily dosage for 104 weeks, assuming dose and time linearity. Mandated limits for NNK and NNN were recommended on the basis of their known toxicity, their variation across brands and information that the levels of these toxicants can be reduced by altering tobacco curing (WHO, 2007). 4-Aminobiphenyl is a human carcinogen (IARC Group 1; IARC, 2006); however, the experimental data on this toxicant do not allow proper calculation of a T25 value.

References

Counts ME et al. (2005) Smoke composition and predicting relationships for international commercial cigarettes smoked with three machine-smoking conditions. *Regulatory Toxicology and Pharmacology*, 41:185–227.

Dybing E et al. (1997) T25: a simplified carcinogenic potency index. Description of the system and study of correlations between carcinogenic potency and species/site specificity and mutagenicity. *Pharmacology and Toxicology*, 80:272–279.

European Commission (1999) *Guidelines for setting specific concentration limits for carcinogens in Annex 1 of Directive 67/548/EEC. Inclusion of potency considerations.* Brussels, Commission Working Group on the Classification and Labelling of Dangerous Substances.

Fowles J, Dybing E (2003) Application of toxicological risk assessment principles to the chemical toxicants of cigarette smoke. *Tobacco Control*, 12:424–430.

Gold LS et al. (1984) A carcinogenic potency database of the standardized results of animal bioassays. *Environmental Health Perspectives*, 58:9–319.

IARC (2006) *Formaldehyde, 2-butoxyethanol and 1-tert-butoxy-2-propanol.* Lyon, International Agency for Research on Cancer (IARC Monographs on the Evaluation of Carcinogenic Risks to Humans, Vol. 88).

Sanner T et al. (2001) A simple method for quantitative risk assessment of non-threshold carcinogens based on the dose descriptor T25. *Pharmacology and Toxicology*, 88:331–341.

Sanner T, Dybing E (2005a) Comparison of carcinogen hazard characterisation based on animal studies and epidemiology. *Basic and Clinical Pharmacology and Toxicology*, 96:66–70.

Sanner T, Dybing E (2005b) Comparison of carcinogenic and *in vivo* genotoxic potency estimates. *Basic and Clinical Pharmacology and Toxicology*, 96:131–139.

Scientific Committee on Cosmetic Products and Non-food Products (2003) *The SCCNFP's notes of guidance for the testing of cosmetic ingredients and their safety evaluation*. 5th revision. Brussels, European Commission.

WHO (2007) *Setting maximal limits for toxic constituents in cigarette smoke*. Geneva, World Health Organization, Study Group on Tobacco Product Regulation. http://www.who.int/tobacco/global_interaction/tobreg/tsr/en/index.html.

Annex 3.4 Correlation of toxicant yields from international brands, Canadian brands and Canadian brands with less than 100 ng/mg nicotine in the modified intense smoking regimen with machine measurement

Table A4.1.
Correlation coefficients: international brands, modified intense machine regimen

	(1)	(2)	(3)	(4)	(5)	(6)	(7)	(8)	(9)
(1) Acetaldehyde	1.000								
(2) Acrolein	0.949	1.000							
(3) Benzene	0.760	0.764	1.000						
(4) Benzo[*a*]pyrene	–0.272	–0.208	–0.266	1.000					
(5) 1,3-Butadiene	0.852	0.855	0.874	–0.401	1.000				
(6) Carbon monoxide	0.830	0.761	0.673	–0.369	0.807	1.000			
(7) Formaldehyde	0.156	0.244	0.081	0.340	0.094	–0.111	1.000		
(8) NNK	0.010	–0.111	0.002	–0.393	–0.051	0.214	–0.639	1.000	
(9) NNN	0.103	–0.014	0.042	–0.476	0.062	0.252	–0.717	0.853	1.000

NNN, *N*′-nitrosonornicotine; NNK, 4-(*N*-nitrosomethylamino)-1-(3-pyridyl)-1-butanone

Table A4.2.
Multiple r^2: international brands, modified intense machine regimen

Constituent	Multiple r^2
Benzo[*a*]pyrene	0.44
Formaldehyde	0.63
NNK	0.79
Benzene	0.81
Carbon monoxide	0.82
NNN	0.82
1,3-Butadiene	0.91
Acrolein	0.92
Acetaldehyde	0.93

NNK, 4-(*N*-nitrosomethylamino)-1-(3-pyridyl)-1-butanone; NNN, *N*′-nitrosonornicotine

Table A4.3.
Correlation coefficients: Canadian data (NNN limited), modified intense machine regimen

	(1)	(2)	(3)	(4)	(5)	(6)	(7)	(8)	(9)
(1) Acetaldehyde	1.000								
(2) Acrolein	0.792	1.000							
(3) Benzene	0.957	0.779	1.000						
(4) Benzo[*a*]pyrene	0.810	0.474	0.859	1.000					
(5) 1,3-Butadiene	0.953	0.836	0.944	0.765	1.000				
(6) Carbon monoxide	0.949	0.848	0.972	0.810	0.949	1.000			
(7) Formaldehyde	0.844	0.568	0.867	0.912	0.827	0.810	1.000		
(8) NNK	0.707	0.426	0.762	0.817	0.627	0.744	0.710	1.000	
(9) NNN	0.454	0.128	0.462	0.464	0.376	0.447	0.347	0.774	1.000

NNK, 4-(*N*-nitrosomethylamino)-1-(3-pyridyl)-1-butanone; NNN, *N*′-nitrosonornicotine

Table A4.4.
Multiple r^2: Canadian data (NNN limited), modified intense machine regimen

Constituent	Multiple R^2
NNN	0.82
Formaldehyde	0.90
Acrolein	0.91
NNK	0.92
Benzo[*a*]pyrene	0.93
Acetaldehyde	0.94
1,3-Butadiene	0.96
Benzene	0.97
Carbon monoxide	0.98

NNN, *N*′-nitrosonornicotine; NNK, 4-(*N*-nitrosomethylamino)-1-(3-pyridyl)-1-butanone

Table A4.5.
Correlation coefficients: Canadian data (all), modified intense machine regimen

	(1)	(2)	(3)	(4)	(5)	(6)	(7)	(8)	(9)
(1) Acetaldehyde	1.000								
(2) Acrolein	0.720	1.000							
(3) Benzene	0.921	0.752	1.000						
(4) Benzo[*a*]pyrene	0.630	0.490	0.753	1.000					
(5) 1,3-Butadiene	0.941	0.776	0.940	0.633	1.000				
(6) Carbon monoxide	0.945	0.798	0.934	0.680	0.936	1.000			
(7) Formaldehyde	0.511	0.555	0.658	0.895	0.565	0.559	1.000		
(8) NNK	0.574	0.137	0.567	0.385	0.532	0.569	0.138	1.000	
(9) NNN	0.270	–0.197	0.109	–0.258	0.192	0.166	–0.498	0.657	1.000

NNN, *N*′-nitrosonornicotine; NNK, 4-(*N*-nitrosomethylamino)-1-(3-pyridyl)-1-butanone

Table A4.6.
Multiple r^2: Canadian data (all), modified intense machine regimen

Constituent	Multiple r^2
NNK	0.81
Acrolein	0.86
NNN	0.88
Benzo[*a*]pyrene	0.91
Formaldehyde	0.91
Acetaldehyde	0.94
1,3-Butadiene	0.94
Benzene	0.94
Carbon monoxide	0.96

NNK, 4-(*N*-nitrosomethylamino)-1-(3-pyridyl)-1-butanone; NNN, *N*′-nitrosonornicotine

Table A4.7.
Correlation matrix for all constituents per milligram of nicotine: Philip Morris international brands (Counts et al., 2004), modified intense machine regimen

Constituent	Tpm	Water	Carbon monoxide	Acetaldehyde	Acetone	Acrolein
Tar puff count	.	.	.	.	.	.
Tpm	1.000	.	.	.	.	.
Water	0.958	1.000	.	.	.	.
Carbon monoxide	0.656	0.707	1.000	.	.	.
Acetaldehyde	0.597	0.611	0.830	1.000	.	.
Acetone	0.563	0.585	0.817	0.983	1.000	.
Acrolein	0.565	0.585	0.761	0.949	0.936	1.000
Butyraldehyde	0.533	0.524	0.781	0.967	0.951	0.931
Crotonaldehyde	0.482	0.427	0.558	0.844	0.860	0.869
Methyl ethyl ketone	0.438	0.397	0.609	0.889	0.919	0.844
Propionaldehyde	0.617	0.622	0.804	0.984	0.970	0.948
Formaldehyde	0.065	0.028	-0.111	0.156	0.204	0.244
Acrylonitrite	0.321	0.322	0.694	0.545	0.511	0.487
Benzene	0.365	0.346	0.673	0.760	0.785	0.764
1,3-Butadiene	0.421	0.457	0.807	0.852	0.857	0.855
Isoprene	0.266	0.318	0.755	0.624	0.609	0.588
Styrene	0.429	0.372	0.501	0.723	0.723	0.742
Toluene	0.359	0.335	0.610	0.719	0.719	0.683
Ammonia	0.410	0.349	0.115	0.074	0.008	0.050
Total hydrogen cyanide	0.567	0.597	0.852	0.672	0.627	0.620
Impinger hydrogen cyanide	0.517	0.549	0.819	0.646	0.606	0.594
Pad hydrogen cyanide	0.647	0.669	0.882	0.693	0.641	0.644

Nitric oxide	0.364	0.403	0.604	0.413	0.381	0.288
Nitrogen oxides	0.392	0.429	0.615	0.429	0.395	0.310
1-Aminonaphthalene	0.292	0.196	-0.105	-0.037	-0.065	-0.117
2-Aminonaphthalene	0.330	0.269	0.020	0.140	0.127	0.069
3-Aminobiphenyl	0.393	0.304	0.101	0.280	0.267	0.196
4-Aminobiphenyl	0.420	0.353	0.242	0.411	0.398	0.319
Benzo[*a*]pyrene	0.032	-0.067	-0.369	-0.272	-0.320	-0.208
Catechol	-0.088	-0.218	-0.431	-0.142	-0.156	-0.144
m- and *p*-Cresol	0.030	-0.137	-0.481	-0.260	-0.282	-0.291
o-Cresol	-0.049	-0.225	-0.539	-0.325	-0.334	-0.359
Hydroquinone	0.153	0.008	-0.245	0.115	0.078	0.113
Phenol	-0.129	-0.309	-0.561	-0.388	-0.413	-0.419
Resorcinol	0.258	0.203	0.220	0.338	0.297	0.366
Pyridine	0.462	0.338	0.263	0.424	0.416	0.422
Quinoline	-0.015	-0.196	-0.534	-0.446	-0.480	-0.503
NNN	0.230	0.230	0.252	0.103	0.089	-0.014
NNK	0.209	0.222	0.214	0.010	0.005	-0.111
NAT	0.194	0.220	0.318	0.144	0.140	0.012
NAB	0.135	0.150	0.225	0.111	0.104	-0.030
Mercury	0.308	0.342	0.704	0.743	0.740	0.621
Cadmium	0.110	0.072	0.130	0.090	0.112	0.029
Lead	0.234	0.225	0.220	0.229	0.211	0.081
Smoke pH	0.446	0.507	0.737	0.819	0.842	0.809
.	.	.	.	.	.	.
Tpm, total particulate matter	.	.	.	.	.	.

Constituent	Butyraldehyde	Crotonaldehyde	Methyl ethyl ketone	Propionaldehyde	Formaldehyde	Acrylonitrite
Tar puff count	.	.	.	.	.	.
Tpm	.	.	.	.	.	.
Water	.	.	.	.	.	.
Carbon monoxide	.	.	.	.	.	.
Acetaldehyde	.	.	.	.	.	.
Acetone	.	.	.	.	.	.
Acrolein	.	.	.	.	.	.
Butyraldehyde	1.000	.	.	.	.	.
Crotonaldehyde	0.876	1.000	.	.	.	.
Methyl ethyl ketone	0.885	0.914	1.000	.	.	.
Propionaldehyde	0.965	0.853	0.878	1.000	.	.
Formaldehyde	0.137	0.348	0.354	0.188	1.000	.
Acrylonitrite	0.610	0.324	0.385	0.514	-0.369	1.000
Benzene	0.825	0.731	0.762	0.760	0.081	0.762
1,3-Butadiene	0.846	0.692	0.740	0.810	0.094	0.734
Isoprene	0.657	0.408	0.441	0.559	-0.307	0.889
Styrene	0.810	0.831	0.773	0.746	0.245	0.472
Toluene	0.798	0.665	0.716	0.728	-0.042	0.763
Ammonia	0.049	0.026	-0.093	0.078	-0.554	0.158
Total hydrogen cyanide	0.695	0.436	0.400	0.655	-0.455	0.818
Impinger hydrogen cyanide	0.678	0.407	0.388	0.632	-0.483	0.841
Pad hydrogen cyanide	0.697	0.476	0.405	0.672	-0.372	0.729
Nitric oxide	0.413	0.144	0.204	0.399	-0.662	0.662
Nitrogen oxides	0.429	0.170	0.212	0.419	-0.651	0.661

1-Aminonaphthalene	-0.052	0.036	-0.081	-0.012	-0.379	-0.141
2-Aminonaphthalene	0.105	0.189	0.099	0.149	-0.387	-0.053
3-Aminobiphenyl	0.234	0.314	0.294	0.268	-0.333	0.049
4-Aminobiphenyl	0.377	0.403	0.397	0.388	-0.378	0.217
Benzo[*a*]pyrene	-0.237	-0.164	-0.215	-0.197	0.340	-0.401
Catechol	-0.159	0.010	0.072	-0.111	0.550	-0.581
m- and *p*-Cresol	-0.257	-0.059	-0.140	-0.213	0.152	-0.587
o-Cresol	-0.309	-0.091	-0.140	-0.289	0.207	-0.591
Hydroquinone	0.103	0.242	0.298	0.148	0.602	-0.341
Phenol	-0.351	-0.173	-0.235	-0.364	0.089	-0.519
Resorcinol	0.329	0.222	0.277	0.346	0.246	0.103
Pyridine	0.514	0.631	0.505	0.439	-0.055	0.373
Quinoline	-0.418	-0.262	-0.322	-0.417	0.030	-0.450
NNN	0.076	-0.044	-0.047	0.069	-0.717	0.334
NNK	-0.030	-0.180	-0.111	0.013	-0.639	0.285
NAT	0.125	-0.045	-0.015	0.107	-0.714	0.416
NAB	0.088	-0.064	-0.004	0.071	-0.735	0.380
Mercury	0.758	0.518	0.653	0.710	-0.152	0.711
Cadmium	0.161	0.115	0.150	0.118	-0.293	0.386
Lead	0.205	0.058	0.205	0.254	-0.205	0.279
Smoke pH	0.798	0.696	0.701	0.775	0.205	0.550
.	.	.	.	.	.	.
Tpm, total particulate matter	.	.	.	.	.	.

Constituent	Benzene	1,3-Butadiene	Isoprene	Styrene	Toluene	Ammonia
Tar puff count	.	.	.	.	.	.
Tpm	.	.	.	.	.	.
Water	.	.	.	.	.	.
Carbon monoxide	.	.	.	.	.	.
Acetaldehyde	.	.	.	.	.	.
Acetone	.	.	.	.	.	.
Acrolein		.	.	.	.	.
Butyraldehyde	.	.	.	.	.	.
Crotonaldehyde	.	.	.	.	.	.
Methyl ethyl ketone	.	.	.	.	.	.
Propionaldehyde	.	.	.	.	.	.
Formaldehyde	.	.	.	.	.	.
Acrylonitrite	.	.	.	.	.	.
Benzene	1.000	.	.	.	.	.
1,3-Butadiene	0.874	1.000	.	.	.	.
Isoprene	0.737	0.845	1.000	.	.	.
Styrene	0.800	0.635	0.439	1.000	.	.
Toluene	0.931	0.741	0.669	0.849	1.000	.
Ammonia	-0.029	-0.066	0.038	0.001	0.079	1.000
Total hydrogen cyanide	0.628	0.683	0.811	0.451	0.630	0.394
Impinger hydrogen cyanide	0.643	0.672	0.813	0.435	0.654	0.389
Pad hydrogen cyanide	0.566	0.672	0.768	0.464	0.551	0.385
Nitric oxide	0.381	0.363	0.586	0.164	0.468	0.513
Nitrogen oxides	0.389	0.368	0.581	0.185	0.475	0.532

1-Aminonaphthalene	-0.135	-0.262	-0.212	0.033	-0.009	0.670
2-Aminonaphthalene	0.040	-0.091	-0.094	0.150	0.164	0.684
3-Aminobiphenyl	0.159	0.069	0.020	0.255	0.252	0.657
4-Aminobiphenyl	0.302	0.226	0.185	0.351	0.388	0.640
Benzo[*a*]pyrene	-0.266	-0.401	-0.581	-0.034	-0.214	0.029
Catechol	-0.266	-0.332	-0.640	-0.034	-0.241	-0.209
m- and *p*-Cresol	-0.451	-0.515	-0.627	-0.170	-0.399	0.220
o-Cresol	-0.445	-0.523	-0.621	-0.169	-0.401	0.087
Hydroquinone	-0.022	-0.088	-0.452	0.233	0.006	-0.110
Phenol	-0.481	-0.541	-0.572	-0.252	-0.448	0.123
Resorcinol	0.239	0.298	0.085	0.324	0.236	0.089
Pyridine	0.534	0.333	0.317	0.768	0.620	0.338
Quinoline	-0.507	-0.600	-0.562	-0.254	-0.423	0.195
NNN	0.042	0.062	0.317	-0.096	0.118	0.699
NNK	0.002	-0.051	0.204	-0.150	0.121	0.568
NAT	0.100	0.122	0.408	-0.083	0.170	0.586
NAB	0.087	0.062	0.354	-0.099	0.180	0.615
Mercury	0.691	0.691	0.682	0.561	0.725	-0.020
Cadmium	0.321	0.032	0.148	0.372	0.493	0.328
Lead	0.198	0.053	0.071	0.176	0.378	0.242
Smoke pH	0.714	0.881	0.686	0.576	0.568	-0.098
.	.	.	.	.	.	.
Tpm, total particulate matter	.	.	.	.	.	.

Constituent	Total hydrogen cyanide	Impinger hydrogen cyanide	Pad hydrogen cyanide	Nitric oxide	Nitrogen oxides	1-Aminonaphthalene
Tar puff count	.	.	.	.	.	.
Tpm	.	.	.	.	.	.
Water	.	.	.	.	.	.
Carbon monoxide	.	.	.	.	.	.
Acetaldehyde	.	.	.	.	.	.
Acetone	.	.	.	.	.	.
Acrolein	.	.	.	.	.	.
Butyraldehyde	.	.	.	.	.	.
Crotonaldehyde	.	.	.	.	.	.
Methyl ethyl ketone	.	.	.	.	.	.
Propionaldehyde	.	.	.	.	.	.
Formaldehyde	.	.	.	.	.	.
Acrylonitrite	.	.	.	.	.	.
Benzene	.	.	.	.	.	.
1,3-Butadiene	.	.	.	.	.	.
Isoprene	.	.	.	.	.	.
Styrene	.	.	.	.	.	.
Toluene	.	.	.	.	.	.
Ammonia	.	.	.	.	.	.
Total hydrogen cyanide	1.000	.	.	.	.	.
Impinger hydrogen cyanide	0.993	1.000	.	.	.	.
Pad hydrogen cyanide	0.967	0.930	1.000	.	.	.
Nitric oxide	0.813	0.835	0.728	1.000	.	.
Nitrogen oxides	0.825	0.844	0.745	0.998	1.000	.

1-Aminonaphthalene	0.102	0.095	0.112	0.230	0.247	1.000
2-Aminonaphthalene	0.196	0.200	0.177	0.337	0.354	0.931
3-Aminobiphenyl	0.239	0.238	0.229	0.386	0.397	0.804
4-Aminobiphenyl	0.387	0.392	0.360	0.484	0.494	0.741
Benzo[*a*]pyrene	-0.409	-0.426	-0.354	-0.482	-0.471	0.084
Catechol	-0.609	-0.623	-0.549	-0.598	-0.600	0.129
m- and *p*-Cresol	-0.431	-0.457	-0.356	-0.354	-0.343	0.583
o-Cresol	-0.518	-0.543	-0.441	-0.424	-0.422	0.470
Hydroquinone	-0.416	-0.437	-0.350	-0.511	-0.502	0.112
Phenol	-0.471	-0.489	-0.409	-0.380	-0.379	0.445
Resorcinol	0.135	0.118	0.163	-0.128	-0.127	-0.010
Pyridine	0.400	0.385	0.413	0.246	0.266	0.375
Quinoline	-0.419	-0.437	-0.360	-0.316	-0.316	0.520
NNN	0.507	0.520	0.456	0.723	0.716	0.518
NNK	0.403	0.434	0.317	0.731	0.721	0.363
NAT	0.563	0.584	0.492	0.788	0.779	0.422
NAB	0.504	0.538	0.407	0.806	0.793	0.480
Mercury	0.699	0.716	0.628	0.654	0.651	-0.103
Cadmium	0.298	0.334	0.209	0.504	0.504	0.178
Lead	0.271	0.303	0.192	0.587	0.581	0.244
Smoke pH	0.584	0.566	0.595	0.234	0.247	-0.164
.	.	.	.	.	.	.
Tpm, total particulate matter	.	.	.	.	.	.

Constituent	2-Aminonaphthalene	3-Aminobiphenyl	4-Aminobiphenyl	Benzo[*a*]pyrene	Catechol	*m*- and *p*-Cresol
Tar puff count	.	.	.	.	.	.
Tpm	.	.	.	.	.	.
Water	.	.	.	.	.	.
Carbon monoxide	.	.	.	.	.	.
Acetaldehyde	.	.	.	.	.	.
Acetone	.	.	.	.	.	.
Acrolein	.	.	.	.	.	.
Butyraldehyde	.	.	.	.	.	.
Crotonaldehyde	.	.	.	.	.	.
Methyl ethyl ketone	.	.	.	.	.	.
Propionaldehyde	.	.	.	.	.	.
Formaldehyde	.	.	.	.	.	.
Acrylonitrite	.	.	.	.	.	.
Benzene	.	.	.	.	.	.
1,3-Butadiene	.	.	.	.	.	.
Isoprene	.	.	.	.	.	.
Styrene	.	.	.	.	.	.
Toluene	.	.	.	.	.	.
Ammonia	.	.	.	.	.	.
Total hydrogen cyanide	.	.	.	.	.	.
Impinger hydrogen cyanide	.	.	.	.	.	.
Pad hydrogen cyanide	.	.	.	.	.	.
Nitric oxide	.	.	.	.	.	.
Nitrogen oxides	.	.	.	.	.	.
1-Aminonaphthalene	.	.	.	.	.	.
2-Aminonaphthalene	1.000	.	.	.	.	.
3-Aminobiphenyl	0.897	1.000	.	.	.	.

4-Aminobiphenyl	0.865	0.971	1.000	.	.	.
Benzo[*a*]pyrene	-0.067	-0.125	-0.239	1.000	.	.
Catechol	0.034	0.058	-0.069	0.702	1.000	.
m- and *p*-Cresol	0.403	0.374	0.229	0.508	0.680	1.000
o-Cresol	0.277	0.284	0.129	0.500	0.724	0.957
Hydroquinone	0.044	0.155	0.069	0.650	0.886	0.578
Phenol	0.231	0.236	0.099	0.485	0.659	0.933
Resorcinol	-0.058	0.045	0.041	0.372	0.353	0.181
Pyridine	0.417	0.528	0.562	-0.082	-0.098	0.113
Quinoline	0.281	0.232	0.090	0.487	0.570	0.869
NNN	0.556	0.576	0.608	-0.476	-0.491	-0.038
NNK	0.415	0.390	0.393	-0.393	-0.464	-0.129
NAT	0.469	0.491	0.547	-0.573	-0.582	-0.147
NAB	0.549	0.598	0.641	-0.532	-0.498	-0.103
Mercury	0.060	0.232	0.393	-0.480	-0.389	-0.468
Cadmium	0.260	0.297	0.350	-0.156	-0.338	-0.258
Lead	0.328	0.369	0.388	-0.107	-0.036	-0.084
Smoke pH	-0.009	0.115	0.268	-0.412	-0.322	-0.409
.	.	.	.	.	.	.
Tpm, total particulate matter	.	.	.	.	.	.

Constituent	*o*-Cresol	Hydroquinone	Phenol	Resorcinol	Pyridine	Quinoline	NNN	NNK	NAT	NAB
Tar puff count	.	.	.	.	.	.	.	.	.	.
Tpm	.	.	.	.	.	.	.	.	.	.
Water	.	.	.	.	.	.	.	.	.	.
Carbon monoxide	.	.	.	.	.	.	.	.	.	.
Acetaldehyde	.	.	.	.	.	.	.	.	.	.
Acetone	.	.	.	.	.	.	.	.	.	.
Acrolein	.	.	.	.	.	.	.	.	.	.
Butyraldehyde	.	.	.	.	.	.	.	.	.	.
Crotonaldehyde	.	.	.	.	.	.	.	.	.	.
Methyl ethyl ketone	.	.	.	.	.	.	.	.	.	.
Propionaldehyde	.	.	.	.	.	.	.	.	.	.
Formaldehyde	.	.	.	.	.	.	.	.	.	.
Acrylonitrite	.	.	.	.	.	.	.	.	.	.
Benzene	.	.	.	.	.	.	.	.	.	.
1,3-Butadiene	.	.	.	.	.	.	.	.	.	.
Isoprene	.	.	.	.	.	.	.	.	.	.
Styrene	.	.	.	.	.	.	.	.	.	.
Toluene	.	.	.	.	.	.	.	.	.	.
Ammonia	.	.	.	.	.	.	.	.	.	.
Total hydrogen cyanide	.	.	.	.	.	.	.	.	.	.
Impinger hydrogen cyanide	.	.	.	.	.	.	.	.	.	.
Pad hydrogen cyanide	.	.	.	.	.	.	.	.	.	.
Nitric oxide	.	.	.	.	.	.	.	.	.	.
Nitrogen oxides	.	.	.	.	.	.	.	.	.	.
1-Aminonaphthalene	.	.	.	.	.	.	.	.	.	.
2-Aminonaphthalene	.	.	.	.	.	.	.	.	.	.

3-Aminobiphenyl	.	.	.	.	.	.	.	.	.	.
4-Aminobiphenyl	.	.	.	.	.	.	.	.	.	.
Benzo[*a*]pyrene	.	.	.	.	.	.	.	.	.	.
Catechol	.	.	.	.	.	.	.	.	.	.
m- and *p*-Cresol	.	.	.	.	.	.	.	.	.	.
o-Cresol	1.000	.	.	.	.	.	.	.	.	.
Hydroquinone	0.607	1.000	.	.	.	.	.	.	.	.
Phenol	0.967	0.542	1.000	.	.	.	.	.	.	.
Resorcinol	0.162	0.458	0.131	1.000	.	.	.	.	.	.
Pyridine	0.138	0.149	0.083	0.143	1.000	.	.	.	.	.
Quinoline	0.908	0.475	0.916	0.073	0.158	1.000	.	.	.	.
NNN	-0.110	-0.505	-0.079	-0.138	0.229	-0.003	1.000	.	.	.
NNK	-0.176	-0.514	-0.190	-0.227	0.136	-0.060	0.853	1.000	.	.
NAT	-0.220	-0.594	-0.184	-0.175	0.187	-0.111	0.971	0.864	1.000	.
NAB	-0.169	-0.498	-0.129	-0.233	0.208	-0.066	0.917	0.831	0.939	1.000
Mercury	-0.496	-0.178	-0.496	0.082	0.307	-0.521	0.228	0.183	0.350	0.370
Cadmium	-0.235	-0.215	-0.245	-0.176	0.434	-0.111	0.347	0.401	0.356	0.404
Lead	-0.102	0.008	-0.158	-0.122	0.160	-0.021	0.274	0.443	0.318	0.445
Smoke pH	-0.463	-0.092	-0.494	0.255	0.275	-0.548	0.049	-0.140	0.119	0.033
.	.	.	.	.	.	.	.	.	.	.
Tpm, total particulate matter	.	.	.	.	.	.	.	.	.	.

Constituent	Mercury	Cadmium	Lead	Smoke pH	Methyl ethyl ketone	Chromium	Nickel	Arsenic	Selenium
Tar puff count	.	.	.	.	.	.	.	.	.
Tpm	.	.	.	.	.	.	.	.	.
Water	.	.	.	.	.	.	.	.	.
Carbon monoxide	.	.	.	.	.	.	.	.	.
Acetaldehyde	.	.	.	.	.	.	.	.	.
Acetone	.	.	.	.	.	.	.	.	.
Acrolein	.	.	.	.	.	.	.	.	.
Butyraldehyde	.	.	.	.	.	.	.	.	.
Crotonaldehyde	.	.	.	.	.	.	.	.	.
Methyl ethyl ketone	.	.	.	.	.	.	.	.	.
Propionaldehyde	.	.	.	.	.	.	.	.	.
Formaldehyde	.	.	.	.	.	.	.	.	.
Acrylonitrile	.	.	.	.	.	.	.	.	.
Benzene	.	.	.	.	.	.	.	.	.
1,3-Butadiene	.	.	.	.	.	.	.	.	.
Isoprene	.	.	.	.	.	.	.	.	.
Styrene	.	.	.	.	.	.	.	.	.
Toluene	.	.	.	.	.	.	.	.	.
Ammonia	.	.	.	.	.	.	.	.	.
Total hydrogen cyanide	.	.	.	.	.	.	.	.	.
Impinger hydrogen cyanide	.	.	.	.	.	.	.	.	.
Pad hydrogen cyanide	.	.	.	.	.	.	.	.	.
Nitric oxide	.	.	.	.	.	.	.	.	.
Nitrogen oxides	.	.	.	.	.	.	.	.	.
1-Aminonaphthalene	.	.	.	.	.	.	.	.	.
2-Aminonaphthalene	.	.	.	.	.	.	.	.	.
3-Aminobiphenyl	.	.	.	.	.	.	.	.	.

4-Aminobiphenyl	.	.	.	.	.	.	.	.	.
Benzo[*a*]pyrene	.	.	.	.	.	.	.	.	.
Catechol	.	.	.	.	.	.	.	.	.
m- and *p*-Cresol	.	.	.	.	.	.	.	.	.
o-Cresol	.	.	.	.	.	.	.	.	.
Hydroquinone	.	.	.	.	.	.	.	.	.
Phenol	.	.	.	.	.	.	.	.	.
Resorcinol	.	.	.	.	.	.	.	.	.
Pyridine	.	.	.	.	.	.	.	.	.
Quinoline	.	.	.	.	.	.	.	.	.
NNN	.	.	.	.	.	.	.	.	.
NNK	.	.	.	.	.	.	.	.	.
NAT	.	.	.	.	.	.	.	.	.
NAB	.	.	.	.	.	.	.	.	.
Mercury	1.000	.	.	.	.	.	.	.	.
Cadmium	0.449	1.000	.	.	.	.	.	.	.
Lead	0.506	0.592	1.000	.	.	.	.	.	.
Smoke pH	0.662	-0.056	-0.008	1.000	.	.	.	.	.
.	.	.	.	.	.	.	.	.	.
Tpm, total particulate matter	.	.	.	.	.	.	.	.	.

Table A4.8.
Correlation matrix for all constituents per milligram of nicotine reported to Health Canada for cigarette brands with NNN levels less than 100 ng/mg nicotine (Health Canada, 2004), modified intense machine regimen

Constituent	Carbon Monoxide	Ammonia	1-Aminonaphthalene	2-Aminonaphthalene	3-Aminobiphenyl	4-Aminobiphenyl
Carbon Monoxide	1.000					
Ammonia	0.625	1.000				
1-Aminonaphthalene	-0.338	-0.594	1.000			
2-Aminonaphthalene	0.859	0.804	-0.514	1.000		
3-Aminobiphenyl	0.307	-0.155	0.550	0.047	1.000	
4-Aminobiphenyl	0.877	0.790	-0.500	0.985	0.154	1.000
Benzo[*a*]pyrene	0.810	0.847	-0.613	0.959	-0.155	0.926
Formaldehyde	0.810	0.817	-0.516	0.878	-0.071	0.852
Acetaldehyde	0.949	0.645	-0.362	0.858	0.239	0.879
Acetone	0.935	0.477	-0.119	0.756	0.452	0.780
Acrolein	0.848	0.306	0.065	0.568	0.624	0.607
Propionaldeyde	0.944	0.579	-0.257	0.816	0.397	0.853
Crotonaldehyde	0.863	0.578	-0.179	0.817	0.250	0.807
Butyraldehyde	0.959	0.620	-0.267	0.871	0.307	0.883
Hydrogen cyanide	0.945	0.746	-0.441	0.929	0.202	0.951
Mercury	0.674	0.161	0.133	0.341	0.466	0.405
Lead	0.892	0.657	-0.535	0.919	0.728	0.927
Cadmium	0.249	-0.178	0.502	0.015	0.603	0.035
Nitrogen oxides	0.890	0.552	-0.374	0.838	0.264	0.864
Nirogen oxides	0.902	0.585	-0.404	0.868	0.232	0.886

NNN	0.447	0.480	-0.438	0.588	0.138	0.634
NNK	0.744	0.666	-0.573	0.902	0.078	0.904
N′-Nitrosoanabasine	0.573	0.500	-0.433	0.715	0.152	0.734
N′-Nitrosoanatabine	0.737	0.678	-0.483	0.854	0.151	0.870
Pyridine	0.830	0.712	-0.286	0.814	0.310	0.839
Quinoline	0.205	0.538	-0.362	0.527	-0.463	0.453
Hydroquinone	0.733	0.577	-0.187	0.772	0.103	0.715
Resorcinol	0.765	0.724	-0.531	0.885	-0.107	0.861
Catechol	0.619	0.606	-0.388	0.766	-0.211	0.685
Phenol	-0.389	-0.033	0.130	-0.114	-0.419	-0.199
m- and *p*-Cresols	-0.055	0.282	-0.144	0.271	-0.457	0.184
o-Cresol	-0.273	0.079	0.046	0.025	-0.442	-0.063
1,3-Butadiene	0.949	0.652	-0.323	0.796	0.266	0.815
Isoprene	0.918	0.785	-0.483	0.915	0.090	0.926
Acrylonitrile	0.938	0.725	-0.489	0.864	0.253	0.901
Benzene	0.972	0.719	-0.401	0.892	0.206	0.901
Toluene	0.864	0.711	-0.389	0.872	0.280	0.893
Styrene	0.045	-0.067	0.012	-0.051	-0.204	-0.080
Puff count	0.847	0.453	-0.202	0.777	0.375	0.790

Constituent	Benzo[a]pyrene	Formaldehyde	Acetaldehyde	Acetone	Acrolein	Propionaldeyde
Carbon Monoxide						
Ammonia						
1-Aminonaphthalene						
2-Aminonaphthalene						
3-Aminobiphenyl						
4-Aminobiphenyl						
Benzo[*a*]pyrene	1.000					
Formaldehyde	0.912	1.000				
Acetaldehyde	0.810	0.844	1.000			
Acetone	0.675	0.740	0.944	1.000		
Acrolein	0.474	0.568	0.792	0.912	1.000	
Propionaldeyde	0.746	0.788	0.972	0.974	0.860	1.000
Crotonaldehyde	0.762	0.844	0.887	0.894	0.801	0.886
Butyraldehyde	0.805	0.828	0.976	0.965	0.843	0.974
Hydrogen cyanide	0.885	0.844	0.932	0.855	0.720	0.910
Mercury	0.315	0.419	0.675	0.759	0.797	0.708
Lead	0.911	0.852	0.879	0.888	0.885	0.896
Cadmium	-0.081	-0.008	0.067	0.313	0.526	0.195
Nitrogen oxides	0.766	0.638	0.849	0.800	0.670	0.835
Nirogen oxides	0.801	0.679	0.860	0.805	0.671	0.841
NNN	0.464	0.347	0.454	0.322	0.128	0.424
NNK	0.817	0.710	0.707	0.609	0.426	0.690

N′-Nitrosoanabasine	0.596	0.476	0.520	0.449	0.258	0.523
N′-Nitrosoanatabine	0.770	0.668	0.756	0.689	0.455	0.749
Pyridine	0.746	0.771	0.817	0.803	0.682	0.830
Quinoline	0.621	0.516	0.259	0.099	-0.051	0.182
Hydroquinone	0.757	0.773	0.713	0.727	0.649	0.691
Resorcinol	0.925	0.835	0.781	0.672	0.493	0.723
Catechol	0.811	0.750	0.607	0.542	0.418	0.554
Phenol	-0.025	-0.073	-0.348	-0.384	-0.379	-0.372
m- and *p*-Cresols	0.356	0.261	-0.002	-0.107	-0.203	-0.054
o-Cresol	0.119	0.062	-0.221	-0.282	-0.317	-0.254
1,3-Butadiene	0.765	0.827	0.953	0.925	0.836	0.935
Isoprene	0.905	0.884	0.954	0.848	0.689	0.900
Acrylonitrile	0.811	0.806	0.924	0.855	0.729	0.914
Benzene	0.859	0.867	0.957	0.915	0.779	0.934
Toluene	0.802	0.785	0.871	0.834	0.749	0.871
Styrene	0.017	0.053	-0.011	-0.021	-0.118	-0.043
Puff count	0.695	0.679	0.851	0.896	0.847	0.885

Constituent	Crotonaldehyde	Butyraldehyde	Hydrogen Cyanide	Mercury	Lead	Cadmium
Carbon Monoxide						
Ammonia						
1-Aminonaphthalene						
2-Aminonaphthalene						
3-Aminobiphenyl						
4-Aminobiphenyl						
Benzo[*a*]pyrene						
Formaldehyde						
Acetaldehyde						
Acetone						
Acrolein						
Propionaldeyde						
Crotonaldehyde	1.000					
Butyraldehyde	0.944	1.000				
Hydrogen cyanide	0.855	0.936	1.000			
Mercury	0.637	0.683	0.584	1.000		
Lead	0.906	0.920	0.951	0.868	1.000	
Cadmium	0.315	0.217	0.133	0.431	0.523	1.000
Nitrogen oxides	0.734	0.863	0.886	0.536	0.878	0.199
Nirogen oxides	0.757	0.876	0.903	0.521	0.891	0.193
NNN	0.274	0.411	0.541	-0.030	0.706	-0.213
NNK	0.643	0.717	0.818	0.157	0.894	0.040

N′-Nitrosoanabasine	0.437	0.532	0.638	0.057	0.822	0.086
N′-Nitrosoanatabine	0.676	0.761	0.814	0.342	0.918	0.078
Pyridine	0.814	0.859	0.866	0.520	0.895	0.290
Quinoline	0.407	0.286	0.368	-0.109	0.014	-0.287
Hydroquinone	0.792	0.765	0.730	0.357	0.673	0.188
Resorcinol	0.734	0.775	0.814	0.347	0.679	-0.110
Catechol	0.700	0.648	0.646	0.171	0.252	-0.055
Phenol	-0.053	-0.280	-0.280	-0.382	-0.514	-0.145
m- and *p*-Cresols	0.226	0.051	0.087	-0.254	-0.295	-0.234
o-Cresol	0.061	-0.158	-0.143	-0.316	-0.402	-0.152
1,3-Butadiene	0.850	0.936	0.889	0.703	0.780	0.132
Isoprene	0.852	0.933	0.954	0.598	0.885	-0.013
Acrylonitrile	0.799	0.907	0.940	0.544	0.859	0.080
Benzene	0.884	0.962	0.949	0.634	0.921	0.197
Toluene	0.822	0.884	0.887	0.508	0.775	0.165
Styrene	0.005	-0.004	0.003	0.059	-0.049	0.064
Puff count	0.828	0.890	0.793	0.604	0.795	0.278

Constituent	Nitric oxide	Nitrogen oxides	NNN	NNK	*N′*-Nitrosoanatabine	*N′*-Nitrosoanabasine
Carbon Monoxide						
Ammonia						
1-Aminonaphthalene						
2-Aminonaphthalene						
3-Aminobiphenyl						
4-Aminobiphenyl						
Benzo[*a*]pyrene						
Formaldehyde						
Acetaldehyde						
Acetone						
Acrolein						
Propionaldeyde						
Crotonaldehyde						
Butyraldehyde						
Hydrogen cyanide						
Mercury						
Lead						
Cadmium						
Nitrogen oxides	1.000					
Nirogen oxides	0.997	1.000				
NNN	0.585	0.588	1.000			
NNK	0.804	0.831	0.774	1.000		
N′-Nitrosoanabasine	0.723	0.737	0.856	0.918	1.000	
N′-Nitrosoanatabine	0.844	0.856	0.828	0.923	0.917	1.000

Pyridine	0.782	0.801	0.498	0.743	0.637	0.806
Quinoline	0.196	0.233	0.204	0.384	0.190	0.324
Hydroquinone	0.549	0.590	0.187	0.593	0.316	0.477
Resorcinol	0.700	0.726	0.405	0.716	0.476	0.639
Catechol	0.482	0.523	0.230	0.590	0.305	0.443
Phenol	-0.396	-0.374	-0.262	-0.204	-0.291	-0.247
m- and *p*-Cresols	-0.042	-0.013	0.011	0.152	0.005	0.100
o-Cresol	-0.268	-0.243	-0.194	-0.079	-0.190	-0.111
1,3-Butadiene	0.763	0.778	0.376	0.627	0.429	0.652
Isoprene	0.837	0.856	0.478	0.736	0.526	0.753
Acrylonitrile	0.847	0.860	0.606	0.800	0.650	0.788
Benzene	0.881	0.898	0.462	0.762	0.597	0.790
Toluene	0.781	0.801	0.457	0.767	0.563	0.720
Styrene	0.062	0.062	-0.006	-0.041	0.064	0.069
Puff count	0.762	0.774	0.286	0.654	0.456	0.627

Constituent	Pyridine	Quinoline	Hydroquinone	Resorcinol	Catechol	Phenol
Carbon Monoxide						
Ammonia						
1-Aminonaphthalene						
2-Aminonaphthalene						
3-Aminobiphenyl						
4-Aminobiphenyl						
Benzo[*a*]pyrene						
Formaldehyde						
Acetaldehyde						
Acetone						
Acrolein						
Propionaldeyde						
Crotonaldehyde						
Butyraldehyde						
Hydrogen cyanide						
Mercury						
Lead						
Cadmium						
Nitrogen oxides						
Nircgen oxides						
NNN						
NNK						
N′-Nitrosoanabasine						
N′-Nitrosoanatabine						
Pyridine	1.000					
Quinoline	0.236	1.000				
Hydroquinone	0.667	0.456	1.000			

Resorcinol	0.645	0.614	0.744	1.000		
Catechol	0.476	0.771	0.843	0.852	1.000	
Phenol	-0.320	0.727	0.055	0.033	0.372	1.000
m- and *p*-Cresols	-0.031	0.927	0.293	0.383	0.644	0.912
o-Cresol	-0.200	0.811	0.150	0.144	0.459	0.983
1,3-Butadiene	0.779	0.218	0.731	0.744	0.618	-0.341
Isoprene	0.820	0.421	0.725	0.857	0.683	-0.236
Acrylonitrile	0.829	0.245	0.655	0.763	0.587	-0.380
Benzene	0.882	0.265	0.730	0.790	0.626	-0.351
Toluene	0.851	0.307	0.765	0.750	0.623	-0.243
Styrene	-0.025	-0.050	-0.143	-0.039	-0.060	-0.108
Puff count	0.746	0.196	0.727	0.694	0.592	-0.260

Constituent	*m*- and *p*-Cresols	*o*-Cresol	1,3-Butadiene	Isoprene	Acrylonitrile	Benzene	Toluene	Styrene	Puff count
Carbon Monoxide									
Ammonia									
1-Aminonaphthalene									
2-Aminonaphthalene									
3-Aminobiphenyl									
4-Aminobiphenyl									
Benzo[*a*]pyrene									
Formaldehyde									
Acetaldehyde									
Acetone									
Acrolein									
Propionaldeyde									
Crotonaldehyde									
Butyraldehyde									
Hydrogen cyanide									
Mercury									
Lead									
Cadmium									
Nitrogen oxides									
Nirogen oxides									
NNN									
NNK									

N′-Nitrosoanabasine									
N′-Nitrosoanatabine									
Pyridine									
Quinoline									
Hydroquinone									
Resorcinol									
Catechol									
Phenol									
m- and *p*-Cresols	1.000								
o-Cresol	0.956	1.000							
1,3-Butadiene	-0.034	-0.239	1.000						
Isoprene	0.132	-0.104	0.930	1.000					
Acrylonitrile	-0.031	-0.271	0.919	0.921	1.000				
Benzene	-0.004	-0.225	0.944	0.952	0.941	1.000			
Toluene	0.061	-0.131	0.856	0.884	0.866	0.881	1.000		
Styrene	-0.064	-0.086	-0.035	-0.034	0.002	0.063	-0.395	1.000	
Puff count	0.005	-0.163	0.821	0.796	0.763	0.833	0.890	-0.279	1.000

NNK, 4-(*N*-nitrosomethylamino)-1-(3-pyridyl)-1-butanone; NNN, *N′*-nitrosonornicotine

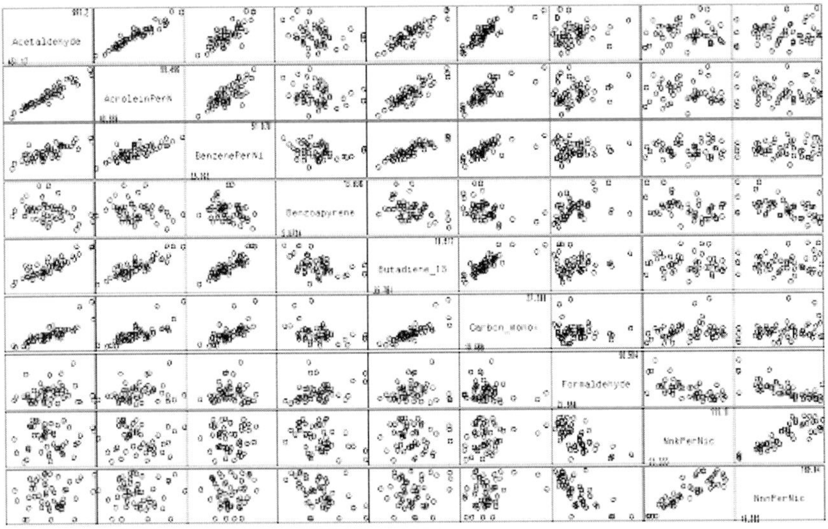

Figure A4.1
Correlation scatterplot matrix: international brands, modified intense machine regimen

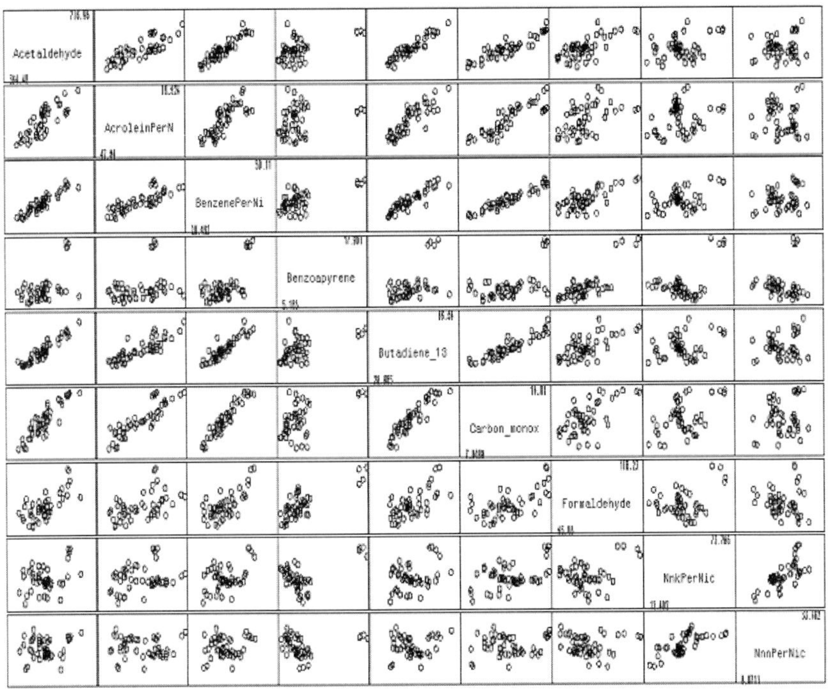

Figure A4.2
Correlation scatterplot matrix: Canadian data (NNN limited), modified intense machine regimen
NNN, N´-nitrosonornicotine

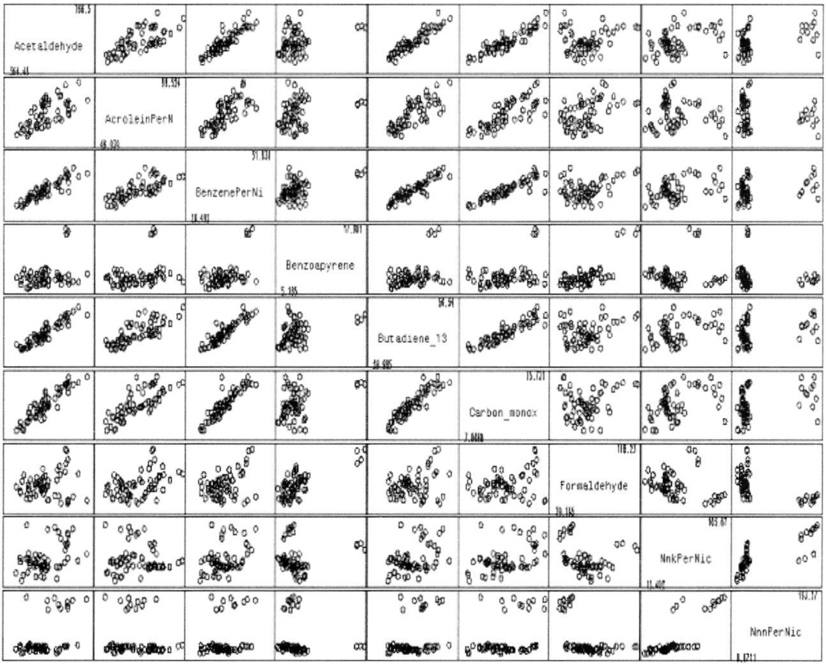

Figure A4.3
Correlation scatterplot matrix: Canadian data (all), modified intense machine regimen

Annex 3.5 **Variation in yield of selected toxicants by brand**

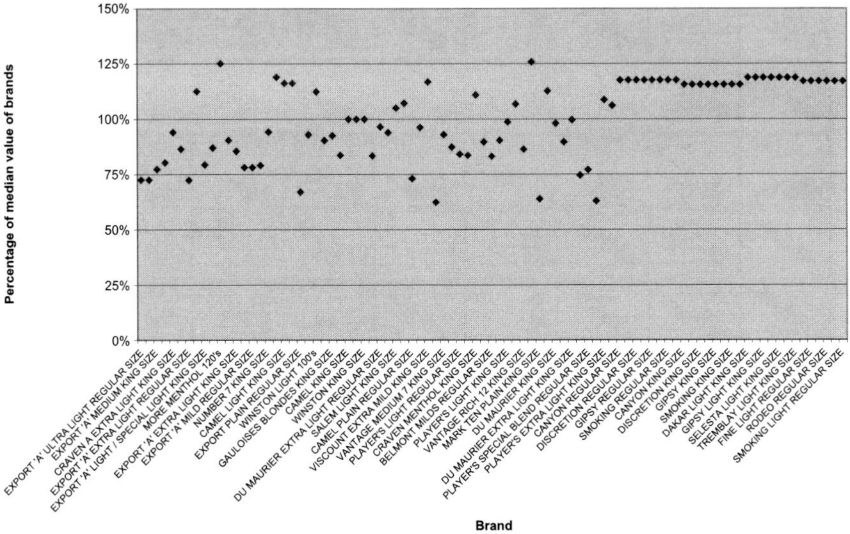

Figure A5.1
Carbon monoxide per milligram of nicotine yield by brand as a percentage of the median yield from brands reported to Heath Canada (2004)

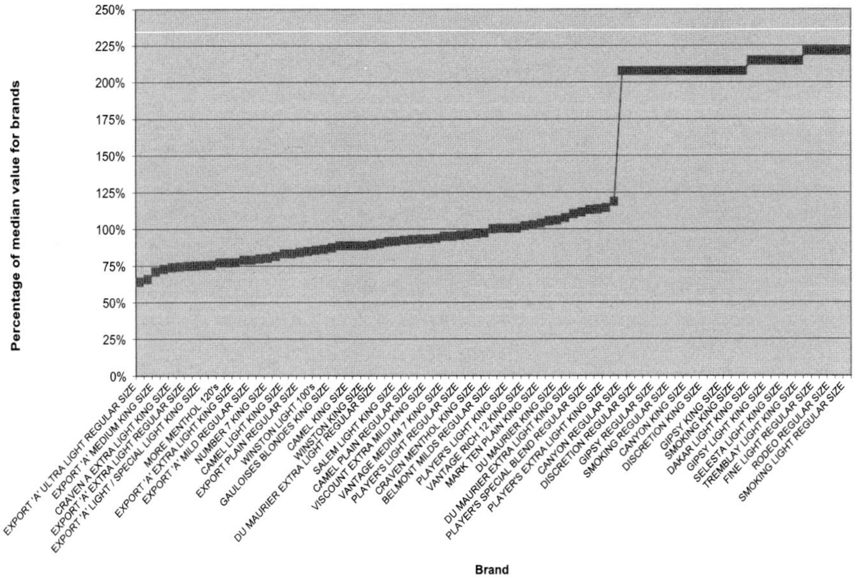

Figure A5.2
Benzo[a]pyrene per milligram of nicotine yield by brand as a percentage of the median yield from brands reported to Heath Canada (2004)

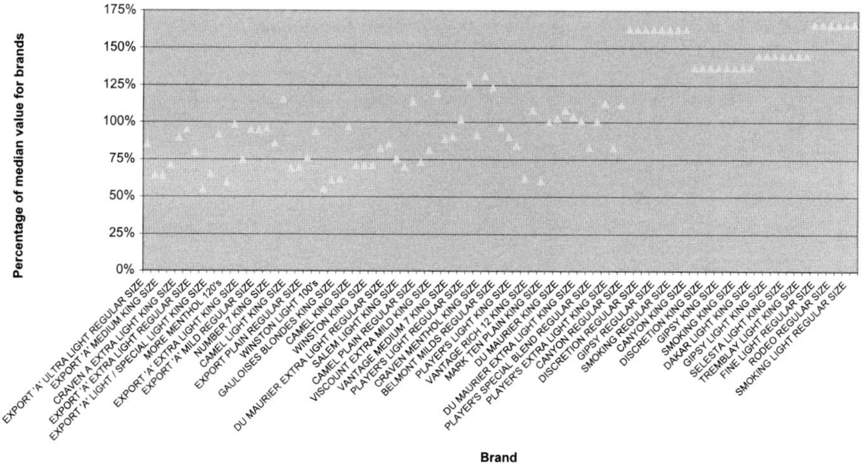

Figure A5.3

Formaldehyde per milligram of nicotine yield by brand as a percentage of the median yield for brands reported to Health Canada (2004)

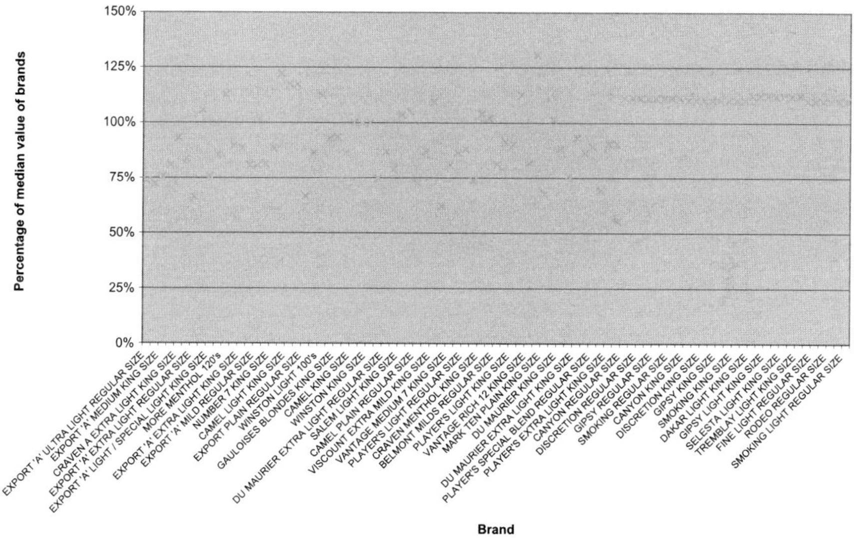

Figure A5.4

Acetaldehyde yield per milligram of nicotine by brand as a percentage of the median yield for brands reported to Health Canada (2004)

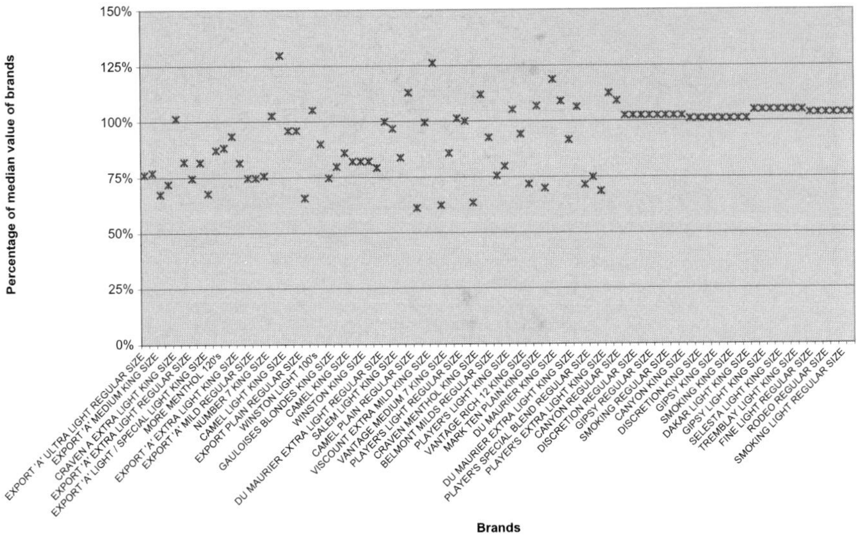

Figure A5.5
Acrolein yield by brand per milligram of nicotine as a percentage of the median yield for brands reported to Health Canada (2004)

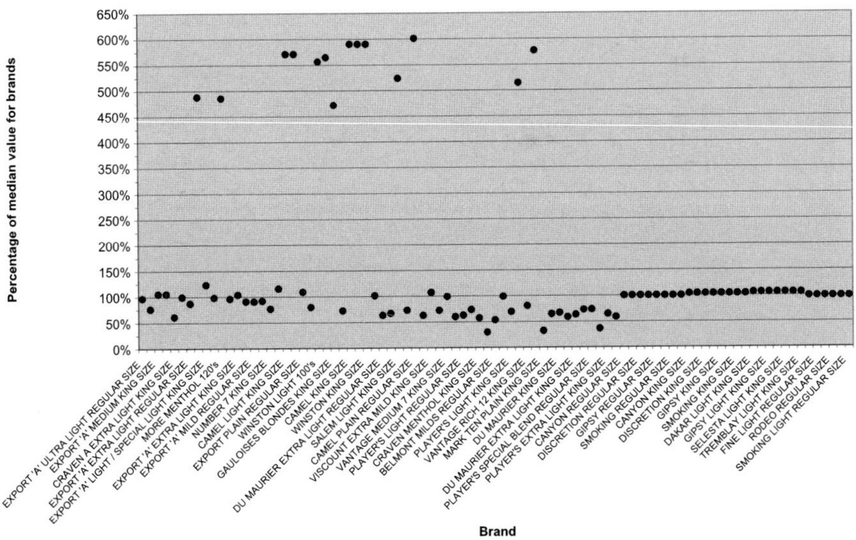

Figure A5.6
NNN yield by brand per milligram of nicotine as a percentage of the median yield for brands reported to Health Canada (2004)
NNN, N′-nitrosonornicotine

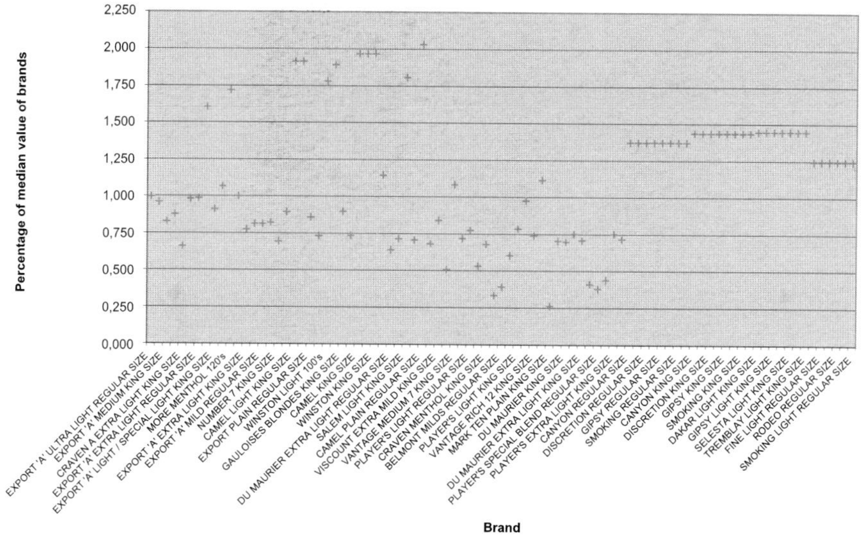

Figure A5.7
NNK yield by brand per milligram of nicotine as a percentage of the median yield for brands reported to Health Canada (2004)
NNK, 4-(N-nitrosomethylamino)-1-(3-pyridyl)-1-butanone

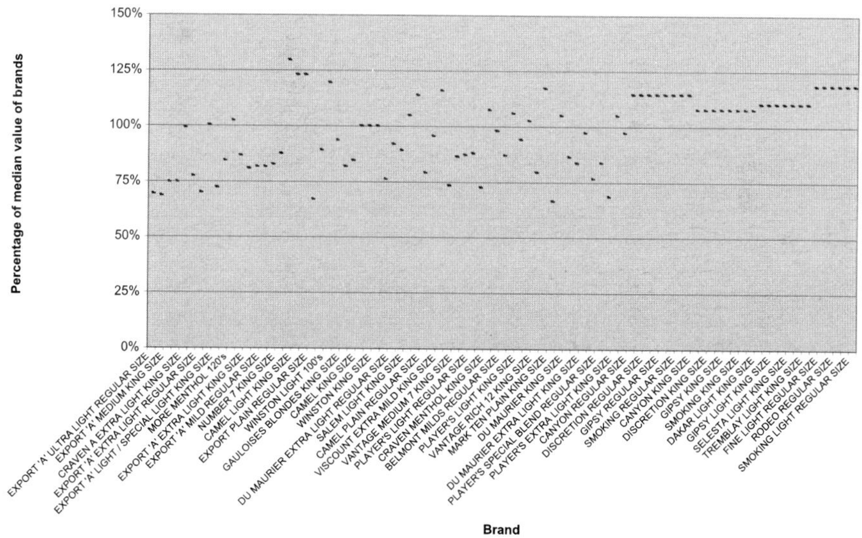

Figure A5.8
1,3-Butadiene yield by brand per milligram of nicotine as a percentage of the median yield for brands reported to Health Canada (2004)

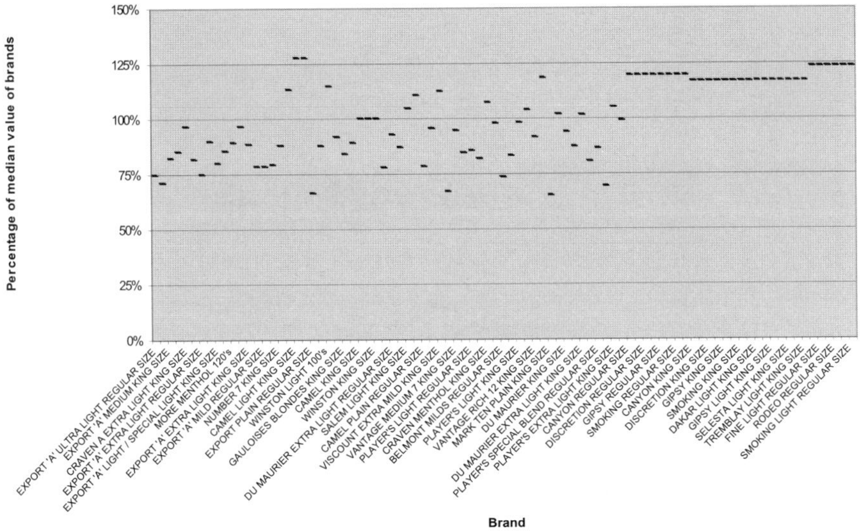

Figure A5.9

Benzene yield by brand per milligram of nicotine as a percentage of the median yield for brands reported to Health Canada (2004)

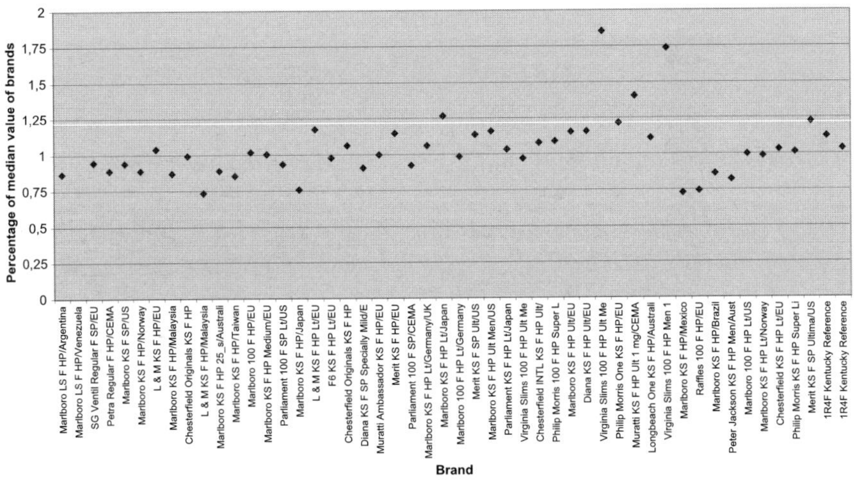

Figure A5.10

Carbon monoxide per milligrams of nictone yield as a percentage of the median yield for Philip Morris International Brands

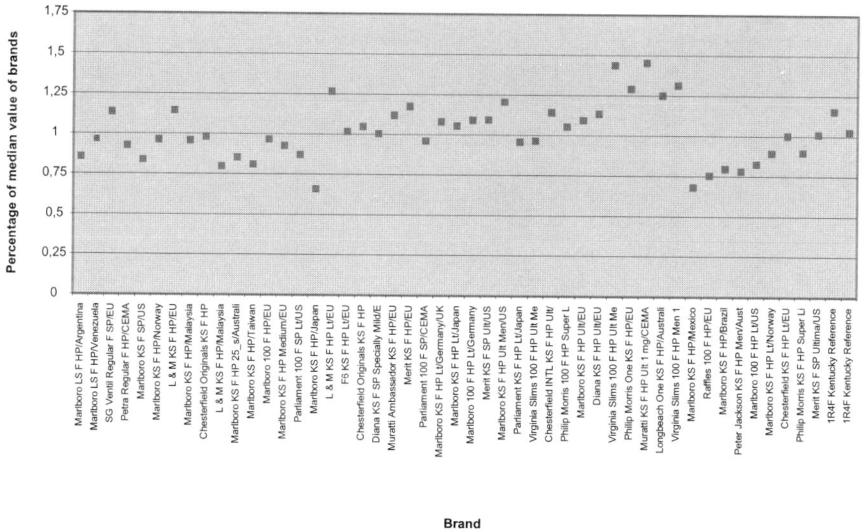

Figure A5.11

Acetaldehyde per milligrams of nictone yield as a percentage of the median yield for Philip Morris international brands

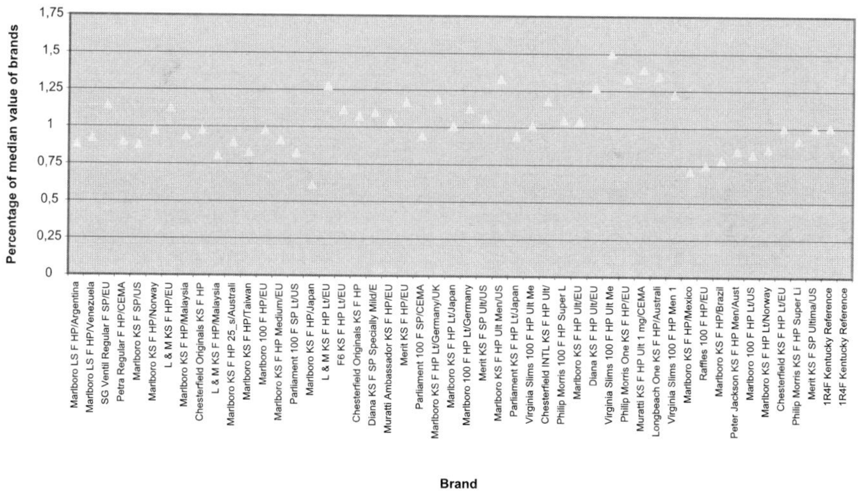

Figure A5.12

Acrolein per milligrams of nictone yield as a percentage of the median yield for Philip Morris international brands

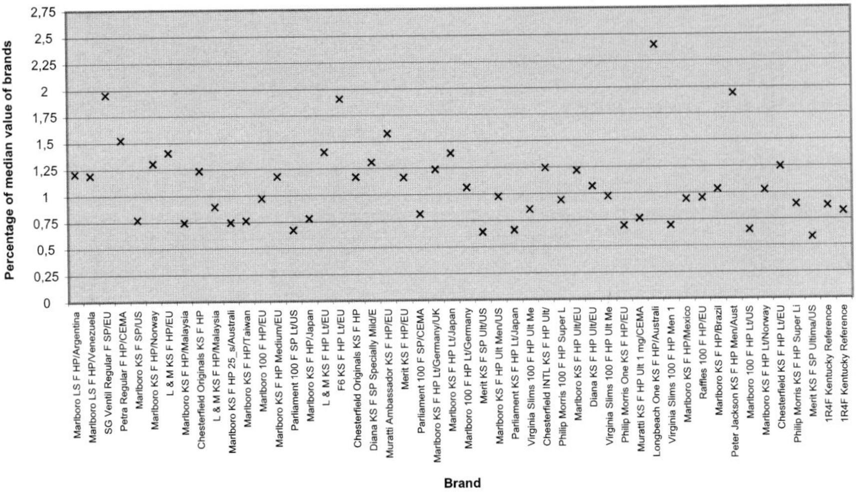

Figure A5.13
Formaldehyde per milligrams of nictone yield as a percentage of the median yield for Philip Morris international brands

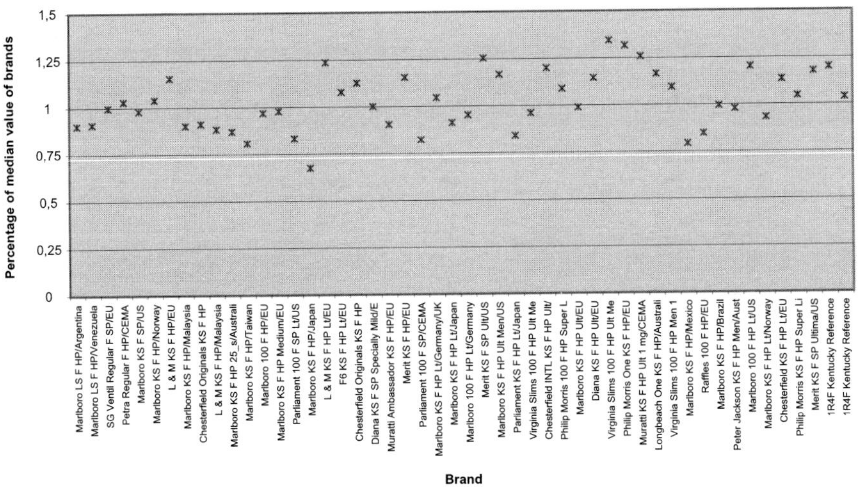

Figure A5.14
Benzene per milligrams of nictone yield as a percentage of the median yield for Philip Morris international brands

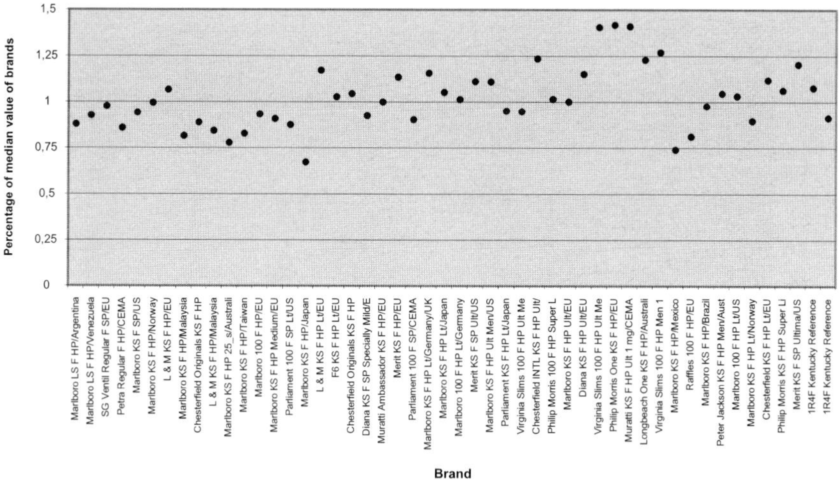

Figure A5.15
1,3-Butadiene per milligrams of nictone yield as a percentage of the median yield for Philip Morris international brands

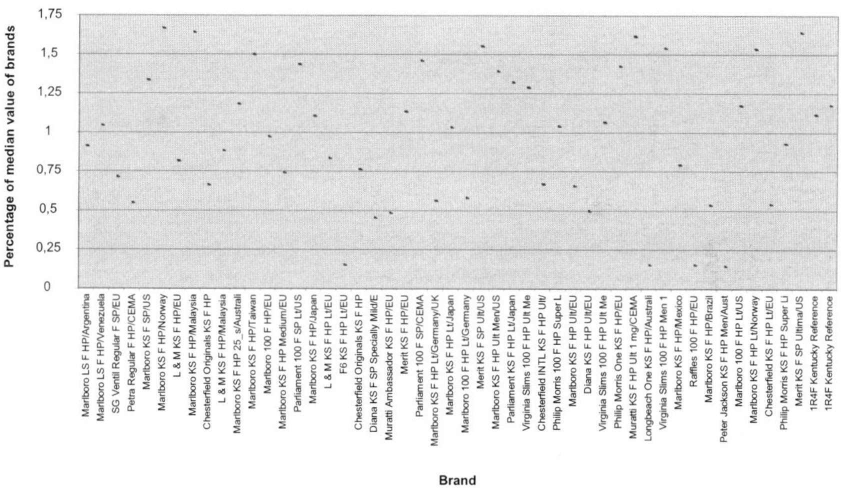

Figure A5.16
NNN per milligrams of nictone yield as a percentage of the median yield for Philip Morris international brands
NNN, N´-nitrosonornicotine

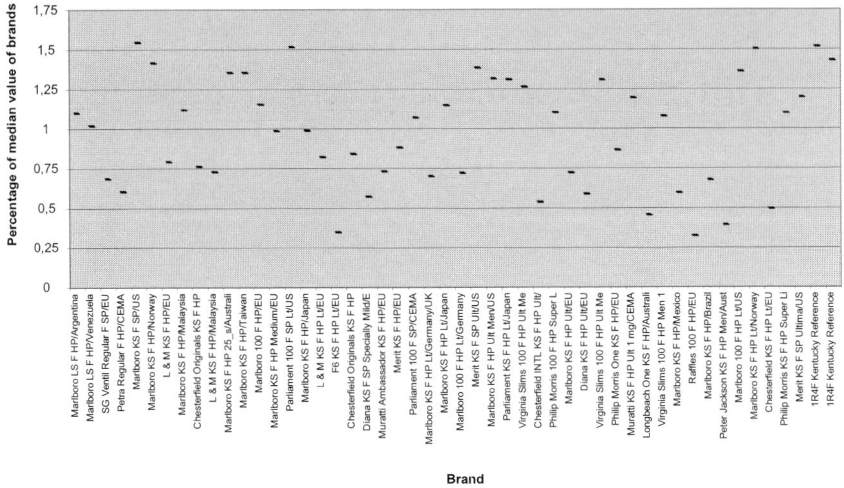

Figure A5.17
NNK per milligrams of nictone yield as a percentage of the median yield for Philip Morris international brands
NNK, 4-(N-nitrosomethylamino)-1-(3-pyridyl)-1-butanone

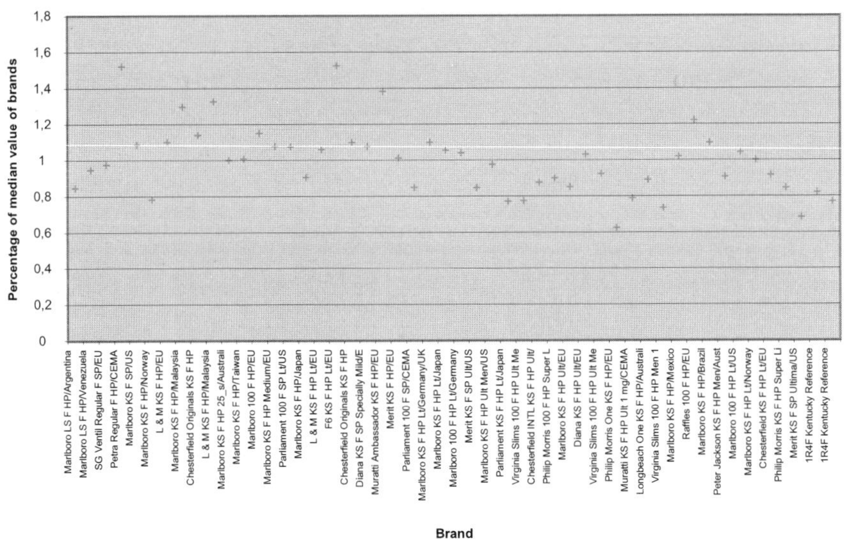

Figure A5.18
Benzo[a]pyrene per milligrams of nictone yield as a percentage of the median yield for Philip Morris international brands

4. Recommendation on cigarette machine smoking regimens

Tobacco product characterization is an essential element of tobacco product control and should be an integral part of comprehensive tobacco control programmes. Assessment of the toxicity of tobacco products allows application of regulatory strategies similar to those used for other consumer products, including informing regulatory agencies about the levels of toxicants in tobacco product content and emissions and reducing the levels of known toxicants present in the emissions, while not requiring measurement of exposure of human populations.

The Scientific Advisory Committee on Tobacco Product Regulation established by WHO held its first meeting in October 2000. In November 2003, the Director-General of WHO changed its status from an advisory committee to a study group, and it is now known as the WHO Study Group on Tobacco Product Regulation (TobReg). The Director-General reports to the Executive Board on the results and recommendations of the Study Group in order to draw the attention of Member States to WHO's efforts in tobacco product regulation. The objective of TobReg is to make scientifically sound recommendations to WHO Member States on the most effective, evidence-based means for filling regulatory gaps in tobacco control and for establishing a coordinated regulatory framework for tobacco products. TobReg's members comprise national and international experts on product regulation, treatment of tobacco dependence, laboratory analysis of tobacco contents and emissions, and design features.

An advisory note from the WHO Scientific Advisory Committee on Tobacco Product Regulation in 2003, entitled *Recommendation on health claims derived from ISO/FTC method to measure cigarette yield*, concluded that the current standard method for measuring tar, nicotine and carbon monoxide in cigarette smoke with the single International Organization for Standardization (ISO)/US Federal Trade Commission (FTC) machine smoking regimen is unacceptable for public health. TobReg examined the scientific evidence and found that the tar, nicotine and carbon monoxide yields per cigarette measured by machine under the existing ISO regimen are not valid estimates of human exposure or of the exposure deriving from smoking different brands of cigarettes. Communication of such measures to smokers creates harm by misleading them into believing that their exposure and risk can be reduced if they switch to cigarette brands with lower machine-measured yields, and by offering the products as an alternative to cessation.

The meeting of the ISO Technical Committee (TC) 126 in Las Vegas, USA, on 22–23 May 2006, which discussed harmonized, international standards for tobacco and tobacco products, recognized that misuse of machine-measured yields can result in false information to consumers. It passed a formal resolution, adopting the following statements as the rationale for all machine smoking regimens:

> *"No machine smoking regime can represent all human smoking behaviors;*
>
> *"Methods are recommended which test the product under conditions of different intensities of machine smoking testing in order to collect main stream smoke;*
>
> *"Machine smoking testing is useful to characterize cigarette emissions for design and regulatory purposes, but communication of machine measurements to smokers can result in misunderstanding about differences in exposure and risk across brands; and*
>
> *"Smoke emission data from machine measurements may be used as inputs for product hazard assessment, but they are not intended to be nor are they valid measures of human exposure or risks. Communicating differences between products in machine measurements as differences in exposure or risk is a misuse of testing using ISO standards."*

In order to address Articles 9 and 10 of the WHO Framework Convention on Tobacco Control on regulation of the contents, emissions and design features of tobacco products and of tobacco product disclosures, the Conference of Parties at its first session in Geneva, 6–17 February 2006, created a working group to draft guidelines for implementation of those articles. At its second meeting in Ottawa, Canada, 26–28 October 2006, the working group requested WHO's Tobacco Laboratory Network (TobLabNet) to evaluate the technical advantages and disadvantages of the current ISO method, the Canadian 'intense' method, the method of the State of Massachusetts (USA), and the 'compensatory regime'. TobLabNet, a global network of government, academic institutions and independent laboratories administered by the WHO Tobacco Free Initiative, met in Beijing, China, 20–22 November 2006 to fulfill that task. TobReg considers that the discussion clearly favoured the Canadian 'intense' method, which includes a more intense machine smoking regimen and is the most useful single regimen for assessing emissions. Nevertheless, TobReg and TobLabNet recognize that more than one machine regimen is needed to characterize smoke emissions adequately.

At the second session of the Conference of Parties, in Bangkok, Thailand, 30 June–6 July 2007, the possibility of working with ISO TC126 to validate methods for measuring the contents of tobacco products was discussed as a problematic but potentially valuable approach. ISO TC126 formed Working Group 10, which is a forum for the exchange of information between ISO and WHO, including issues related to deliberations by WHO or the Conference of Parties on standard setting for product regulation in general and the design and validation of test methods in particular. ISO TC126 exchanges information with WHO in order to conform to the needs of the Conference of Parties, if that body chooses to exercise its competence in standards development for tobacco products, specifically in the design and validation of tobacco testing and measuring methods.

On the basis of existing scientific evidence, TobReg at its meeting in Stanford, California, 25–27 July 2007, made the following recommendation through the Head of the Convention Secretariat of the WHO Framework Convention on Tobacco Control, the Tobacco Free Initiative, to the Conference of Parties working group mandated to prepare guidelines for Articles 9 and 10:

> *TobReg recommends that the Conference of Parties Working Group finalize its decision on a machine smoking regimen and recommends that the regimen selected be the Canadian 'intense' regimen. To assist Parties in strengthening the regulation of the content of tobacco products, the working group on Articles 9 and 10 established by the Conference of Parties at its first session to develop prepare for implementation of Articles 9 and 10 of the Framework Convention, charged the Tobacco Free Initiative to work with TobLabNet to identify the method of choice for each of the three groups of chemicals in cigarette tobacco and for the emissions of four groups of chemicals in mainstream cigarette smoke. TobLabNet is prepared to carry out the mandated method validation but requires a decision from the Conference of Parties concerning finalization of the machine smoking regimen and any need for interaction with ISO.*
>
> *In this regard, TobReg considers that use of the Canadian 'intense' regimen would reflect the yields resulting under intense smoking conditions and would also form a basis for preventive public health strategies. The yields derived from this regimen could be used, for example, in setting product performance standards.*

After this recommendation was written, the working group on Artices 9 and 10 included in its progress report to the third session of the Conference of Parties in Durban, South Africa (17–22 November 2008), a recommendation for use of two smoking regimens—the ISO regimen and an intense regimen—for validation of the test methods outlined in their report. The working group identified three sets of contents (ammonia, nicotine and humectants) and four sets of emissions (tobacco-specific nitrosamines, benzo[*a*]pyrene, aldehydes and volatile organic compounds) for method validation. The report recommended that the Conference of Parties, through the Convention Secretariat, request WHO's Tobacco Free Initiative to validate the analytical chemical methods for testing and measuring the cigarette contents and emissions identified as priorities in its report, using the two smoking regimens set out in paragraph 18 of the report and to inform the Conference of Parties through the Convention Secretariat of the progress made on a regular basis. The first smoking regimen is ISO 3308:2000, which defines a routine analytical cigarette smoking machine used under standard conditions, with a 35-ml puff volume, a puff frequency of one every 60 s and no modification to ventilation holes. The second is similar but with a 55-ml puff volume, a puff frequency of one every 30 s and blocking of all ventilation holes with Mylar adhesive tape.

The Conference of Parties at its third session deliberated on the progress report and mandated the working group to continue its work, elaborating guidelines step-by-step, and to submit a first set of draft guidelines to the Conference of Parties for consideration at its fourth session. In addition, the Conference of Parties requested the Convention Secretariat to invite WHO's Tobacco Free Initiative to undertake the following work:

(1) submit a report for consideration by the Conference of Parties at its fourth session, which:

  (a) identifies best practices in reporting to regulators as regards contents, emissions and product characteristics, including electronic systems;

  (b) identifies best practices in informing the public; and

  (c) collects information on legal cases and analyses the legal issues related to tobacco product disclosures;

(2) validate, within 5 years, the analytical chemical methods for testing and measuring the cigarette contents and emissions identified as priorities in the progress report of the working group (FCTC/COP/3/6), using the two smoking regimens set out in paragraph 18 of that report, and to inform the Conference of Parties through the Convention Secretariat on a regular basis of the progress made.

5. Overall recommendations

5.1 Harm reduction and smokeless tobacco products: regulatory recommendations and research needs

Main recommendations

The objective of harm reduction in relation to tobacco is to decrease morbidity and mortality among continuing tobacco and nicotine users who are unwilling or unable to quit, with due consideration of effects at the population level. Cigarette smoke is the most hazardous form of nicotine intake, and medicinal nicotine is the least hazardous. Among the smokeless tobacco products on the market, products with low levels of nitrosamines, such as Swedish *snus*, are considerably less hazardous than cigarettes, while the risks associated with some products used in Africa and Asia approach those of smoking. The finding in Sweden that long-term use of smokeless tobacco by men reduces cigarette smoking has not been replicated in other countries where smokeless tobacco has been widely available. The Swedish experience may not therefore be generalizable, and it would be premature to use it as a basis for public health recommendations.

It is recommended that research be conducted to determine whether and under what conditions smokeless tobacco might be used as an aid in smoking cessation and whether marketing smokeless tobacco as a method for harm reduction would encourage initiation of smoking and smokeless tobacco use. The evidence that use of smokeless tobacco leads to cessation of cigarette smoking is inconclusive, although survey data from Sweden suggest that this may have occurred. The evidence that initiation of smokeless tobacco use leads to a higher prevalence of use of combustible tobacco products is conflicting. In view of the wide diversity in the composition, toxicity and patterns of use of smokeless tobacco products by geographical region, it is inappropriate to consider smokeless tobacco as a single product.

Significance for public health policies

All smokeless tobacco products should be subjected to comprehensive regulatory control by an independent, scientific government agency. The control must include and require disclosure of ingredients by manufacturers. As claims for reduced exposure might be interpreted as claims for harm reduction, the former must be based on evidence of reduced risk.

In view of the wide variety of smokeless products with respect to composition, patterns of use, history of use and user characteristics, public health policy must cater for different populations. Continued testing and measurement of the contents and emissions of smokeless tobacco products must be conducted in order to identify regional variations. Careful attention should be paid to product characteristics and risks, the pattern of tobacco use in the population, social and cultural differences and marketing messages in order to evaluate the potential of specific smokeless tobacco products to reduce harm.

Implications for WHO programmes

The wide range of smokeless tobacco products and use characteristics means that WHO should support individual and population-based research on specific products. Better knowledge about the effects and mechanisms of action of smokeless tobacco products and about what modifications can be made to alter the effects is needed so that governments can implement the WHO Framework Convention on Tobacco Control. WHO should continue research on the health hazards and risks to individuals and populations due to use of smokeless tobacco products.

5.2 'Fire-safer' cigarettes: approaches to reducing ignition propensity

Main recommendations

Fires due to cigarettes and the related deaths are a major global public health problem. In view of the role of cigarettes as the source of residential fires and resulting deaths, public health policy is required to reduce the number of such incidents over time.

Techniques for reducing ignition propensity are available and are used. An ignition propensity performance standard has been established for cigarettes which makes them significantly less likely to cause fires if left unattended. It is recommended that standards such as that of the National Institute of Standards and Technology in the USA be implemented in Member States.

Research is needed to ensure the effectiveness of regulations for reduced ignition propensity and on the effects of changes in cigarette design to provide the basis for further policies. As in countries that already have reduced ignition propensity policies, others should require tobacco manufacturers to test ignition strength, report to the appropriate authority and cover the costs of research and implementation.

Significance for public health policies

Adequate, appropriate monitoring, reporting and archiving is needed of the effectiveness of techniques for reducing ignition propensity for reducing deaths, injuries and property damage due to cigarette-induced fires. Such monitoring will increase public assurance and lead to more effective policies.

Claims that use of products with reduced ignition propensity will reduce risk should not be allowed, as they could lead consumers to perceive a lowered overall health risk. Public education programmes should be continued, to inform consumers that tobacco products are lethal and that smokers should quit. Such programmes should also include education campaigns to teach the public how to prevent fires.

Implications for WHO programmes

As techniques for reducing ignition potential are available and may be beneficial, Member States should require cigarettes with reduced ignition potential based on the National Institute of Standards and Technology standard or any other standard that has been shown to be effective. Countries and jurisdictions within countries should retain the right to alter the standard on the basis of population-based data on the effectiveness of the standard. Policies should require tobacco manufacturers to commission testing by independent laboratories that have been accredited in accordance with ISO standard 17025, *General requirements for the competence of calibration and testing laboratories*. WHO should facilitate implementation of such policies and support the development of more effective means of redcuing the damage due to cigarette-ignited fires.

5.3 Mandated lowering of toxicants in cigarette smoke: tobacco-specific nitrosamines and selected other constituents

Main recommendations

Communication of machine-measured tar, nicotine and carbon monoxide yields per cigarette as a measure of human exposure or difference in risk between products is currently misleading smokers to believe that low yield cigarettes have less risk and are a reasonable alternative to cessation. The scientific capacity to assess human exposure and harm from use of different products for use in regulation remains incomplete. In the interim, a new strategy for regulation is proposed which establishes product performance standards, requires disclosure of emissions, and mandates a lowering of the toxicant levels generated under standardized conditions by prohibiting the sale of brands that do not meet established levels of these standards. This approach is similar to the regulation of most consumer products where toxicant levels present in the product are reduced to the extent possible as part of good manufacturing processes. An essential component of this recommendation is the regulatory prohibition of the communication of these measures to the public as measures of human exposure or risk, and of any ranking of products by their toxicant yields.

Toxicant levels would be compared using units per mg nicotine in order to focus on the toxicity of cigarettes under standardized conditions and avoid their use as measures of exposure. Toxicants were selected based on multiple criteria, the most important of which was evidence of toxicity.

The primary goal of the proposed regulatory strategy is to reduce the levels of toxic constituents measured under standardized conditions in the smoke of cigarettes allowed on the market. A secondary goal is to prevent the introduction into a market of cigarettes with higher levels of smoke toxicants than are present in brands already on the market.

Significance for public health policies

Regulatory bodies should consider adoption of the new regulatory strategy in order to avoid the continuing harm resulting from communication of tar, nicotine and carbon monoxide values per cigarette and as a means of reducing the toxicants known to be present in smoke in a manner similar to that used to regulate toxicant levels in other consumer products. The recommended regulatory strategy should be implemented in phases beginning with a period of required annual reporting of toxicant levels by cigarette manufacturers to the regulatory authority. This should be followed by the promulgation of the levels of toxicants above which brands cannot be offered for sale. Finally, the established levels would be enforced and violating brands banned from the market.

Any regulatory approach based on yields under standardized conditions should prohibit the use of testing results, ranking of brands by testing levels, or statements that the brand has met governmental regulatory standards as indicators of risk or exposure. Regulatory authorities have an obligation to ensure that the testing results are not used to mislead the public, which has occurred previously.

Implications for WHO programmes

In view of the harmful effects of the present approach, which allows communication of measurements of emissions per cigarette, WHO should promote the prompt replacement of that approach with the recommended regulatory strategy. Mandated lowering of levels of toxicants per mg nicotine in cigarette smoke will make regulation of cigarettes consistent with other regulatory approaches which mandate reduction of known toxicants in products used by humans. The WHO Framework Convention on Tobacco Control recognizes the need for tobacco product regulation in Articles 9 and 10.

5.4 Cigarette machine smoking regimens

Main recommendations

The Conference of the Parties at its second session acknowledged the potentially value of working with the International Standards Organizations (ISO) Technical Committee 126 to establish an ISO standard for a machine smoking regimen. The recommendation for a new regimen is based on a scientific consensus that a new, more intense smoking regimen is needed to characterize better the composition of tobacco smoke produced by cigarettes under conditions reflecting the upper range of intensities of the patterns of their use. After evaluation of several machine-smoking regimens, TobReg recommends that the ISO select the Canadian 'intense' regimen.

Significance for public health policies

Continued misuse of the 'per cigarette yields' generated with the current ISO regimen is harmful to public health and results in inadequate characterization of the smoke generated by different products. In the Canadian 'intense' regimen, more intense smoking conditions are tested, resulting in better characterization of cigarette smoke for use in public health. The yields derived from this regimen can be used, for example, to set product performance standards.

Machine smoking testing is useful for characterizing cigarette emissions for design and regulatory purposes; however, it is not intended to be and is not a valid measure of human exposure or risk. Care should be taken that the measures are not misinterpreted by consumers as differences in exposure or risk.

Implications for WHO programmes

Accurate characterization of tobacco products and disclosure to regulatory agencies are essential for tobacco product control, as outlined in Articles 9 and 10 of the Framework Convention. Machine smoking regimens that allow better characterization of the smoke generated by different products are essential for improving public health and might result in reductions in the levels of known toxicants in emissions. WHO must continue to support TobReg's recommendation that a new machine smoking regimen be standardized.